The Vivette Voyages

The Vivette Voyages
Adventures in a 25ft Sailing Cutter

Down Channel in the Vivette

Through Holland in the Vivette

E. Keble Chatterton

The Vivette Voyages:
Adventures in a 25ft Sailing Cutter
by E. Keble Chatterton

First published under the titles
Down Channel in the Vivette
and
Through Holland in the Vivette

Leonaur is an imprint
of Oakpast Ltd

Copyright in this form © 2009 Oakpast Ltd

ISBN: 978-1-84677-780-6 (hardcover)
ISBN: 978-1-84677-779-0 (softcover)

http://www.leonaur.com

Publisher's Notes

In the interests of authenticity, the spellings, grammar and place names used have been retained from the original editions.

The opinions of the authors represent a view of events in which he was a participant related from his own perspective, as such the text is relevant as an historical document.

The views expressed in this book are not necessarily those of the publisher.

Contents

Down Channel in the Vivette — 7

Through Holland in the Vivette — 163

Down Channel in the Vivette

Contents

Preface	11
Introduction	15
From The Crouch To The Medway	24
From the Medway to Ramsgate	37
From Ramsgate to Newhaven	49
From Newhaven to Hamble	55
From Hamble To Poole	60
From Poole to Weymouth	65
From Weymouth to Dartmouth	72
From Dartmouth To Salcombe	84
From Salcombe to Plymouth Sound	98
From Plymouth Sound to Fowey	107
From Fowey to Falmouth and Back	115
From Fowey to Salcombe	126
From Salcombe to Torquay	134
From Torquay to Lulworth	139
From Lulworth to Swanage, and Hamble	152

Preface

Most of the best logs remain unprinted. I heard the other day of the cruise of a small yacht, whose dimensions are such that she would make a nice, convenient-sized craft for sailing about on the Serpentine. She went away from her home port for her annual summer outing, and came back after some weeks. All the time she was sailed entirely single-handed, with only her owner aboard. When she returned someone asked him where he had been. He answered that he had been down the Channel, round Land's End, and across to Ireland.

"Have any adventures?" inquired his friend.

"No—just ordinary cruising."

"How did you get on in the Irish Channel? Plenty of wind?"

"Yes, plenty of wind."

"How long were you crossing? "

"Oh—not a quick passage. You see," he explained reluctantly, "I was hove-to for two days during that breeze—you remember?"

That is the type of yachtsman—and there are many of them—who would as soon think of publishing their logs as of publishing their private diaries. It is a justifiable question for the reader who takes up the present book to ask: "Then, why do you not follow so excellent an example when you have done less than they?" I answer that, lacking the essential modesty which characterises these splendid sailor-men, I have dared to rush into print where angelic yachtsmen fear to tread, in the hope that they may be induced to spin their much better yarns for the interest and benefit of the least adventurous. Good wine needs no bush, but a good yarn does need publicity: otherwise it dies with the man, and his interesting exploits are buried with him. There is not a supply of these published logs sufficient to meet the demands of most sailing men, who enjoy nothing better than to read the experiences of other amateur sea-farers. Of course there is the Superior Person in the yacht club as there is everywhere else, and to him I know that this little book can make no appeal. But I venture to hope that those others with whom I enjoy a similarity of tastes, and a sympathetic interest in the matters which are herewith recorded, may find some little pleasure in reading what I have set forth. At least, perhaps, they may find some pleasure in glancing at the illustrations, for the making of which I have again to thank my friend and cruising-mate, Mr. Norman S. Carr.

May 1910.

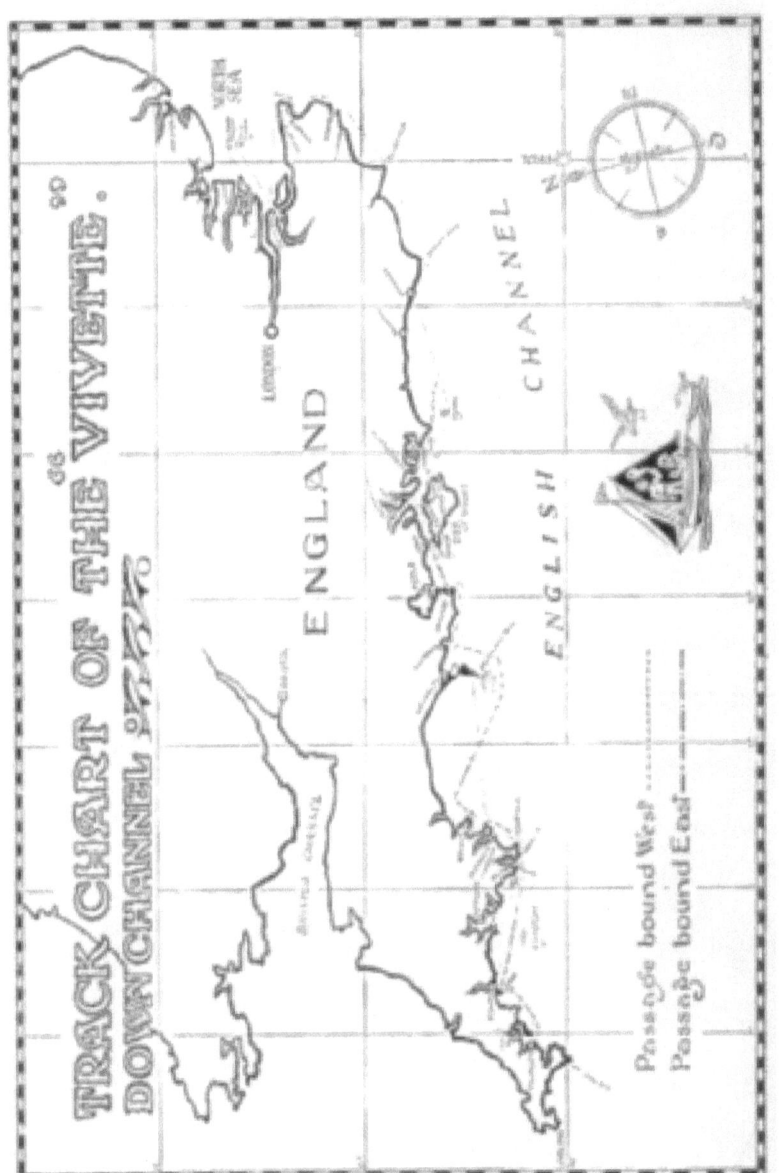

Track Chart of the *Vivette*

Introduction

We had come in from the open sea, which all the day had been doing its utmost to make itself just as trying and difficult to live with as ever. With every one of our four reefs tucked in to the mainsail, and nothing but a spitfire of a jib at the end of the bowsprit, we had rounded in between the high piers at the conclusion of our passage, and tied up in a snug corner of the sheltered harbour: for the next few days it was going to blow "some," and the seas would be far too treacherous for our little craft. As we lowered sail, a paid-hand on the next yacht anticipated our wish, and stood by to catch our line preparatory to making fast alongside the quay.

During the ensuing days we became great friends with our neighbour. His owner had left the yacht to go inland, so that the man was alone, and welcomed the arrival of a stranger as someone to talk to. It was not long before we discovered that he was different from the ordinary type of yacht's hand one meets sometimes up and down the coast, the product of having too little work to do and of receiving too much wages in return for the little that has to be done.

There was something about this man which seemed to stamp him with a clearly-cut character of his own, and as we got to know each other better during the time that we were kept in port, while the wind blew across the harbour, and the angry, torn clouds scudded over the sky, he began gradually to unburden himself. It was then that we learnt that most of his life had been spent in deep-sea sailing vessels, voyaging into every corner of the seven seas, round the Horn, the Cape, and elsewhere. He used to spin us yarns sometimes of those real experiences which can only be obtained on the old-fashioned sailing ship, but happen somehow differently on the steamer, even though she be but a rusty, ill-found tramp, painfully grinding out her miserable nine knots an hour.

One sunset, just before he went below and squeezed himself through the narrow forehatch into the kennel of a fok'sle, he halted, and turning round to me in a sudden spasm of confidence said—

"Look 'ere, sir, if I 'ad the chance I'd let the sea alone—that I would."

I looked at him and smiled, for I knew he was but exercising the sailor's historic privilege of grumbling.

"And if you did," I replied, "what then?"

"What then? Why, I'd go an' live in the country—right away from the coast; get a little bit of a place somewhere and a few cocks 'n 'ens, and I wouldn't want nothing else then. Oh, it's a dog's life going to sea," he growled despairingly.

Somehow he didn't meet with the sympathy he had expected, for—

"Well, supposing you did," I argued, "supposing you got your nice little place in the country, your garden and a few cocks and hens, how long do you think you'd tolerate it all?"

He didn't answer at first. Then—

"Oh—dunno," he muttered half audibly.

"You might stand it a few months, or you might have had

enough in a few weeks," I submitted, "and all the time you'd be thinking not about your garden and your fowls—your mind would be away from the land right across to the sea—and before long you'd have given up the shore life, and gone back to look for a ship again."

He looked thoughtfully across the harbour for a minute, drew the back of his strong, brown hand over his mouth, and, resting his weight on his arms, leaned out on to the deck.

"Yes—well, I suppose you're about right," he agreed at length. "I can see myself doing it all over again. When I come home at the end of a voyage," he continued, "the first week's all right, an' so's the second. But after that, sir, it seems to get a bit old-fashioned like, and I've had enough. It's always the same every time, and I'm thankful when my time's up. Seems a funny thing, but there it is," he concluded. [1]

Had he been a little more of a philosopher, this British sailor-man would have admitted that it was but the spirit of his fathers manifesting itself in him in spite of himself; the instinct of an island race, of the sons of the sea, that is every bit as truly existing to-day, though not as openly shown, as in the days of the Elizabethan seamen, and further back still to the times that followed after the coming of the Vikings to instil what we had yet to learn, but have never since lost, the fascination which is found in ships and the sea.

For it is true enough that the professed object of those sixteenth-century sailors when they manned their capstans and

---

1. The sensationalism of coincidence is remarkable. I had not seen or heard anything of this yacht or its paid-hand for nearly eighteen months when, the morning after the above words had been written, the following significant intelligence was published from Lloyd's:—

"—— (6-tons), of ——, sank after being on fire in the Downs last night. Crew of three men, including her owner, were saved by the North Deal lifeboat, and landed at Ramsgate this morning." I can see my friend clambering out of the sinking yacht into the lifeboat, and murmuring to himself again, in his own quiet way, something about a "dog's life" and "letting the sea alone."

But I wonder now whether he is any nearer to his country ideal, or whether, by the time these lines are in print, he has signed on again aboard a big ship and "gone foreign"—"right away from the coast"?

unfurled their sails to go to sea was plainly and clearly to obtain wealth. They roamed the ocean expressly to catch the Spanish treasure frigates and relieve them of their valuable gold and silver and spices for the aggrandisement of themselves. But at the back of that sordid sense was the sea-sense, and many of the merchant-adventurers had in them less of the merchant and more of the adventurer.

They were prompted by that restless force which is indescribable, and scarcely capable of analysis except on the supposition that it is the reappearance of that part of human nature which is still linked most closely to the primitive man. Even in those for whom the sea has little or no attraction that same yearning comes out in a Selous, a Sven Hedin, or a Roosevelt. The ex-President of the United States in the first words of his account relating his experiences in the heart "of Central Africa, himself remarks that "the great world movement which began with the voyages of Columbus and Vasco da Gama, and has gone on with ever-increasing rapidity and complexity until our own time, has developed along a myriad lines of interest. In no way has it been more interesting than in the way in which it has resulted in bringing into sudden, violent, and intimate contact, phases of the world's life-history which would be normally separated by untold centuries of slow development."

Even today in this age of ultra-civilisation man feels that he must go forth and contend for something. Even if it is not for fortune, it is for fame or fun. That, surely, is the only way in which Arctic and Antarctic expeditions have had their birth. It is nothing less than a continuous war which has gone on uninterruptedly down the ages between man and the superior forces of nature. He likes to strive in the contest and show his worth, if not to the satisfaction of the whole world, at least to those whose applause is to him the most acceptable.

For nothing is so gratifying to the weak as to be able to attain even a temporary triumph over a greater power. The woman, who knows she is in strength, at least, the inferior of the man, exults in achieving some little thing in which the other sex has not succeeded. And so man puts out to sea to wrestle with waves that could swallow him up any moment, with winds that can blow him miles from his course, with tides that can cast him and his ship helpless on to sand or coral.

It is in the full knowledge and realisation of these potentialities that he delights to match his weakness and limited power. He goes out because he has in mind the coming back—the joy of having dodged his enemy, outwitted him not by superiority of power, but by skilfulness of strategy: he knows he is weak, and yet he is strong in resource.

But today there is so little of the world to be explored; there are so very few shores of the sea that have not seen man and his ships go past. There are but a handful of pirates anywhere, and perhaps, like the diminishing wild animals of Central Africa, they will soon be protected from being chased, and preserved as curiosities to wander as they please within certain limits. We cannot, like the Elizabethans, go out to capture a *Madre de Dios* and bring her into Dartmouth Harbour with her rich spoil: International Law has tamed us too much to do that.

But though we cannot all be Scotts or Shackletons, or Pearys or Nansens, yet we keep that spirit alive in a smaller way by sending our whalers out for many months in the year, and in despatching the fine, daring fishermen in their able vessels from Brixham, Yarmouth, and elsewhere to find their way through fogs and gales in order to gather the harvest of the sea. And, in a manner smaller still, this primitive instinct is kept from being extinguished utterly by the yachtsmen, fettered to the city as they are for most of the year, who break their irksome bonds and hurry to the coast to match their town-bred weakness and amateur skill against the tyranny of the narrow seas.

In the extremely kind and favourable reviews which greeted the publication of my *Sailing Ships and their Story*, some of the critics in applauding what they were pleased to call the writer's "passion for the sea" referred to this as being a virtue that is rare among our fellow-countrymen. But whilst I take advantage of this opportunity to express my thanks for the generous reception which my efforts received, I cannot allow the last remark to pass unchallenged. To do so would be to acquiesce in an injustice dealt to those hundreds of amateur sailing men who are now found coasting along our shores in almost every part of our isles.

In them the old Elizabethan spirit is displayed every week end: in them the fascination of the sea has an overwhelming influence, and it is these enthusiasts who keep alive much of the original "passion for the sea," and the old seamanship which is destined to be swept away by the coming of the steamer and motor craft.

Ever since the close of the Crimean War the custom of doing on the sea for sport what others are doing for their livelihood has been obtaining a strong hold over men who saw in all other recreations a limit too close and a freedom from danger too clearly defined; so that now there is scarcely a port or an estuary in the kingdom which has not its flourishing sailing or yacht club with a membership of keen, eager sailing men. For some time the queen of sports was confined to those who alone possessed the income of a monarch. Up till the 'seventies it was almost exclusively the recreation of the rich, and not till after the 'eighties was room made for the poor man and his small yacht.

By the end of the last century, however, he had proved that to be a good sea-sportsman it was not essential that his ship should carry a large crew, nor in fact any crew at all save himself and his friends. And by now the Corinthian sailor, profiting by the experience of others, knows that apart from the freedom of expense which he enjoys in working his vessel with an amateur crew, he is learning all the time something which he would have taken far longer to acquire under constant tutelage—that feeling of self-reliance and cool confidence in making his little voyages down the narrow seas. Side by side with this new enthusiasm was growing up ready to meet it a fuller knowledge and more scientific study of the architecture of small yachts, so that now, at the end of the first decade of the twentieth century, the small yacht-owner is able to put to sea in a craft that is proportionately as well built and designed as those bigger and more aristocratic sisters carrying their gold-laced skippers and innumerable hands to do the work on board them.

The following pages, then, contain a faithful record of a cruise from one end of the English Channel to the other in as small a vessel as most people, perhaps, would care to embark on for such a voyage. No claim, however, is made that anything in the least wonderful was achieved thereby. Vessels as small as *Vivette* have even crossed the Atlantic, and the famous little *Tillikum,* in which Captain Voss sailed around the world, is nothing more than a decked dug-out. The first part of the cruise appeared in two numbers of *The Yachting Monthly,* and has since been revised and largely rewritten. But sailors, yachtsmen, and others, some of whom were complete strangers to me, have asked for more, so that it has seemed desirable to publish in an improved and more permanent form what has gone before, with the addition of the completion of the cruise which was made the following year.

The publication of yachtsmen's logs is of only recent date, but most members of this sport find that their voracious appetite is not satiated by the few which make their appearance at rare intervals. There is a keen delight in reading of the adventures which greeted a fellow-sportsman, and in learning how an exit was made from an exciting difficulty.

Apart from the mild thrill which is to be obtained by following another's exploits, there results sometimes an addition of knowledge based on the experiences and experiments which others have made in their effort to contend with the great forces of nature. There are some yachtsmen, too, who find their enjoyment almost exclusively in going in and out of their own port without troubling to follow the coast past the next headland. But there is so much fresh pleasure in finding a new anchorage every night, in entering new harbours and estuaries, in negotiating other channels, that it is hoped the following narrative may tempt them to break from their tradition, leave their moorings, and see other corners of this fair isle of Albion.

Nevertheless, it is not exclusively for the yachtsman that this record has been written. The success of the travel book within the last two or three years has shown conclusively that there is a large public among the class known usually as the general reader, that prefers to do its voyaging vicariously without having to stir outside the four walls of the room. Perhaps to these there may be some pleasure in seeing with the author the coast-line of the English Channel, not, as is usual, from the land side, but from the sea, as Cæsar saw it, and the Vikings, and Phœnicians, the French, the Dutch, the Spanish Armada, and other invaders of our shores have seen it. The holiday-maker who is set down at the end of a long journey through the country at a seaside town knows nothing of the continuity of his country's coast-line. Beyond the two headlands that bound the bay he knows that land and sea stretch away until the next port is reached. But of the unceasing panorama, changing every minute as you fly on before the wind, of the succession of lighthouses and lightships, cliffs and ravines, of beautiful and peaceful red-tiled villages nestling under the shelter of a craggy mountain, of fields yellow with harvest abutting on to the sea, of creeks harbouring a few weatherworn fishing-boats, of the multifarious line of shipping that passes you by day and by night, he has only a vague and disjointed notion.

To the stay-at-home, then, I hope that I shall succeed in presenting a new picture to his imagination; to the yachtsman accustomed to sail only in his own home waters I trust I shall hold out a temptation to cruise farther along; in those who have already been down Channel perhaps I may awake happy memories; while to none I trust I shall seem wearisome in recounting one of the most interesting and attractive forms of travel which can be obtained without needing the assistance of a comfortable train, a luxurious liner, or a high-powered motor-car.

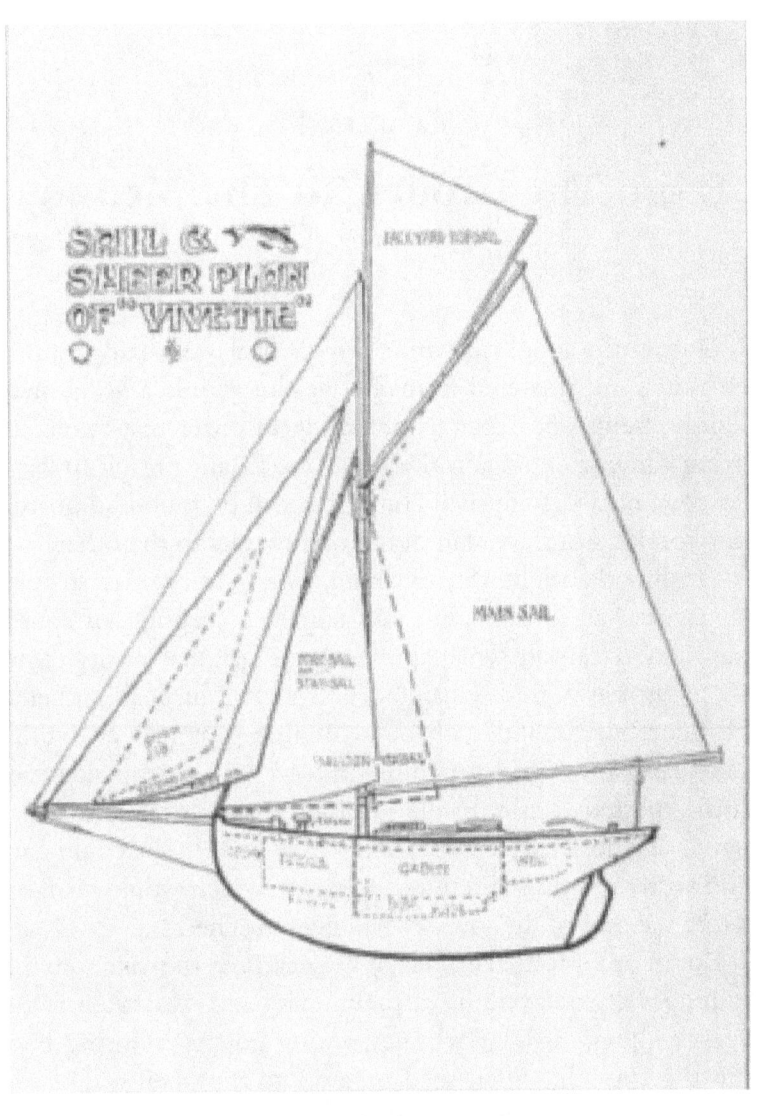

Sail and Sheer Plan of the *Vivette*

CHAPTER 1

From The Crouch To The Medway

During the long, sad winter *Vivette* had been hauled out of the water and sheltered from the weather, while a good many improvements and repairs were made in order that when the spring came round again she might be fit and strong to carry her crew of two, with such comfort as can be found on board a four-tonner, from one end of the narrow seas to the other.

Finally, one bright May morning, with her new mast stepped, her rigging all in place, her sails tanned (excepting, of course, the balloon canvas, which preserves its original purity), with her ballast clean, freshly painted, and stowed in position below the floor boards, and with new running gear and everything ship-shape and "Bristol-fashion," *Vivette's* white top-sides and varnish glistened gaily in the sunshine. She was ready to begin her voyage down west and to show how bravely she could contend with the waves and tides and winds which would assail her before the end of the journey had been reached.

But in order to make a test of her gear, and to make sure that nothing was still wanting, a preliminary sail was taken at the week-end; and a few days later, letting go the mooring-buoy into the Crouch, *Vivette* sped on away to the open sea, leaving Burnham and the dreary Essex flats astern. As we go down with the strong tide and light wind, let me explain a little more fully the nature of the ship and her equipment.

Vivette had been designed and built by Messrs. E. J. & W. Goldsmith, Ltd., the well-known firm of barge builders of Grays, Essex, and many a sailor-man, amateur and professional, has since admired alike the strength and generous amount of wood that was put into her. For some years, under her previous ownership, she was well known cruising up and down the east coast, but my thoughts turned westwards to the fascinating waters of the Wight, the bold cliffs of Dorset, the deep coves and creeks of Devon and Cornwall.

I wanted, therefore, a vessel of such a design and build that could be managed alone, if necessary, without the burden and nuisance of a paid-hand; she must be comely in appearance, with plenty of freeboard, and a nice comfortable little cabin below. Primarily she was to be a good bad-weather craft, with the best possible speed that could be obtained when the other conditions had been fulfilled.

She was not to be a flier, but a wholesome cruiser, so that if caught in a blow she would render a good account of herself. In every respect *Vivette* satisfied my requirements. The value of carrying a considerable amount of internal ballast, after the fashion of the famous Bristol Channel pilot-boats, instead of having it all on the keel, was proved over and over again down Channel. A bulb-keeled boat would have possibly gone through some of the have been far less habitable, and at the same time far wetter.

Cruising for weeks on a small vessel like ours, with only two all told aboard, doing day and night passages along the coast, watching out for a sudden change of weather, keeping care-

GETTING UNDER WEIGH, BURNHAM-ON-CROUCH, ESSEX

ful compass courses and attending to the navigation of bays and channels, reefing and setting sail, getting up or laying out anchors, cooking and sketching or doing a hundred odd jobs whilst being tumbled about by the uncertainty of the sea, make a serious strain on the physical endurance of even the strongest and keenest of us. Every little thing, therefore, that tends to the increased comfort of the crew of a small vessel and is a saving in labour cannot be lightly dispensed with.

Although *Vivette* was surprisingly fast, yet she had a full-bodied design that materially assisted her stability, even if it somewhat retarded her speed. Only twenty-five feet over all and twenty-one feet on the water-line, she measures an extreme beam of seven and a half feet, being thus rather more than three beams to her length. Her draught of four feet three inches enables her to get a good grip on the water, yet to enter many snug little creeks which would be impossible to deeper-draught vessels. It means, too, that in bad weather a slightly more sheltered anchorage can often be obtained by going a little farther into the land, and it permits of one navigating channels, having only a fathom, with full confidence, except in very disturbed weather.

Her planking is of yellow pine, an inch and a quarter thick, while her timbers are of American elm, an inch and an inch and a half in thickness. The keel, also, is of elm, but the stem and stern-post are of English oak. She carries two tons of lead on her keel, while inside she has about another ton of ballast. Her appearance forward shows a cut-away bow with steep sides, a somewhat full-bodied midship section below the water-line with a decidedly pretty entrance, and the short elliptical counter which the intrepid M'Mullen adopted in his *Orion,* and is so frequently seen today on some of the coasters which come into the Mersey from the Irish Sea.

To have had the long, overhanging counter that one sees on some of the pretty toys of the Solent would have been utterly out of place both in a following sea (giving it an opportunity of lifting the stern up and depressing the bows) and in occasions when, pitching fore and aft in the trough of the Channel, the stern comes down with an alarming crash on to the wave. Experience has taught one that for weatherliness the so-called canoe-stern is hard to beat, but the counter is far superior in appearance. The elliptical stern, therefore, as in *Vivette*, forms a happy compromise.

To describe a vessel by her tonnage is scarcely less deceptive than it was in mediaeval times. *Vivette* is only four tons according to Thames measurement, but her accommodation below is the equivalent of many seven-tonners. She has a cabin-top which is only a few inches above the gunwale, giving four and a half feet of headroom below, and in such a way that one can sit up in comfort under the decks, a possibility that is frequently missing in craft of even larger tonnage. Below the bunks, which are on either side, there is plenty of room for stores, while as you enter down the companion at the stern large roomy cupboards face each other capable of stowing more than enough provisions for two people for over a week.

Above the cupboards are sideboards for books and navigation instruments, and higher still are racks for drinking glasses and odds and ends. Outside in the well, and underneath the seats, are the tanks for the fresh water, holding sufficient for two men for three to four days, including an adequate supply for washing. Thus, with her water and stores aboard, *Vivette*, in spite of her size, can keep the sea, totally independent of the shore, for at least three or four days, as we have proved in practice.

Before we come on deck let us point out the large locker at the extreme stern where a good forty-fathom warp and a light kedge are always in readiness for emergencies, together with a slightly shorter line for harbour work. All sorts of gear, such as a canvas sea-anchor, a spare pump in case the other should clog, tools, putty, oakum, marlin spikes, fog-horn, spare compass, and other items of her "furniture," are carried, besides spare blocks, marlin, and a host of those articles which accumulate year by year, and in spite of their uselessness become so dear to one's heart that one hesitates to throw them overboard as one ought. A large, full-sized lifebuoy is carried instead of one of those pretty little things so many small yachts have on board. It is a stupid mistake to suppose that the smaller the yacht the smaller should be the amount of buoyancy required for the support of her crew in the time of need. This buoy fixes on to the cabin hatch and keeps the chart in place, and is always ready for any serious emergency, which, I am thankful to say, we have never yet experienced. Forward, a handy little brass-domed capstan saves considerable labour in breaking out the anchor.

She carries a mainsail, topsail, staysail, and has three jibs, as well as trysail, spinnaker, and balloon staysail. The latter proved itself to be in suitable winds the most useful extra sail on board, and on many an occasion added at least a knot per hour to our speed. The mainsail is reefed with Turner's patent reefing gear, which, in spite of certain defects, is wonderfully handy; and the convenience of being able to reef down snug in a couple of minutes or less was appreciated over and over again. If the wind and sea suddenly get too much for us we stow the staysail, lashing it down so as not to blow loose again, and roll in as much of the mainsail as need be.

The two fears that one always had were, first, lest the claw-ring should rip up the sail; secondly, lest the gear should give at the gooseneck. The reefing gear adopted by the Bristol Channel pilot-cutters is excellent, both as to the way in which it is made fast to the mast, and because of the abolition of the claw-ring, the sheet being attached to the extremity of the boom. The only drawback would seem to lie in the fact that the boom must be of such a length as not to project farther aft than the counter. There is also the additional possibility of the boom breaking because of the strain being nowhere in the middle, but confined to the end; and the introduction of this gear among the Bristol pilots has in fact led to more snapped spars than was previously the case.

The compass in *Vivette* is affixed to a wooden bracket which is on the starboard bulkhead in the well. When doing a passage this bracket can be slid out into the centre, but when in port it is pushed back out of the way. Reaching not quite up to the height of the cabin-top, it is protected to some extent from spray coming aboard, whilst at the same time it is high enough to allow us to take cross-bearings clear of interruption. Except in very short, choppy seas this compass was never too lively. After swinging the ship on several points I found that the greatest deviation did not exceed a quarter of a point, which is about the same amount of error expected on a torpedo-boat.

For the most part I used admiralty large scale charts, being careful always to have all courses carefully marked out the night before sailing from an anchorage or harbour. There are times, of course, when one has to modify one's plans owing to the variation of winds and tides, but anyone who has tried to use his parallel rulers on the cabin table of a small yacht when the little ship was trying to stand first on her head, then on her tail, knows that the operation of drawing only a straight line is not easy.

The shrouds of *Vivette* are made fast by means of rigging-screws, which enable one to tighten up in a few seconds, and do not need the attention which the old-fashioned rope lanyards require. At the same time the latter have the advantage of giving a little play to the rigging, which many authorities deem expedient when the ship is being pressed; and there is the further disadvantage to be taken into account in the case of rigging-screws, that the full strain comes on to the thread instead of elsewhere. Instances are not wanting of the thread being pulled right off and the rigging becoming useless to support the mast; and I know of one serious case which occurred while racing, and unless the yacht had been put about on the other tack her mast would have gone by the board.

In order to counteract the possibility of such a catastrophe, when at length we had adjusted the rigging-screws to their proper extent we spliced on little wire lanyards, which in case of accident would have held until we were able to replace with spare rigging-screws carried ready in the boatswain's locker. Round the deck, extending from about midships, runs a wire life-line, stretched on brass stanchions. Besides adding considerably to our safety when moving about, it was most useful as affording something to lean against when sitting on deck.

From the stanchions two small brackets project, hollowed something like a rowlock, on which rest the spars not in use, such as the topsail-yard and dinghy mast. These are usually on the starboard side, while the long ash sweep is kept on the port deck. Forward two anchors are carried, whilst a lighter kedge is stowed in the after-locker.

Below in the cabin, immediately under the small companion, is the tap connecting with the water-tanks. Above the bunks canvas cots fold up, when not in use, against the side of the ship. At the forward end, on the port side, is a wardrobe, which is a great convenience for keeping dry one's shore-going clothes. Its door contains a cheval mirror, and reflects some of the light which comes through the skylight of the cabin. On the starboard side is a stove for heating the cabin in cold weather, and burns peat.

Even during the so-called summer it was not without use sometimes, and dried our damp clothes in the absence of the sun that should have appeared. Thence a sliding door gives access into the forecastle, which contains a handy kitchen table coming out from the side for cutting lip meat and for other uses connected with cooking. Opposite is room for another bunk in case of emergency, with lockers underneath for peat, &c. Right forward is the lamp locker and oil room, while below is the chain locker. All the cooking is done on a couple of primus stoves, which as long as they are kept clean do excellent service. The ship's crockery fits into racks on the starboard side of the forecastle, and shelves are suitably placed to prevent the knives and forks from rolling on to the floor.

With such an introduction to the ship and her accommodation, let us proceed on deck again as we find ourselves going down the Crouch and gradually nearing Foulness.

It was a curious, uncertain kind of weather that was hovering about. The previous day had been squally, the sky had gone as black as ink, and a thunderstorm had vanished as quickly as it had come. On the morrow we were up betimes so as to start at high water, but unfortunately a fog hung heavily and obliterated everything within a few yards. But as soon as the ebb set in came a little breeze from the east yet very faint, going round presently to the south.

We were informed that a tempest would probably follow. The wind eventually backed to the south-east, but before we had got clear of the river it had dropped, and we were becalmed off Holywell Point. By half-past ten a nice little sailing breeze came along, and we ran ahead of the yacht *Merlin*, which was bound for Gravesend; but she, setting her topsail, ultimately passed us.

Our intention was to make for the Isle of Wight by easy weekend stages, and later to the westward, having a good look round the interesting ports on the way. No paid-hand or pilot was ever employed, except once when entering a strange harbour at midnight against a strong ebb and headwind, where uncertain, baffling puffs and cross-currents usually necessitate employing either a pilot or tug: but this incident will be related in due course, and the employment of a pilot was less for navigational than for other reasons. But apart from this we went from Essex to Cornwall and back to the Solent always with a crew of two, and both amateurs.

The charts and sailing directions in common use were sufficient aid, assisted by local information occasionally picked up at various places as we went along. One of the most helpful books carried was a book of tidal streams based on the time of high water, Dover. Consequently, wherever we were along the coast we knew exactly in what direction the tide was setting us. The value of this when doing a night passage across a wide, open bay, or in a fog, will be readily apparent.

I know that there are some casual people who boast of sailing without such aids. But to neglect to avail oneself of such aids as exist is to display a conceit and foolishness which would be condemned by any true sailor. To hazard your own life and that of your ship unnecessarily is mere folly: it is neither smart nor good seamanship, and such a reputation may be remembered when the yacht's insurance is about to be renewed.

Having set a course from Holywell Point E. by N., we had passed the West Buxey Buoy by eleven, and were just able to close-haul to the Ridge Buoy. The sun burst out, *Vivette* gently heeled to the breeze that came forth from the cloudless sky, and already we were on our way to the coast where the waters are bluer, mud-banks fewer, and the atmosphere warmer. Half-an-hour later we had passed the Ridge Buoy, and overtook a hay-barge that had started ahead of us from the Crouch.

By midday we had brought the South Buxey Buoy abeam, and presently, when the South Whitaker bore due S., went about on the other tack and cut across the Whitaker Spit. We had thus carried the last of the ebb out of the Crouch into the broader Swin Channel, where the flood-tide, making to the southward, had barely begun. For a time a curious mirage hung over the water, but there was a change coming.

The wind gradually freshened as we set a course SW.½ W., and here we were in the great thoroughfare which leads to the London river. Yachts and barges, tramps, liners, full-rigged ships, and vessels of every kind were passing. We were the smallest of the fleet as we sped gaily on with a freshening breeze, and a nasty wash from a couple of steam fish-carriers racing abreast of each other for the Billingsgate market kept us busily on the *qui vive*.

We passed the Swin Lightship as she was swinging to the tide. Just beyond here the channel gives a sudden turn in a more southerly direction, and the space between the NE. Maplin and

SWIN MIDDLE LIGHTSHIP

the SW. Middle Buoys is something like going through a gateway none too wide for the amount of traffic which is always going up and down. By a quarter to two in the afternoon we were abreast of the Maplin Light—the "Sheers," as it is known among-sailing men—and were making good time with the assistance of the strong tide now under us and a nice breeze above.

After being some time at SE. the wind gradually veered to S. and presently to SW. Before we had reached the Mouse Lightship it had gone right ahead, had freshened considerably, and with wind against tide the nasty hollow sea which is so notorious at the mouth of the Thames got up. Three yachts astern of us which were apparently racing from Burnham to Southend lost no time in shortening canvas, taking in topsails and flying-jibs with some haste. The smallest of the three also stowed his staysail, and we, after carrying on for some time, had to do likewise when the spray began to come aboard in bucketfuls, to be followed by one or two "green uns."

It was annoying to have the wind head us like this after wasting so much time earlier in the day through fog and calms, but we had started out for Port Victoria, and there we were going if we could get. The landsman who looks at the map of England imagines that the Thames estuary is one vast sheet of water; so, indeed, it is, but in many places the water barely covers the treacherous, wreck-strewn banks, so that a great part of this space is unnavigable and separated into channels. In the olden days, before surveys were made and charts issued, the Thames entrance must have been a series of deathtraps to the unwary, but from the very earliest times sailors relied on their lead and line more extensively than we are accustomed nowadays, knowing at a glance with the chart in front of one exactly the amount of water below one's keel.

But in spite of the considerable width of the Swin in the vicinity of the Mouse Lightvessel it was remarkable how all the traffic within sight somehow converged to one point. The full-rigged ship that we had first seen as we came across the Whitaker, and, as long as the breeze was moderate, we had out-sailed, now came up on us: the three racing yachts and ourselves were tacking all of a bunch, while into the midst of us all came a big black steam yacht flying the white ensign. The weather looked like being a repetition of yesterday as the sky began to seem highly ominous and to take on a depressing curtain of black. Giving my mate the helm I went below and looked at the glass, finding to my discomfort that it had dropped three-tenths, so the sooner we got to our destination the better.

The day was getting on, the tide would soon be done, and the wind and sea were increasing. To be boxing about here among banks and buoys and all manner of night traffic would not be pleasant, and my friend had an important engagement in town in the morning. We ought to have reefed, but under mainsail and jib we sloshed along, and this being the first time since I bought *Vivette* that I had seen her in anything "popply," gave me the greatest confidence in her. We were doing a long leg and a short, making good tacks between the Maplins and the Kentish shores, but the sun was getting lower and lower ahead of us, and the sky was taking on a depressing look.

At last we sighted the Nore Lightship, the farthest outpost of our port. The wind coming more westerly, I thought that by standing in nearer to the Isle of Sheppey we might find easier water, but there was no appreciable difference. The *Walton Belle*, full of trippers bound for London, passed us as we were over this side, and at length with an ever-slackening tide we came abreast of the Nore and entered the beautifully buoyed channel leading into the Medway. Past the fort we went about as we got alongside H.M.S. *Dreadnought*, looking a most formidable and interesting mass of complications with her triple masts and wireless telegraph gear aloft.

Sheerness, with her warships and mammoth mooring buoys scattered all over the water, is, from a shipping point of view, scarcely less fascinating than Portsmouth; but it is no place for a small yacht with its exposed anchorage, so we were bound a little farther up the river to a little bight called somewhat magnificently Port Victoria.

We saw a small forest of masts in the direction where our resting place should be, and finding a vacant mooring went about in midstream, lowered main and ran down comfortably under jib, picking up the buoy just as the ebb was making and the ships were swinging, eleven hours out from Burnham. We could not boast of having had the conditions favourable for a quick passage, but we had got in and saved our tide literally with a margin of a few seconds. Had we been a little later and encountered both adverse tide and contrary wind outside we should at least have spent a most uncomfortable night. But as it was, exhilarated with the punch to windward, and our faces encrusted white with sea-salt, we "made good," as the Americans say, by cooking ourselves a mess of meat, and then unable to keep awake any longer hung out the riding-light, let down the cots, and tumbled into our blankets.

Vivette rolled gently as the ebb sluiced by and cradled us to sleep.

ENTRANCE TO THE MEDWAY

Chapter 2

From the Medway to Ramsgate

I heard a story once of an owner who, having left his yacht all the week at Port Victoria, came down one summer night not a little pleased to find that life afloat was free from the annoyance of insects which on land had been making themselves heard as well as felt. Coming out on deck in the cool of the evening, he turned to his man who was sitting forward smoking discontentedly.

"There don't seem to be any wasps down here, John," he remarked; "we've had a plague of them in town."

"No, sir," answered the man quietly, removing his pipe, and shifting his position, "I don't wonder at that; there ain't nothing down 'ere for the poor things to eat."

It is not unfair, in fact, to describe Port Victoria as one of the dreariest and most melancholy habitations in our country. If you sum it up by saying that it consists of a striking yacht club, a mean-looking building called an hotel, and a railway station pier, you have said everything that could be pleaded on its behalf. From the land side all around is unending and monotonous marshland, variegated here and there by a chimney or two from some brick-works or chemical factory. As the last expression of the abomination of desolation other places must be given only a second place. But with your back to the shore the picture is different: it is one continually moving panorama of shipping, both naval and mercantile.

Battleships and cruisers, destroyers and torpedo-craft, fussy little pinnaces, tugs, colliers, Medway barges with their Dutch-like hulls and sprits, come past your cabin-door in a long pageant of interest. It is one of the finest free-shows in the world, and gains rather than loses by contrast with the dull shores through which it passes. Wyllie and others have depicted this so well, that to emphasise it the more is unnecessary. I had left *Vivette* in charge of the waterman of the Royal Corinthian Yacht Club, and coming down a few days later, since the tides were not favourable for continuing our voyage, it was decided to explore the Medway, which for years I had longed to do.

There was a little black yacht astern of us slightly bigger than ourselves, and the owner hearing we had good charts for the river came aboard in the evening. This was Mr. Percy Unna, who had recently bought *Lona II.* , one of the finest little six-tonners ever seen on the east coast. We found that he was bound south also, and single-handed, so we decided to cruise in company. But there had been a possibility of *Lona* not performing the voyage with her present owner, for a few weeks earlier, while lying at her moorings in the Orwell, she had been stolen by a bargee and a navvy, and with this quaint crew was bound away: unfortunately for the culprits, however, she stuck on the mud up the Stour, where she was subsequently found, and the men arrested.

PORT VICTORIA
H.M.S. *VICTORIA AND ALBERT* ALONGSIDE THE PIER

Mr. Unna told us he was about to attend the police-court on the following Monday, and the magistrate's sentence materially delayed the voyage which had been contemplated by these two rascals to Cardiff. Fortunately, though a certain amount of damage was done to the yacht, it was not considerable.

It was while our visitor was aboard in the evening, and the three of us were chatting in the cabin, that I thought I heard shouts outside. On rushing out I found that a thick, heavy fog had dropped down over everything, and one could see but a very few yards ahead. Right alongside *Vivette* was a torpedo-boat. Her red port light glaring into my face, and the sound of the ticking of her engines below, gave me quite a shock. It was her skipper who was hailing us.

"That white light ahead, sir—is that Port Victoria Pier?"

"Good heavens, no. That's a yacht's riding-light. Better leave that well to port, or you'll be on top of the pier."

And so expressing his thanks he started his engines and disappeared again into the fog, as I heard one of his men suggesting it would be advisable to go well to starboard in order to avoid a wreck that lay just past the pier. Scarcely had we recovered from this surprise when a deep-voiced siren rose sounding up from the sea, and presently what must have been a big cruiser or battleship grunted her way slowly up with the tide. Instantly all the shipping in the Medway began to ring their fog-bells like timid creatures alarmed by the approach of a voracious monster. There were several big coal-hulks and an immense repair-ship as big as a liner out in the fairway, and there were some obsoletes lying farther up the river.

The nerve of the man who dared to navigate such a ship up the Medway, with its twists and turns, on such a night, with a spring floodtide, was admirable. Though we could see nothing, we could almost feel her going by in the blackness. We were thankful that we were snugly riding in the little bay which Port Victoria makes; but since one torpedo-boat had lost her way, we began to wonder whether we should be roused by a sudden, sickening crash against our sides, the splintering, snapping of wood, followed by the gurgling inrush of the water. With these pleasant thoughts we went to sleep, but not before several times we had paid a visit to the bows to make quite sure the riding-light was burning brightly.

By the morning all trace of fog had disappeared, and in its stead came a delightful sailing breeze, with glorious, hot sunshine. *Lona* suggested our sailing with him, so, leaving the *Vivette* at her moorings, we took advantage of the flood, set spinnaker when we were in the fairway, and had a delightful trip up to Chatham as far as Upnor Castle, admiring alike the natural beauty of the river here and the business-like activities of the naval dockyards. Catching the ebb back we tacked down Gillingham Reach, where, in Elizabethan times and later, our men-of-war used to lie moored after being built at the Deptford Royal Dockyard. Nice and quiet they would have lain here while the sixteenth-century barges that had loaded up with guns and war stores from the Tower of London, having dropped down with the tide to the entrance of the Medway, came up the river alongside the big ships and discharged their cargo.

It was a week later when I rejoined *Vivette* to take her on a stage farther. During the week the craft off Port Victoria had been joined by the arrival of His Majesty's yacht *Victoria and Albert*, which was moored just above us alongside the pier, and at ten that night the train, bringing the King and Queen, drew up alongside the yacht. High water next morning was at 5.15, and we wanted to make an early start, so as to carry the ebb down to the North Foreland. I looked out at four o'clock, when the weather seemed anything but tempting. The Royal Yacht had just hoisted her white ensign at the stern and the Royal Standard at the main, and was getting under way for Reval. She would get a bit of a dusting when she got outside, and this we learned from the papers afterwards was the case.

It was not a tempting morning to go outside, but after waiting some time *Lona* put to sea, and at 9.15 we followed also. The glass was not optimistic, and there would be plenty of wind about during the day. However, as we were anxious to get on, and the wind was NW., we set forth, although we should have only two and a quarter hours of ebb-tide with us. We carefully inspected the reefing gear to see that it was working satisfactorily, for we should have to rely on it before we got into port again; and rolling in the equivalent of one reef in the main, we hoisted No. 2 jib, slipped our moorings, tore down the Medway past Sheerness Fort, and out into the Nore. There was a goodly lop on again. The wind came down in squalls, and although the sea was in the same direction, everywhere around were white horses and nasty steep seas.

Just as we had entered Sheerness, so as we left, the sky was lurid and threatening, with anything likely to happen. But we were tearing along now, and there was to be no going back. It was a picture reminiscent of some of Turner's earlier works, with the shipping and craft, the sea pea-green where it was deeper, and the whitened crests where it ran shallow, but there was little opportunity now for such thoughts as these. We were bound down through the four-fathom channel. *Lona* had decided to go by a slightly longer route, the Prince's Channel, but he got deeper water and better seas, and though my way was the shorter, I regretted before long to have chosen this.

The Four-Fathoms Channel is rather a misnomer: it does not contain such a depth except at high water. Consequently, with most of the ebb run out, there was far less water when we began to negotiate it. At dead low water there is an average depth of about twelve feet only. This way down to the Foreland might be likened to the narrow path which leads up to a house through a back garden. It is used by trading barges, as its counterpart on land would be used by tradesmen's boys. Its boundaries are indicated by buoys of different shapes and patterns, not always easy to see, and sometimes confusing when discovered bobbing up and down among the waves.

Leaving the main channel at the Cant Buoy, we cut across the back garden, so to speak, and laying a course SE. ½ E. for the Spile Buoy, which guards the entrance to the four-fathom way, duly allowed for the direction of the tide setting us to the eastward. With the wind NW. we were now practically running free, and as soon as we got into the shallow water we began to realise pretty fully what was in store for us. The sea rolled up astern, threatening to come aboard every minute, but nothing except a little spray reached us.

With the wind right aft and the tiresome little seas it was only with some difficulty that I could keep the yacht on her course, whilst it was very necessary that we should not fail to pick up the Spile Buoy. However, we found it all right, and laying a course E. by S. ½ S. with the tide in the same direction, and therefore nothing to allow for it, we were heading for the West Middle Buoy. It was when we were distant about three-quarters of a mile that we suddenly bumped heavily, to our dismay. I looked at the chart again, and saw that we ought to be in ten feet of water at low water springs. Now as this was neaps, and there were still an hour and a half before low water, it seemed inexplicable.

We wondered if the incident were going to be repeated, but happily the suspense was not long, for we never touched again. The chart gave the bottom as mud, and the nature of the bump seemed to indicate this. Had it been of harder substance—some of the cement boulders, for instance, which a little farther on are scattered about—and had the depth shallowed just a little bit more, we should certainly have been in a serious condition, going at the pace we were. To find a reason for having touched at all, some allowance must be made of course for the scend of the sea; but, as stated already, *Vivette* draws only four and a quarter feet, and with the condition of the tide there must have been a good thirteen feet depth, or at least eight feet of water under our keel. How was it, then, that we touched? I think it was partly owing to the scend of the sea and partly to the fact that the Spile Bank, which the Admiralty chart states to be extending eastward, must also have extended slightly to the southward.

To clear the East Spaniard Shoals we had to close-haul, and so bad was the sea that I hesitated for a while whether to stand farther out and join the Prince's; but as we could sail her presently with a freer wind again I kept to the original plan, and steered SE. to allow for the tide which was now flooding.

The West Last Buoy for which we were now making was about four and a half miles distant, bearing SE. by S. I had thus allowed the extra point to counteract the flood, and this course eventually brought us within about a mile of the West Pan Sand Buoy, which resembles the West Last so closely that it is unfortunate the Admiralty do not put a St. Andrew's Cross on the top instead of merely changing the colour, for with the spray dashing over it, and the variations of the atmosphere, it is not easy to discriminate.

It was from about this point that the wind and sea conspired to joke with us right heartily. We rolled in as much as three reefs, and away we rushed with the sea swishing over us. It was in one of these moments that the glasses which I was wearing disappeared, and this happening to be the only occasion when I had omitted to bring a spare pair on board, the rest of the day's sail was one of considerable discomfort. For instance, such prominent landmarks as Reculvers Towers, which are invaluable for leading down to the buoy we were making for, were not visible to me, so I relied on the new mate who had joined me at Port Victoria to keep a smart look-out. But he, partly owing to the fact that we had not broken our fast for about six hours or more, and partly because of the tossing about of the ship, began to show signs indicative of *mal de mer*.

So I gave him the tiller, shot into the cabin for some preventative which I always carry, and dosed him, much against his will. It was effectual, however, in doing what it ought, and prevented me from being absolutely singlehanded without a pair of eyes to keep the lookout. In a few minutes he was asking for food, and so from the chaos of cushions, and books, and all sorts of ropes and gear which had joined the general confusion reigning below, some damp ship's biscuits and some very salt bloater-paste were extracted and handed out into the dripping well.

By now we had entered the narrow Horse Channel leading into the Gore Passage between the mainland and the treacherous

Margate Hook sands, on which many a vessel has come to grief. This sand dries to the extent of three and five feet at the lowest tides, and has been the scene of many a rescue from shipwreck, sad and terrible, in the winter gales. But there is on record the story of the young guardsman (which is doubtless entirely untrue), who with greater daring than knowledge had chartered a yacht and unhappily got stuck on the Margate Hook. This was espied by the Margate men as a sure and certain chance of earning salvage money, so the *Friend to All Nations* put out from the shore and was soon alongside the gallant young officer.

"What the blazes do you want?" he shouted angrily as they came on with the confidence of a pack of wolves sure of their prey.

"You're ashore where you are," they shouted back, "an' we've come to get you off. But you don't need to worry, sir," solaced the sharks; "we knows this bit of sand all right, don't we, Bill? We'll come aboard to get you off when the tide rises."

The offer, however, was not received in quite the same tone with which it was made.

"I'm not ashore, you something idiots—I've come here to play go'f. Can't I go where I like without your confounded interference? Come aboard at your peril, but . . ."

And with that the salvage job that might have been was not, while the *Friend to All Nations*, full of all uncharitableness, went back against wind and tide to Margate.

I had hoped that the wind being still NW. we might find the sea a little less turbulent under the lee of the Margate Hook, but the reverse was rather the case, for the flood was coming up against the wind. Getting an impetus through sliding over the watershed, and impelled by the wind, the seas came rolling on to our quarter in a manner quite unpleasant enough. Just astern of us came the s.s. *Koh-i-noor* and another passenger boat, rolling about quite a little bit.

As we gradually drew out of the Gore the waves became longer but the hollows deeper, and as we passed Margate and began to approach the North Foreland we had a fairly exciting time. First of all the fore-hatch, which had been carelessly left without its iron bar over it, got adrift, but we soon secured that. Then the little eight-foot *pram* dinghy towing astern, which had rushed up hills and down valleys for some time, now suddenly broke adrift, but there was far too much popple to turn back and endeavour to rescue her, and she only just cleared the starboard paddle of one of the oncoming passenger steamers that had put in to Margate and was proceeding to Ramsgate. It was a pity to have lost the boat when so near to our destination, but the wind and tide were setting in the direction of the shore, so I hoped that she would find her way to the beach, but there, perhaps, to be pounded quickly to pieces.

In order to give the shore a fairly wide berth, and get perhaps smoother water, we went nearly out to the Long Nose Buoy, and at last, with the Foreland opening out sufficiently to bear away, gibed her in a smooth, having previously rolled in the last reef, rushing on at a good pace past Broadstairs, where a couple of ketches brought-up were rolling wildly. As we approached Ramsgate we saw one of the big smack-like pleasure yachts, which had just come out of harbour, immediately run back to the shelter she had left. In order to cheat the tide we ran on past the entrance to the harbour, and then quietly tacked in, the mate, who was now recovered from his previous indisposition, being of great assistance with his local knowledge.

The usual pilots rowed out to meet us, but declining their services, we ran up the West Gully, mooring alongside *Lona*, seven hours out from Port Victoria, making an average of over five knots an hour, which, considering that we had the tide against us for most of the way, was not slow. The assistant harbour-master told us that we must have "got it a bit bad "round the Foreland, as he said the *Koh-i-noor* had arrived with her decks wet all over.

This was the day when, during the race from Harwich to Burnham of the 15-metres and 52-footers, a heavy squall struck *Ma'oona* off the Gunfleet, and her mast went by the board, and she was taken in tow by the *Lucida* and *Mariska* to Port Victoria. During the same afternoon the *Norge* had capsized near the Chapman Light, and her crew were rescued with great difficulty. The next issue of *The Daily Graphic* contained a long account of this, the first trip of the season of the *Koh-i-noor*, almost all of her passengers having been seasick and bitterly cold during the journey.

We ourselves, wet through to the skin and our teeth chattering, were not sorry to have a good hot meal and our clothes dried ashore.

Lona also, we learned, had had plenty of fun. Arriving off Ramsgate ahead of his tide, he had dropped anchor outside, where the jib had thrashed itself into such damage before it could be taken in that it had to be replaced with a new one. But his voyage had been done singlehanded, and was a thing to be proud of. I reported the loss of my dinghy to the coastguard, and indicated as nearly as possible where this had taken place, asking that the Margate coastguards might be informed.

The next morning at six the same red-faced official woke me up from my peaceful slumbers to say that we could not have lost her off a better place. She had been seen by the Foreness coastguards, and picked up two hours after the incident, and was now in their keeping. Later in the day I called on Captain Nicholson, R.N., in command of the Coastguard District, who very kindly put every facility in my way for regaining the truant.

The Foreness coastguards were rung up on the telephone, and the same afternoon I walked over and found her not only undamaged in the slightest, but without even her bailer missing. After arranging for her to be delivered by cart next day in Ramsgate Harbour, I settled the whole matter for the sum of fifteen shillings. The coastguards informed me that when they saw the dinghy separate, they thought we had purposely cut her adrift owing to the sea running.

Next morning the dinghy duly arrived on the top of a cart, and I amused myself sailing her up and down the harbour for the rest of the day. It was with no little gratification that both yacht and her satellite had come round so well, and that *Vivette*

Entrance to Ramsgate Harbour

had for the second time shown herself to be so efficient in sea-going qualities, and so easy to handle in a sea-way.

CHAPTER 3

From Ramsgate to Newhaven

The first attempt to set forth from Ramsgate was unsuccessful. Having left the yacht in the inner harbour during my absence, in company with some half-dozen others of all sizes, a few days later we solemnly processed out of the lock gates, and at the conclusion of the weekend recessed back. Only one yacht dared to venture outside, and she just escaped being smashed to pieces on the north pier by a matter of inches, with the sheet of her jib carried away and the sail flapping madly in the south-west wind, which blew hard. However, we were very snug inside, and the tedium of waiting was dispelled by the kind hospitality of the owner of the *Moretta* (18 tons cutter, R.T.Y.C.).

During the afternoon we watched the race of the 23-metre yachts, the schooner class, the 15-metre, and the old "fifty-twos" as they came past Ramsgate to Deal. Outside the Goodwins they had all the sea they cared about. It was a fine sight to see the finest of our fleet punching against wind and sea, and in the evening I counted seventeen yachts and traders brought up in the Downs, where bad weather was brewing. Two or three, including *Lucida* and *Shimna*, ran into the East Gully. The former had evidently strained herself in the tumble off the sands, judging by the appearance of her seams; but no one who saw her looking so trim and otherwise smart suspected that a few weeks later she would be lying in Ostend, damaged beyond repair and abandoned to the underwriters.

June 20 saw us up betimes and cleared out of the harbour by

8.30, four hours after high water, Dover, so as to catch the first of the west- going tide. The wind was in the very quarter we had been hoping for—north-east. With a rising glass and a nice smart breeze, under whole main, foresail, and No. 2 jib, we set a course due south to the Deal Bank Buoy, followed half-an-hour later by *Lona*. It was grand to feel one's freedom again and to be clear of Ramsgate Harbour.

The sun came out and brightened the chalk cliffs and speckled the sea. Now and again a wave of a cross sea came dancing over *Vivette's* quarter, though nothing to hurt, but a gradual sense of disinterestedness in the scenery showing itself on the part of the mate, the useful remedy was brought out, with the same wholesome effect as before.

Knowing that the tide was setting me down on to the South Foreland, where a green lightship was standing sentinel over a wreck, I stood out from the shore, half to a whole point; then I laid a course SW. by W. ½ W. to fetch Dungeness, presently altering this to a half-point farther south in order to allow for the tide setting me into Dungeness Bay. Dover was passed at 10.45, so we knew we were wasting no time. Astern of us came *Lona*, like ourselves, rolling a bit, but just before Dungeness, which we reached at 1.45, she came abreast and passed us.

It was about this time that a fleet of Rye fishing-luggers came tacking out from Dungeness Roads, the foremost boat heading on a course that I could see would bring him right across our bows. Running free, it would, of course, have been my duty to give way to him. I had calculated the gap between, so that, holding on my present course, I should clear him by several lengths, which I eventually did. Had I altered my helm, I should have had to gybe, a proceeding that I did not care about till absolutely necessary, as the ship was rolling a good deal. However, the lugger did not seem over pleased, and kindly favoured us with his opinion that "we ought to have known better."

The weather seemed to have made up its mind to be fine, but from the sky I thought we should have more wind. This came in a sudden squall in Rye Bay, in which we had to luff up speedily, but we soon got the foresail off her and reefed the main. For a few moments it was exciting, and we saw *Lona*, who had been ahead some distance to leeward, run right up on our weather and reef. But it was glorious going with the *Vivette* riding the seas now like a duck and as comfortable under snug canvas as ever man could wish.

We tore past Hastings and Bexhill at a good eight knots. Below the mate was sleeping, ahead the brown sails of *Lona* were bobbing up and down on the endless green sea, while a couple of fishing-boats at anchor, with the mizen set, were tumbling about to leeward. I sat on the weather deck, my back against the wire lifelines that run round the *Vivette*, and wondered why, when nature's pleasures were so inexpensive, we were the only two little craft running down Channel under such ideal conditions. It was a day that will live in my memory as long as ever I shall remember anything at all.

But, as if this enjoyment was likely to become monotonous, when we had cleared the Royal Sovereign Lightship, so that it was just past our beam, and with Beachy Head bearing W. by S., the waves at last became too much for the dinghy's painter, and for a second time she broke adrift. It was very annoying, as we were making an excellent passage and shortly should pick up our tide again to get us past Beachy Head; but though it hurt my feelings terribly to leave her alone, to be blown perhaps across to France, or perhaps to be stove in during the night by another vessel, yet I felt that it would be better to lose her than try to rescue her under those conditions.

So, after having carefully taken a bearing and noted the exact conditions of wind and tide, I looked round the sea astern for a sign of any other craft, and hoped that one of the fishing-boats might perhaps pick her up. But for that incident the voyage so far had been perfect. I had taken the precaution before setting out from Ramsgate to give her a strong rope and not too short, but there had been such a continuous series of jerks on the tow-rope all day, that at last it had to give somewhere near the overfalls at that spot marked on the chart as the Horse of Willingdon.

By 6.30 p.m. we had Beachy Head astern of us, and, setting the yacht on a course N.W. by W., made for Newhaven, accomplishing the last eight miles within the hour. Off Hope Point, the wind falling- lighter, we shook out all our reefs and set foresail, passing inside Newhaven piers a few minutes after *Lona*, having accomplished the seventy-three miles from Ramsgate in eleven hours, making an average of over six and a halt miles an hour. Finally, in a light air, we tacked up the harbour and berthed at No. 9 stage alongside *Lona*.

Again I sought out the coastguard, who promised to telephone to Beachy Head, who in turn telephoned along the coast eastward. We spent. the day following our arrival on the magnificent downs overlooking the sea. A perfect day, with hardly a ripple on the sea, we lay basking in the sun watching a big, white, full-rigged ship approach the land flying her national ensign, having come "from foreign." Presently a tug came snorting out and, after the usual haggling as to price, took her in tow.

A little breeze came up to help the trawlers on the horizon, a few open boats in the foreground of the picture moved to the gentle swell of the emerald-blue sea, while in the middle distance a white steam yacht, a red-sail yawl, and a tubby old tramp added new colour to the picture. Summer was here with all its glory on sea; ashore it had covered the never-ending downs with a soft carpet of purple and green. We came down from the

BEACHY HEAD AND LIGHTHOUSE

cliffs to a little white speck below that had carried us to this fair spot, and went on board to lunch.

Presently the coastguard, smart and spruce in white-topped cap and gold braid, came aboard, too, to say that Bexhill had that morning reported a fishing-smack R 77 at daybreak going east, towing a white dinghy astern answering to our description.

I suggested that the trawler, wishing to land his fish as early as possible, would not care to plug against a north-easter too long. Although a Ramsgate boat, she might put in either to Hastings or Folkestone, or even Dover, to which the coastguard agreed. Accordingly I wired to the Receiver of Wrecks for that district asking him to let me know details of the trawler; for it was significant that trawlers' dinghies are not as a rule painted white, nor do they tow them at sea, but carry them on deck. Therefore my hopes rose high until the reply came back from the Receiver of Wrecks (to whom, of course, she would have been handed over), "Know nothing of R 77 or dinghy."

Leaving the mate in charge of the yacht till I should return at the end of the week, I went up to town and informed the Insurance Company of my loss. A few days later the mate sent me the welcome information that the dinghy had been found, and was now lying at the Customs House, Shoreham. Thither I journeyed the following day, only to find that, it being the King's birthday, the building was closed; and, though I searched all Shoreham and the neighbourhood for any of the officials, the only news I could get was from a kindly old sail-maker who was stitching away close by the harbour, whose evidence gave me absolute assurance that the dinghy locked up in the Government's shed was mine. Presently we were joined by three pilots, with whom I whiled away the time discussing three-point bearing and other interesting branches of navigation. They had taken more than ordinary interest in the wayward 8-footer.

Outside in the offing lay a steamer of about 500 tons that was waiting for tide. In a few moments the pilots were putting out to her to bring her in. It was that ship, in fact, that had rescued our lost appendage, and they very kindly offered to convey a message to the skipper asking him to meet me the next morning- at the Custom House.

In the twilight the s.s. *Webb* came slowly up the harbour.

"Skipper says he'll be there at eleven," came a shout from the bridge as the ship just squeezed through the lock.

"All right! I'll be there."

I stayed the night at a delightful little inn, kept by a retired shipbuilder, overlooking the water, with a nice old bay-window that opened out on to a dozen yachts fitting out for the summer. It was just such a snug little haven as would have delighted the heart of W. W. Jacobs. While we talked in the evening I found that that terrible dinghy was one of the topics of the town. The subject was in every man and boy's mouth. How did I come to lose her? Where was I bound from? And then it all had to be told again over our whisky to those who had missed the beginning of the story. It is wonderful what possibilities lie in eight feet of pinewood. Outside the Custom House was the usual notice announcing the finding of the derelict dinghy. It all seemed far too serious for so small a matter.

The captain of the *Webb* arrived at the appointed time. He had apparently picked the boat up within an hour of our losing her. So, after agreeing to pay a sovereign claimed as salvage and a fee of two shillings to the Board of Trade, and having signed no end of official matter, we shook hands and parted. The dinghy was forthwith carried down to the water, and, having rowed up the harbour, I secured the services of two men and a boy to carry her to the railway station.

Putting her in the guard's van, we got to Newhaven at last, where I launched her into the water just astern of one of the Dieppe steam packets, and surprised the mate by rowing up alongside with the dinghy's thwarts disfigured by luggage-labels.

CHAPTER 4

From Newhaven to Hamble

The weather on the following morning looked anything but promising, and the local seafarers shook their heads ominously. The skipper of a big sailing ship reported that they had had a dirty night in the Channel. However, about eleven o'clock the sky took on a sudden change for the better, and the glass began to go up. So, since the wind was as fair as we could wish, I decided to make a start, and, setting whole main, foresail, and No. 2 jib, we had cleared the Newhaven piers by 11.25 a.m., just ahead of the Dieppe boat. With a delightful wind from the north-east we laid a course W. by S. across a sea resplendent with sparkling sunshine.

The Owers Lightship is about thirty miles from Newhaven

ENTRANCE TO NEWHAVEN HARBOUR

W. ½ S., but I had conceded the extra half-point to allow for in-draught into the bay that extends between Selsey Bill and Beachy Head, and also in order that when I picked up the Owers I might be well to the southward of it. I could not hope to carry a favourable tide any longer than about the time I should reach this point; and, knowing that the direction of the stream would be setting me then on towards the nasty shoals between the lightship and Selsey, I felt justified in keeping thus far away from the land. There was, too, the possibility that the wind might veer round to the south or southwest, for in the direction of the latter there was that curious light on the horizon that usually foretells such a change.

It was to be a delightfully comfortable sail, with a steady though light wind, and overhead a hot, scorching sun. A haze hung over the land, and eventually blotted it out. *Lona* had set out for Bembridge the previous day, so that we were alone again. We steered a steady course, and crossed a little to the south of the track of shipping between Beachy Head and the Owers. German liners, a British gunboat, colliers, tramps, and excursion steamers kept us interested all the time. Far away ahead, hull down on the horizon, I could see a topsail schooner. We found she kept steadily to our course—W. by S.—and mile by mile we got nearer and nearer until we were abreast, when she altered her course to make for the south of the Wight.

At about five o'clock we sighted the Owers on the starboard bow, bearing about NW. by W., distant five to six miles. This was just about where I had calculated to be, so we had made a good landfall. But now the wind dropped, and, with a strong spring tide against us, we only got abreast of the Owers at seven. There we remained almost stationary till nine, the wind coming and going in little puffs that barely enabled us to stem the 2½-knot tide. We rolled uncomfortably, and all the time the tide was setting us on to the lightship, so I was glad we had kept well to the south.

An Antwerp pilot schooner regarded us with extreme curiosity as he cruised about in wait for a liner. Whether we looked too small or too helpless rolling unceasingly in the swell I know not, but all the crew lined up on their weather-deck and did not take their eyes off us until we had got too far away from them.

At sunset I gave the mate the tiller and went below to fetch out the side-lights; then, having fixed them and seen they were burning all right, I kept the riding-light hung up just inside the cabin in case of an overtaking boat coming down on the top of us. Covering it over to hide the glare from the steersman's eyes, I lighted the cabin lamp and spread the admiralty chart on the table, as we should need to avoid any mistake going up Spithead, which I had never navigated before. The lightship with its red and white flashes seemed to get no farther away, but with the turn of the tide came a smart little breeze and away we went, steering NW. ½ W. to pick up the Nab.

"Two quick flashes every 45 sec," said the chart, and at the rate we were going we ought soon to see it, for it is visible for eleven miles. The wind freshened a good deal and became at times squally. The glass had fallen two-tenths and the sunset had been yellow, so, not knowing what the night had to bring forth, we handed foresail and rolled in a bit of the main as we rushed through the darkness like a mad motor, with the powerful electric light of St. Catherine's flashing to leeward. Away to the southwest we could see the long rows of a liner's lights. Then flash, flash! I looked at my compass; *Vivette* was dead on her course.

"Two flashes every 45 sec." Yes, that was the Nab. Nearer and more powerful became the lights, so I left the tiller again and went below to work out a course for Bembridge Harbour, or at least to bring us just southeast of St. Helen's Fort, where we might anchor till daylight. The tide would be ebbing out of Bembridge, which I had never seen and was indifferently charted. But the wind was blowing right into the harbour, and if the lights were showing I thought of having a shot for it. However, in the midst of these reckonings the mate sung out from the cockpit—

"White light ahead!"

I came out of the cabin and, seeing she was a pilot boat, showed the riding-light, which I kept holding up in the air and then concealing. The pilot boat saw it and burnt his flare in response.

"Pilot, ahoy-y-y!" I shouted, and we manoeuvred to get near each other. "Will you take me into Bembridge? "

"Yer can't get in just yet; tide's ebbin'!" came the reply across the waves.

So we decided to push on to Hamble, as we had originally intended. The strong tide was carrying us every moment nearer the Nab Lightship, so, putting her on the same course as before, we soon passed the Warner and Noman's Fort.

Then, steering exactly NW., we passed to leeward of a number of battleships brought up off Spithead, and about to depart for the Naval Manoeuvres. The breeze was moderate, and we should just about save our tide. Going below, I got the primus to work and brewed ourselves some hot cocoa, which was like meat and wine to our tired bodies.

Then the dawn gradually came, gentle and beautiful, over the Hampshire shore. A sweet smell of hay came floating to our

THE PILOT OFF THE NAB

nostrils with the returning light, and in the far distance right ahead gleamed the East Bramble and Calshot lights. We took in the side-lights, shook out the reef, set foresail, and overhauled a ketch. Then just as we reached the mouth of the Hamble the wind died utterly away, till at length with the first of the flood came a gentle zephyr; so we tacked up to Hamble village, lowered main, and ran down to a mooring which we picked up at six o'clock, nineteen hours out from Newhaven. We cooked breakfast, and then tumbled asleep till after midday.

The next few weeks I made Hamble my headquarters, cruising up and down the Solent, visiting Bembridge and Cowes, seeing any amount of racing, the *Indomitable*, fresh from her trip across the Atlantic, and many other fascinating sights. There is nothing like this part of the world for its interesting shipping—yachts, traders, and naval vessels of all kinds. The scenery in- land is beautiful, and I had no end of fun sailing up to Botley and back in my dinghy, or taking her out to Southampton Water to see how much she could stand with wind and tide kicking up a bit of a fuss.

But she flop-flopped through it all beautifully after the manner of her class. Then through the kindness of a friend I was enabled to experience a new sport of motor-boating. I hope and believe that nothing will ever tempt me from sailing to motoring, but I can see now what a fascinating thing it is to steer a motor-craft flying along at delightful speeds; and one day, too, we saw the famous hydroplane *Ricochette* skimming over the top of the water like a wild duck.

But at last, about the middle of August, having shipped a new mate, we turned our faces regretfully from Hamble.

CHAPTER 5

From Hamble To Poole

The Isle of Wight tides take a little understanding, but, after making a careful study of them and deducing a formula therefrom, they were soon quite rational. Taking advantage of a slack in the tide, we started out from Hamble at 10.30 a.m. with a south-east wind, light, under main, No. 1 jib, and foresail. As we cleared the Hamble Spit a big black schooner-yacht got under way, but try all we could, with a strong spring flood-tide against us and a light wind, it was not till 1.30 that we had Calshot Castle astern. The schooner did but little better; the modern flyers gradually forged ahead, but some others, seeing they were making but little headway, ran back to Southampton Water.

After passing Calshot Lightship we had a fair wind for the rest of our journey. A big German-American liner crowded with passengers and emigrants came by, making a picture of dignified beauty with her enormous freeboard and top-hamper. With a 3½-knot tide under us we soon got alone down the Solent, than on either side of which surely no scenery could be fairer, with a wealth of hills, valleys, and rich woods.

Setting a course W. by S. we flew past Yarmouth, looking very snug in its bay, and had a good look at the unfortunate *Gladiator* lying on her side—a sad, miserable object, like an enormous dead whale. In order to avoid being carried down to the Needles by the 5-knot tide, I edged over to the Hurst side with only a light wind and fitful; then, keeping my stern in line with Cliff End Fort and steering NW. by W., we raced through the North

Channel, where the tide soon lost half of its strength. But a nice little breeze came up at the right moment. Away to the south the Shingles stood dry out of the water. The passage by this channel is indeed between the devil and the deep sea, for you must not get too near the Hurst side or you become unmanageable in the strong eddy by the shore, and if you edge just a little too far the other side you get ashore on the Shingles.

Steering the N.W. by W. course till Milford Church tower, just visible in the trees, bore NNE. ½ E., I then altered the direction to W. by S., which allowed half a point for the tide, and would also bring me sufficiently east of the Christchurch Ledge Buoy to avoid the overfalls. We had passed Hurst at 3.45, and the next nine miles were done in an hour and a quarter, for we had the Christchurch Lodge Buoy abeam and nicely to leeward at five o'clock.

I have had occasion to say nothing recently concerning the dinghy. She had lately behaved herself quite nicely, and we had always towed her with a double painter attached to both of the yacht's quarters since the Beachy Head incident. But coming through the race off Hurst she must have shipped some water through the slot for the centreboard, and in Christchurch Bay I noticed she went down at the stern with her bows high up in the air. The strain on the tow ropes was very great, and; being almost awash, she was impeding our way considerably, so I hove-to and with some difficulty got her alongside and emptied most of the water out of her. Under main eased off, with foresail drawing and jib hauled a-weather, *Vivette*, in spite of being cut away considerably at the forefoot, rode hove-to without any heed being paid to the tiller, which I did not lash. This will no doubt be a great convenience some day.

With just so much wind as we could stand without having to reef, we now steered due west for Handfast Point, running dead before the wind, so that with a certain amount of rolling it was not easy to keep the ship from gybing. I had never been into Poole before, but I had met a man who had wrecked his ship just outside, and I had heard tales from others of what the entrance could be like.

But the day was beautifully fine, although there was a good deal of swell, which I under- stand always gets up here when the wind is in the east. We had carried the tide all the way from Calshot, but the ebb was still running out from Poole, so I steered a little to the north-east of Old Harry Rock, then, picking up the Bar Buoy, went straight on for the Marconi telegraph-post, entering Sand-Banks at slack water at 7.30, or six hours from Calshot, including the time hove-to in bailing out the dinghy.

As we got inside the estuary, with its puzzling channels, the leading lights were made visible, so, steering NE. by E. until nearly up to the light, I altered the course to due north, passed Parkstone Pier, and brought up in Parkstone Lake. Entering the latter at dead low water springs in the dark, we got picked up by the mud, although my admiralty chart gave the depth as eleven feet, which is obviously wrong. However, we only remained stuck for about a quarter of an hour.

Here we were made the recipients of the most generous hospitality on the part of the members of the Parkstone Sailing Club, one of the keenest and most sportive lot of yachtsmen I have met. They have a convenient clubhouse at the end of what is practically a private creek, and a useful workshop attached to the building. There is only one drawback to this sweet spot, and that is the lack of water in the lake, but the best water seemed to be about thirty yards inside in midstream.

Poole Harbour, with its wonderful mixture of Italian and Scotch scenery, fascinated me so much that I decided to remain there for the present. Such sunrises, such sunsets, such blues and greens and golden reds I have never seen. From where we were anchored in Parkstone we had the most delightful view imaginable; sandbanks and tufts of green grass to our left, Brownsea Island, with its lofty fir-trees, in front, and behind us a stretch of well-wooded hillocks, while in between was the broad estuary that carried all sorts of craft past our cabin-door.

The Parkstone Sailing Club gave me some excellent racing on board the *Babe*, which I found out later had originally come round from Essex also. Finally, as the autumn was beginning, I laid the *Vivette* up after some weeks, so that this might be a convenient starting-port for my cruise next year, when, if the Fates were kind, I wanted to continue my voyage down Channel to the attractive waters in the Falmouth neighbourhood.

It had been a splendid summer, and I had not a fault to find with *Vivette*. I had been in and out of all sorts of ports without ever a paid-hand or pilot. I had learnt much about human nature, about the sea, about its shipping. I had learnt to love my boat and her little ways, and, finally, to quote Ruskin in words to which I think most yachtsmen will add their agreement—

> *I say, without any manner of doubt, that a ship is one of the loveliest things man ever made, and one of the noblest; nor do I know any lines, out of divine work, so lovely as those of the head of a ship, or even as the sweep of the timbers of a small boat, not of a race boat, a mere floating chisel, but a broad, strong, sea boat, able to breast a wave and break it.*

Poole Fishing Boats
Going out for the night to the fishing grounds

CHAPTER 6

From Poole to Weymouth

I went down to Dorset once during the winter to have a look at *Vivette* snugly housed under her shed till the weather would tempt us afloat again. Further improvements and repairs were made to increase her efficiency, and these included such items as alterations to the rudder- and channel-plates, recaulking deck-seams, adding chocks on the port side in which the bower-anchor rests securely when not in use, while it is ready always for being thrown overboard in a hurry. A new bowsprit, was added, and, instead of the old fixed bobstay, I had it so arranged that, when at anchor or at moorings, this could be hauled up.

Lying in Parkstone Lake the previous summer, when the wind and tide were so disposed, the chafing of the cable against

LAUNCH OF *VIVETTE* AT POOLE

the bobstay was so great that I determined this improvement should be made, and most useful it was found to be, for in the new cruise it was almost always a case of riding to one's anchor instead of being tied up against a quay in harbour. New topmast stays were installed to replace the old ones, new rigging was given *Vivette* wherever any seemed doubtful, and where this was not essential it was thoroughly overhauled.

Spars were cleaned and received three coats of varnish, the ballast again painted with red oxide, the cabin varnished inside and out, the forecastle painted a nice sea-green to add a touch of colour below, while the tanks were cleaned out with lime. In order to make the decks thoroughly tight they were dressed with a preparation of red ochre and oil, which, as soon as it had properly dried, was found to be quite a success. Hitherto the decks had been varnished, but the sea water soon made them bare again. The red ochre colour, however, not only wore well, but was not unsightly, for it matched the colour of *Vivette's* sails, and saved a good deal of work in keeping the ship clean, an advantage that we appreciated many times. The hull of the ship below the water-line was scraped and covered again with anti-fouling composition, while the topsides were rubbed down, and received two coats of white paint and one of enamel, while the dinghy was also cleaned, painted, and varnished.

However, in spite of careful preparations and regard for time, *Vivette* was not ready as soon as she should have been. The winter and early spring had been characterised by a series of cold, easterly winds, which had so thoroughly dried all the craft laid up ashore as to go through them "like a chisel," as the Dorsetshire-men put it. Consequently when the yacht was first launched it was some time before she "took up," and a serious leak manifesting itself, she had to be put on the cradle again and examined. It was soon discovered that the defect came from the gar-board strake, but this was thoroughly caulked, made perfectly tight, and we arrived from town one afternoon at the end of May in time to see her going down the slipway, and take the water again for the continuation of her cruise to the westward. But even then so much had to be done in the way of stowing the ballast properly, as to get her to her right water-line, that all we had time to do was a preliminary sail down to that delightful corner of the many-armed bights and bays of the extensive Poole Harbour known as South Deep, where we anchored for the night.

We returned the next day in a miserable and incessant rain, with the weather cold and depressing. There were still several little things needing the attention of the shipwright, and these were to be seen to against our return in a fortnight. It is better to be sure than sorry, and, next to a seaworthy hull, nothing gives one so much confidence in a breeze as to know that all the gear is good and more than able to bear any reasonable strain to be put upon it.

We found plenty to interest us in the meantime looking round Poole and its shipping, and incidentally much to learn. Even when we came down again, this time to set forth in earnest, there was much to be done in getting a full assortment of all kinds of stores both for the yacht and ourselves; but at last, with lockers and water-tanks well filled, and all gear in the best condition, we dropped down again to Sou' Deep, where we rode to our anchor for another day, hoping that the westerly wind would soon go round so as to allow us a chance of going on to Devonshire.

We were very happy none the less in this quiet, out-of-the-way corner of the world, with none of the sounds of the town,

Sou' Deep, Poole Harbour

but a curious mixture of Broadland and Scotch scenery, high ranges of hills, green and wooded islands, lagoons and stray cottages on one side, but the open sea on the other, with the white cliffs of the Isle of Wight in the far distance.

During the too short time that we spent at this anchorage my new mate—the artist who has here enlivened my dull prose with his spirited sketches—and I enjoyed ourselves to the fullest human capacity. We were going to leave the world and its worries alone, we thought; we would come back here in the winter, build a little hut just above the sandy beach on one of the islets, hew down the pine trees for our fuel, fish in the water for our sustenance, or creep up and down the silent creeks after waterfowl. I went up one day and dared to land at Goathorn Pier to beg a pailful of water with which to make up the amount we had already consumed.

Here a family had lived apart from the doubtful advantages of town life for years, and the proud mother told me she would regret to have to leave what seemed to one a genuine "Peter Pan "kind of cottage among the trees in the very heart of the Never-Never Land. Then there were jolly dinghy sails among these quaint waterways, while the mate sketched and tried to catch the fleeting scenic effects which quickly come and as quickly go. There were night interests too, as, for instance, when smoking on deck, and talking in almost a whisper, we suddenly heard in the distance seaward a puffing and blowing and splashing in rhythmical rotation.

"Porpoises!"

It was a very dark, moonless night, and they were coming up at a great pace against a sluicing ebb-tide. No wonder they are able to give impudence to liners and play saucily round their bows. No wonder porpoises can do their twenty knots. On they came, passing within a few yards of us, holding straight on their course until a loud thrashing and splashing a quarter of a mile ahead told us they had got aground in the shallow water off Goathorn Pier. That was evidently the end of their evening's cruise, for they presently got off and passed again at the same distance, tearing down to the sea with the added force of the tide.

So it came that after an early breakfast we determined to go out to the sea, too. We slipped out of the narrow harbour entrance, past Old Harry, reaching right out to sea on a SSW. course till about nine miles from Handfast Point, getting a "fix" of our position by the cross bearings of Durlstone Head and the distant St. Alban's. But the tide had carried us a good way to leeward, and when we came about on the other tack and close-hauled on a course that would have cleared the outside of the St. Alban's Race and led us on for Weymouth we were making so little headway, the wind gradually headed us so persistently, and the sky began to look so threatening, that we eased our sheets and ran back again to Son' Deep.

But on June 15 we had better fortune. Leaving our anchorage at high water, we had cleared Sand-Banks at 8.30 a.m. Old Harry was abeam at 9, Peveril Ledge at 9.30, and St. Alban's Head an hour later. With a nice whole sail breeze from SE. by E., and a fair tide all the way, we were in Weymouth by 1.30, having covered the whole distance within five hours. We were told beforehand of the surprising beauties of the coast-line from Poole to our new port, and our informants had not exaggerated. Swanage tucked away in its pretty bay, Tilly Whim Caves beyond, then the few miles of rocky scenery with patches of yellow and green above on to the towering St. Alban's Head, followed by the glorious, massive cliffs which bend round in a majestic sweep gradually to form Weymouth Bay.

This was indeed a day of delight, with a powerful sunshine and a fair wind. We set the balloon staysail off Durlstone, and the wind and tide sent us "boosting along," as a Poole fisherman prophesied they would. We had been told that by keeping close into the land off the dreaded St. Alban's Head we should avoid any of the unpleasant race, but we found that to be not so, for though we were so near that we could have thrown the proverbial biscuit on to the rocks ashore, there was a very obvious tide-rip present. Not that there was anything to hurt on so calm and pleasant a day, but the roar of the water, and the curious slap-slap against the dinghy's sides, and the slight difference it made to the steering of the helm, were mildly suggestive of what this locality could be when the race was at its worst and an on-shore gale was blowing in the dark winter days.

For the benefit of the general reader who may not have had intimate experience of a race, I may be permitted to remark that this is a space of disturbed water found off various headlands, caused by the unevenness of the bottom of the sea. Many headlands have a race in a minor or less degree. Flamborough Head in Yorkshire, for instance, Orfordness in Suffolk, Hurst Point opposite the Needles, are among the milder ones, while that which is found in Pentland Firth in Scotland and off Portland Bill in England are at certain times positively dangerous. But even the less excitable tide-races can, when the wind is against tide, make themselves thoroughly objectionable to small craft.

In making the passage with a fair tide, as we did out of Poole bound to the westward, one has to bear in mind and allow for the strength of the stream off the southern arm of Swanage Bay, or one would be set on to the rocks off Peveril Point; but by day this can easily be avoided by keeping outside the black-and-white chequered buoy. Then just round the corner Anvil Point Lighthouse comes into view, looking as if it were trying hard to balance itself on tip-toe near the edge of the cliff.

From there a course of W. by N. leads you to St. Alban's Headland, on which there is not, as perhaps one would have supposed, any sort of light, but a signalling station. And so setting the yacht on a NW. by W.¾ W. course we had got round the head, and sailed gaily past Kimeridge and Warbarrow Bays, with the sea a delicious emerald-green, so clean and clear in comparison with the water off the east coast. Lulworth Cove was soon abeam, and away to the westward the haze lifted and revealed the high land on Portland, looking for all the world like a headland turned round the wrong way—facing inland instead of seaward.

We passed a few fishermen and a big yawl-rigged yacht beating the other way, but otherwise the sea was our own, and holding on our course the distant piers of Weymouth in time showed themselves; so, not having even seen the place before, we lowered staysail as we got to the entrance, and were running comfortably in under jib and main when one of the big Great Western steam packets bound for the Channel Islands was seen to be blocking up the harbour with her thick warp across, so we dodged about beyond the pier outside till she had gone, and then, following the harbourmaster's instructions, ran right up the narrowing gut and moored alongside *Donah*, an auxiliary motor yacht of about our own tonnage.

Vivette and *Donah* lying in Weymouth Harbour

CHAPTER 7

From Weymouth to Dartmouth

Weymouth is a nice old-fashioned watering-place, with plenty to look at in the harbour and a fine front alone the bay, so we spent the time pleasantly here exchanging yarns with the owner of *Donah*, doing a few odd jobs to *Vivette*, refilling her water-tanks and getting stores aboard, going for walks, and two days after we had arrived started off again. We turned out of our cots at 5.30 a.m., had breakfast, and in a heavy mist, which was soon dispersed when the sun got up, cleared the harbour mouth at 7.15 with a gentle wind a little east of north. We were hoping to reach the Bill of Portland when the tide was slack, and to creep inside between the dreaded race and the land. But unless the wind would freshen a bit this did not seem to be likely.

We ran through the spacious Portland Harbour, entering at the northern end and coming out the other side, thus saving at least a mile. It is a vast anchorage, and this morning looked bigger still, for the fleet were away at manoeuvres, and only a few odd ships remained in possession. As we passed through the sun began to warm the atmosphere, a pilot cutter was putting to sea through the eastern entrance, and a yacht was getting her sails up. As soon as we were out through the southern entrance we began to get a better draught of wind. Away over to the southeast we could hear the Shambles Light-vessel blowing her siren in the fog, but we never saw her.

By a quarter past nine, two hours after leaving Weymouth, we had made so much headway that we were at the extremity of Portland Bill, where we found the wind to be northerly and very light indeed. The tide was just slack, so we could not have hit off our time better; indeed, there were a few open boats peacefully fishing off the rocks when we passed.

But the tide would soon be making to the westward, and the race would not delay its coming long. So, with every anxiety to hurry on, we made the best of the light air, which was backing more to NW., and were just able to keep *Vivette* on her course W. by N., with presently a fair tide under us. A Thames barge, bound eastward, was doing her best to creep round the Bill before the tide got too strong, and with all her canvas up, and the wind still backing to the W. of N., she just did it. But two bigger vessels astern of her, seeing they would be too late, bore up and ran out to sea, intending to clear the race to the southward.

About the time we cleared the Bill *Donah* was leaving Weymouth under power, bound for Lyme Regis; but though we watched carefully with our glasses, we failed to see her. At 1 1.23 we took a bearing of the Bill E. by S., and now getting very dim in the mist and distance. At one o'clock the yacht we had seen getting under weigh as we passed through Portland, with a topsail up, came abreast as the wind dropped utterly and we lay becalmed. We hailed each other and found the *Mildred*, an 8-ton, transomed stern cutter, with her owner, a friend, and a couple of paid-hands on board, was, like ourselves, bound for Torquay. Our

BOUND WEST, OFF PORTLAND BILL

log was not working; it had been damaged the first day we had put to sea from Poole, and the spare part which we had wired to town for had not reached us at Weymouth as we had hoped, so our distance had to be done by guesswork and the known rate of the tide.

We estimated we had come about thirteen to fifteen miles from the Bill, and *Mildred*, who had his log out, agreed that the latter was about the correct distance. For most of two hours we were becalmed in the middle of West Bay, with occasional draughts from the westward and north- west. Sometimes we got a little puff, and then it died away again. The day was gloriously hot, but it was tantalising to be here wasting valuable time, making practically no headway, with the useful power of the tide quickly running out.

Mildred went about and stood in for the shore, but it seemed advisable to us to go farther out to sea on the chance of finding more wind, which soon showed itself to be the case, and at 3.15, unable to lie any better than N. by W., and estimating Torbay to bear about WNW., we went about on the other tack and picked up a little breeze. We had clearly done the right thing, for *Mil-*

MILDRED AND *VIVETTE* BECALMED IN WEST BAY

dred was now several miles to leeward.

By 4.30, having stood in to the land so that we could identify Golden Cape, we tacked ship again, and the wind veering so that we could comfortably lie due W., we put her on that course, and the breeze freshening gradually till it was all that we could ask for, *Vivette* heeled to it, and away we went, soon leaving our "chummy" hull-down and out of sight. We had sighted a point to the westward, which we could not identify with any certainty, but supposed it to be Hope's Nose at the northern arm of Torbay, but, as the reader will see presently, we were mistaken, being slightly to southward of the position we had imagined.

We dined very early, and found that the new arrangement of having the primus on gimballs, and swinging quite happily in spite of the angle at which the yacht was now heeling, worked splendidly. When we were about to do a passage, with the chance of not reaching port before nightfall, we usually fill the Wellbank Cooker with meat and vegetables, bring the primus and gimballs into the cabin in readiness, and, when wanted, get the stove to work, and a delicious hot dinner is ready as soon as we are. It is wonderful what amount of new life and energy a hot meal is capable of putting into one, and the pleasures of a night-passage are multiplied a thousandfold.

The brave breeze was now making up for time lost earlier in the day, and we reeled the knots off in excellent style, taking it in turns to relieve each other and go below to the feast awaiting us. An Irish stew, a little weak brandy and soda, some fruit, and a pipe—there is not much more that one wants in order to dine pleasantly, if simply, while the orchestra of the wind through the rigging, and the splashing of the waters as the ship goes through the waves, gladden the heart and mind of man. But nearer in shore, while we were congratulating ourselves, a tragedy was taking place, as we learned afterwards. In one of the little puffs that would come down on us now and again, and cause us to luff up a little, an open sailing craft two miles off Teignmouth capsized, and seven lives were lost, including two local pilots. Of course it was the old story of having made the sheet fast.

As the hour of sunset crew nearer the wind came more off shore and freshened, but the pace was most exhilarating. We passed a few of the fine, big Brixham ketches bound the opposite way: most picturesque they looked with their brown canvas and big staysails pursuing their dignified way over the dark blue waves. There was just a chance that we might save our daylight into Torquay if the wind held, and so, parodying the Gloucester fishermen in "Captains Courageous," we began to sing to ourselves—

Now Thatcher Rock comes into view,
Oh, Hope's Nose Point, and how are you?
Soon the German band we'll hear
At anchor in Torbay.

For the point we had taken for Hope's Nose was coming very near now. It was sixteen or seventeen years since I had last been in this district, and the distinguishing marks of the land were not clearly in my memory. The engraving showing the contour of the coast given at the bottom of the Admiralty chart was confusing in that it omitted to show the day-mark which leads one to the entrance of Dartmouth. Furthermore, the red sunset behind the cliffs made them take on an appearance that was all the more difficult to discriminate. But just as we had got close into the land, and I began to realise that we had overshot our course, a bright light suddenly flashed from what I had taken for Hope's Nose, followed by another flash from a light farther down to the westward.

I knew at once then that the former was Berry Head, and the latter was the Start. We had thus come about a mile beyond the western arm of Torbay. With the twilight came a further increase in the wind from about NW., and the sea became a little bit lumpy. We went about, and began to stand out to sea again, but realising that it would be a beat right into Torquay, and that we now had a strong ebb-tide, after stowing the foresail, and rolling in the equivalent of about a reef and a half in the main, I decided to run for Dartmouth, for which we should have a fair wind and a fair tide as far as the entrance. This was a sudden change of our plans, and we were not prepared for it. I had not counted on entering Dartmouth except by daylight, and intended to have taken it on the way from Torquay. Consequently one had not studied the directions in the pilot book for entering.

But it took only a few minutes to realise that we should find it impossible to get in for some hours yet. The tide would be ebbing pretty hotly, and the wind was blowing right out, and as everyone is aware who has entered Dartmouth, the currents are strong and uncertain, the wind is baffling, and the shore on either side is strewn with dangerous rocks. So on the way down we lighted the binnacle, got the side-lights burning and hung out, and the riding-light kept handy in the cabin entrance.

We knew it would be difficult to endeavour to get in, but we saw a cluster of Brixham "mumble-bees" and ketches making for the entrance, so at nine o'clock, being off Dartmouth, we resolved to follow them in, as they were probably beating in to land their fish before morning. It was fairly exciting work doing tack and tack with a crowd of these heavy craft within a few yards of us all the time. But as we followed them on we soon found that they only approached to a certain distance, and then came out again. Meanwhile the water seemed positively to be thickening: with "mumble-bees."

From out of the darkness they suddenly seemed to spring as if by magic, causing us endless bother in looking out. We had now had a chance of reading up the pilotage directions, from which we gathered that as long as we kept in the leading white light we were in the fairway. As soon as the light showed red we were too far to the starboard shore: when it turned green we were getting among the rocks on the port side of the entrance. In the midst of all this one of the "mumble-bees" came unpleasantly close to us, and addressed us in rich, sonorous Devonshire accent—

"What the something, something did we want?"

We made answer that we were following them in to the harbour.

Another wave of language flowed over from the big black

object to our little, white craft so many feet below. A few moments and we were positively surrounded by "mumble-bees" and ketches. It took us some minutes to realise what was happening, but from both sides they came romping along, most of them with no lights showing. This was becoming interesting. I decided to put out to sea again, and then to alter my course and run for Torbay. Just then a big fellow came ranging up on our starboard side, hanging out his side-lights as he advanced. I suggested to the mate that it would be well to make sure that both ours were burning brightly. He went forward to look.

The starboard one had gone out.

We soon got it to work, however, and stood away from the land, and then keeping just inside a line formed by the lights of Berry Head and Start Point, were able to keep parallel with the shore. We should get into Torquay, even though we should have to beat across the bay, sometime before breakfast time. Then if we got tired of beating we could run back, and make the entrance to Dartmouth in daylight with a flood- tide. But astern of us came the "mumble-bee." He could not manoeuvre so quickly as we, but he footed it faster when he got going. A fine selection of anathemas in advance told us who it was, though the night was very dark, and the cliffs increased the intensity of the blackness. In the first encounter, when we realised that they were going to smash us up if they could, it occurred to me to try a little bluff.

"We've got your number, old skipper; you'll be reported in the morning sure enough."

It was a lie obviously, for we couldn't have read his number nor his name in that lack of light.

But the remark served as fuel to the flames, though the reason was not discovered till afterwards. But now he was clearly determined to stick to us and prevent us getting away. He was to seaward of us, and we were becoming hemmed in far too near to the shore. The Mewstone scarcely showed up against the darkness, and there were other islets and rocks to watch for. Suddenly from the sea a big west-country ketch came in sight.

"What the something, something —?"

The "mumble-bee" shouted across to him, and the bigger vessel altered her course and came dead on for us, handing us a few oaths as we luffed quickly and he shot under our stern, barely clearing the dinghy. We took counsel together, my mate and I. To continue as we were was to pursue an unequal contest. At the very least we should have our dinghy smashed, and very probably the *Vivette* holed and sunk.

We had made enemies—for what reason we knew not—and being in the midst of a hostile fleet, very tired after our fifty-mile run and little sleep the night before, we felt the only thing was to capitulate and make the best terms we could. To keep this chase up all night, along a rocky treacherous coast, every inch and short cut of which were known to these local men, was not welcome, even though delightfully mediaeval in the nature of the sport. Perhaps these were the descendants of the crews of some of the ships that gave the Spanish Armada their whacking, and the same fighting spirit was evidently very much alive.

So we hove-to under the land and parlied.

"' Mumble-bee' ahoy. . . ."

"What d'ye want?"

"What's this game you're playing at?"

"Game . . . ?" Then a splutter of oaths.

"How much longer are you going to ...? Look here, we want a pilot . . . take us into Dartmouth . . . how much?"

There was a sound of subdued murmurings as one of the men walked aft. Then the same deep voice echoed back—

"Take yer in . . . ten bob."

"Give you seven -and-six," was *Vivette*s reply.

The enemy refused to accept our suggestion, so thinking that hostilities would be renewed, we closed with the offer.

"Got a dinghy?" asked the "mumble-bee."

"Yes; but it won't carry you tonight."

No more it would. There was enough motion to make it inadvisable to row about in a little eight-foot *pram* with a great, hefty seaman clambering in her from a heavy trawler, and he might have upset both of us, accustomed only to the heavier, deeper, beamier rowing-boat. So they launched theirs overboard, and soon from the black waves the dark object carrying two men shot out and bumped heavily alongside us. Two pairs of great strong hands gripped *Vivette*s gunwale as their owners stood up in the rowing-boat.

"You said ten bob?" emphasised the familiar voice.

"Ten bob it is—come aboard."

And shouting instructions to the disappearing boat, he stumbled into the well and took the tiller as we made for the harbour entrance again. In the cabin a light was burning dimly—turned low to avoid inconvenience in steering—and the doors were just pulled-to. The pilot had scarcely been aboard when he pushed open the doors and looked in.

"Oh," he said cheerfully, as he withdrew his head, "I see it's all right. We thought you'd got a 'bogey-man' aboard."

We laughed faintly, not understanding the joke.

In the meantime we had begun tacking again off the entrance to the harbour. The stray "mumble-bees" and ketches collected together as they had done before, and came on over the waves like so many black monsters, with red and green eyes gleaming to port and starboard. The oaths began to be hurled at us again, but the pilot shouted back in a similar strain. Then—

"It's all right-t-t-t," he bellowed across to them.

"What's yer name?"

He gave it.

"What's the name of the yacht?"

"Don't answer," I whispered in his ear. He remained silent.

A few more hails from other trawlers, and at length, satisfied as to the identity of their pal, they gradually began to sheer away, and going about their business, left us in peace.

"It's all right, I tell you," he shouted over the side again as we passed the last. "It's all right. I've stole a shirt off the pilot," he remarked gleefully. Then turning to me, "Us fellows 'asn't no right to take you into Dartmouth."

"Oh," I answered. "Then why did you come aboard?"

"We can't take you no farther than the Range; besides, the

ebb won't be done for an hour or two.... Can y' see the buoy yet?"

I went forward and kept a keen lookout, but none of us saw it till we had passed, so dark was it under the high cliffs. We dodged backwards and forwards stemming the tide and making headway slowly, the Brixham man taking us well in- side both the red and green lights, but to him every bit of the entrance was as an open book: he could almost smell the rocks in the night. And so at eleven o'clock we let go anchor off the Pin Rock in about five fathoms, a little distance below where the Pilots' Moorings are marked on the chart, and just inside the red light, so out of the fairway, but sufficiently exposed as to be able to see the Start Light blinking away to the west down the coast. I settled up with the pilot, who seemed anxious to disclaim all knowledge of the first encounter; but his voice betrayed him.

Furthermore, he did protest too much. In point of fact I had been able to discern neither the number nor the name of his ship—though they carry each of these marks of identification—and to ask him bluntly was fruitless. But I was determined to find out none the less; so, taking a roundabout route, beginning by talking generally about the fishing-fleets of the west-country, then coming down to praise the fine ships sailing out of Brixham, narrowing the subject still more to the "mumble-bees," getting him to talk about their build and rig, and so on, I got him off his guard once, and before he had time to realise it he had told me the name of his ship.

I didn't get the number, and he quickly saw that he had already said too much, but it was all that I wanted to know for future remembrance. His own vessel had followed us behind into the Range, and she sent her boat off for him. We gave him a drink before he went over the side again, and one to the younger man in the boat, and away they went back to resume their night's fishing.

Left to ourselves once more, and seeing that the anchor was holding well, though with wind against tide, as soon as the flood made we should certainly sweep round somewhat, we went below and made some good strong cocoa, after which neither of us could keep awake. But with slack water at 3 a.m., and the night nearly ending, we broke out the anchor and sailed in through the high land, between the two picturesque castles, keeping well in the white light of the fairway, and brought up off Kingswear in a little under three fathoms. As we wished to remain here some time we laid out a kedge, so that she was securely moored in case it blew during the next few days. At 5.30, having been out of bed for twenty-four hours exactly, we turned in, and slept peacefully till one o'clock, glad to have crossed West Hay and to have got so far into Devonshire.

Chapter 8

From Dartmouth To Salcombe

The joy of being back again in Devonshire after so many years, and the opportunities afforded of revisiting the nooks and corners so dear to one's youth—the coves where one used to bathe, the shop where one used to buy cream and fruit—made one in no hurry to get away from this landlocked harbour. There was so much to see, re-see, and to think about; we were so hospitably entertained, so fascinated with the contents of the harbour, that we had barely time to get in all that we wished in one week. It was well, too, that we had arrived in a sheltered haven, for the weather broke again, and for several days it blew very hard, and out in the Channel we learned that there was more sea and wind than we wanted. Even the Brixham trawlers went about their work with a couple of reefs tucked in, and

Entrance to Dartmouth Harbour

these dreadnought men aren't exactly wind-shy. But of course they carried their topsails over reefed main: they say it steadies the gaff in a seaway. The complaint of these men is usually that there is not wind enough for them, and it would have to be a very strong gale that saw them douse topsail because of the wind. Those who have ever seen the Brixham men racing round Torbay in a breeze during the annual regatta realise something of their capabilities.

But before the weather got lively we were joined by several other small craft. The *Mooween*, whose owner I had met the previous year at Hamble, came slowly up the harbour after making a long passage from Poole to Dartmouth, including all night. She was followed presently by the *Lady Moll*, who was cruising in company, but had been down to the Start and boxed about uncomfortably in a fog before coming in to Dartmouth. *Mooween* was slightly bigger than *Lady Moll*, and had shipped a paid-hand for this cruise. *Lady Moll* was a little bigger than *Vivette*, being sailed in a most sportive way by her owner and his wife, who set but little account on all-night passages and other minor details of endurance.

Mooween was a sloop, built by Luke of Hamble, with a transom stern, and exceptionally comfortable accommodation for her size. *Lady Moll* was also sloop-rigged, having been designed by Linton Hope, with a plentiful amount of headroom, afforded by means of a curving cabin-top. At first sight she seemed to be far more suitable for Solent cruising, but her ample freeboard and her sea-keeping qualities proved her to be more than a pretty toy.

About the same time arrived also the *Joybird*, a little 6-ton yawl, also cruising with only owner and "owneress" on board. So, forming ourselves into a sort of mutual admiration society, we spent the time very pleasantly visiting each other's yachts, exchanging yachting lies, learning a new idea here, a novel gadget there, and generally confounding the cold, miserable weather which had set in. Although it was the month of June, and we were so far to the south of England, we were not sorry to have the enjoyment of our peat-stove burning away in the cabin at night.

With this little fleet had arrived also the *Iris*, an 100-ton trading ketch, who had come out of Poole with *Mooween* and *Lady Moll*, bound for Plymouth. She had brought up astern of us, but far too near to be pleasant, and more than once, at the turn of the tide, we had to get out from our cots and do some fending off. She carried a skipper, mate, and boy, all of them having taken a keen sporting interest in their race with *Mooween* and *Lady Moll*, from whom the Iris had become separated during the night. They yarned about the Teignmouth disaster, and knew the pilot who had charge of the sunken boat. Weather-bound, like all of us, they busied themselves all the time, and had scraped and varnished mast and topmast, and done a good deal of other work before putting to sea again.

One day, whilst lunching with one of the Harbour Commissioners, and a keen yachtsman, we were relating the experience we had enjoyed off the entrance to Dartmouth, and inquired what the local definition of a "bogey-man" was. In the next few minutes we soon understood why we had been treated by the Brixham trawlers in so curious a manner. It appears that the fishing industry had been getting worse and worse, so, contrary to all regulations forbidding trawling within a line drawn from outside Dartmouth to the Start, the practice had begun of pursuing their industry where we had first discovered them just off the harbour entrance.

Warnings having been disregarded, and fines having been levied without any abatement of the wrongdoing, it was made clear that the next offence would be punished by confiscation of nets and gear. The inspecting official charged with the duty of keeping an eye on delinquents had recently been compelled to go out in a powerful, sea-going tug. But he had been recognised, the "mumble-bees" in their anger had charged straight down on to the powerful tug, and, with their mighty bowsprits, had succeeded in knocking in two of the steel plates, so that the steam vessel had to hurry back to port, and her owners declined to charter her again for a similar purpose. On another occasion the inspector was compelled to beat a very hasty retreat, and it was only by good luck and the condition of the tide that he was able to run his craft in between one of the islands and the land, where the trawler could not follow, that he got back safely. Consequently all sorts of unsuspicious-looking craft had to be employed to outwit the men of Brixham. Another friend of ours, who was peacefully fishing from a motor-boat, was similarly taken for a "bogey-man," and only with difficulty succeeded in convincing the trawlers of his identity.

Knowing not a word of any of these internal troubles, *Vivette* had arrived on the scene that night, and, seeing us dodging about the harbour mouth, where they were illegally trawling, then finding we were standing off and on, whilst we were really waiting for the tide to ease, they had made sure we were none other than the "bogey- man" himself, this time out in the disguise of a yacht, and, in the opinion of myself and mate, confirmed by those to whom we related the incident at Dartmouth, there can be no doubt but that, unless we had hove-to when we did, one of those heavy bowsprits, with ample weight and impetus behind it, was meant to crash through *Vivette* and send us to the bottom.

Having discovered their mistake when too late it would have been easy enough to explain that it was an accident, or that the yacht was in the wrong. Even if we ourselves should have been picked up, would the evidence of the sworn enemies of the "bogey-man" have been on our side? I doubt not. A week or two later one of these trawlers did crash into a big yacht lying anchored off Torquay. It was night, and although the yacht's riding-light was burning brightly and the weather clear, the skipper got confused, cut the yacht down to the water, and only by a miracle of good luck were the owner and his lady got out before the lighter vessel sank to the bottom.

Feeling energetic one day after arriving in Dartmouth I took a delightful walk alone: the coast to Brixham, so timing my arrival as to watch the fishing-fleet getting under weigh in the evening; but some of the ships had just gone round the breakwater, and I could not with any certainty recognise our friend off the "mumble-bee," though I did identify the big ketch that had so closely shaved our stern, for I had noticed a patch in his mizzen of material lighter than the tanned canvas, and there he was this afternoon with sails up, riding to his moorings, curtseying so gently to the swell as if incapable of doing one pennyworth of harm to "bogey-man" or yachtsman alike.

There were enjoyable little voyages, too, in the dinghy, sailing up to Dittisham, and enjoying the famous Devonshire doughnuts and cream, being not a little amused at the seamanship displayed by the cadets from the *Britannia* as they heroically endeavoured to make the prehistoric sailing-boats with which they are still supplied go against wind and tide. But Dartmouth is full

H.M.S. Brittania in the Dart

of interesting obsoletes of all sorts. Apart from the old *Britannia*, there are some fine old hulks, now used for storing coal, but at one time they sailed the seas as gallant clippers, East Indiamen, still picturesque even though covered with coal-dust.

Here, too, somewhere in the stream must have lain the famous old carack, *Madre de Dios*, which readers of Hakluyt will remember was captured by Ralegh's men and brought into Dartmouth. So immense was she that she drew nearly as much as the modern *Mauritania*, but had been so lightened of her rich contents that on running in between the two old castles which guard the Dart she drew only twenty-six feet. Still, this was a big enough draught for a 1 600-ton ship.

"*By which perfect commensuration of the parts*," concludes Hakluyt, "*appeareth the hugenesse of the whole, farre beyond the mould of the biggest shipping used among us either for warre or receit.*"

As we swung to our anchor we used to think many times of the scenes when the great Elizabethan sailors must have attracted the whole population of Dartmouth to the water's side to speed them on their exciting journeys, or to welcome them back with the bells from the old church ringing, streamers flying, men cheering, and women dancing for joy as the big clumsy old ships came carefully in through the narrow entrance towering on either side with rocks and high trees. We walked out to the old castle of St. Petrox, and looked down. But the old high-pooped ship of the sixteenth century was vivid in one's imagination, even if, instead, a smart modern yawl with overhanging bow and stern was coming up the same fairway in which the *Madre de Dios* and thousands of other bluff-bowed ships had pushed their way through the water into the Dart.

We made the acquaintance of the owners of the *Gipsy*, a fine old Fife yacht, now used as a houseboat for summer and winter alike. Sometimes in the winter ships who lay where the *Iris* was brought up showed their respect for a Fife ship by breaking away from their anchors and crashing into the houseboat, to the consternation of its inhabitants.

One of these happened to be a trader, weather-bound, on

The *Madre de Dois* coming into Dartmouth

which the principles of economical living must surely have been carried out with a brilliance rarely found on shore.

"Yus," related the old skipper as he yarned away to the *Gipsies*, "'tain't no sort of weather this. 'Ere we are, me and my mate's been out a fortnight, and it's cost the two of us a big hole in ten bob for grub alone."

It isn't often you can boast of having entered a lady's drawing-room in ancient clothes and heavy sea-boots, but the weather was boisterous, the dinghy full of water, and our host and hostess most charitably gave us a plenary dispensation and the kindliest Devonshire welcome.

Three of the Bristol Channel pilot cutters came in while we were in Dartmouth, and showed how easily they could be handled in a crowded anchorage. We rowed round them admiring their gear, and the mate, making friends with one of them, was asked on board. No yachting-trip this kind of work can be in the winter, when two men race out in each ship round Land's End keen to be the first to get the job of piloting a big steamer into port.

Only two men, and one of them gets the dinghy overboard and rows off to the big liner, clambers in, kicks the dinghy off from the great steel side, leaving the other man to come down presently, heave-to and get the dinghy on board again. Then, literally single-handed, the man that is left sails his ship back day and night to his harbour. No wonder the lead of the ropes

HOUSE-BOAT *GIPSY* WITH *STELLA MARIS* IN FOREGROUND

is made as handy as possible and the value of the Appledore reefing-gear is appreciated.

Presently there was a general consultation between the skippers of the three ships as two of them rowed off to the third. A short delay, and they rowed back hurriedly. The cables were shortened in, up went the mainsails and head-sails, the anchors were broken out, and away they went out into the Channel, but I noticed they did not omit to roll in a reef or two, and the Bristol pilots can stand wind.

But Dartmouth seemed to attract to its shelter all kinds of ships and men. A venerable bishop was seen at the helm of a fast motor-boat, daily besporting himself off the harbour mouth; surely an extraordinary combination of the old and the new. There were steamers of all sizes continually coming in from the sea to take aboard enough coal to carry them on to the end of their journey.

One vessel blew his siren for most of the night as it seemed, but no one came out to pilot him in, although, as we learned, he would have to pay just the same, for Dartmouth is a compulsory pilotage port. By night the whole haven would be illuminated by the flashing searchlight from some millionaire's steam-yacht, producing a weird effect as the beams mounted the tops of the trees on the high hills which look down to the harbour from

BRISTOL CHANNEL PILOT-CUTTER
IN DARTMOUTH WITH SCHOONER YACHT *ORELIA* TO THE RIGHT OF THE PICTURE. INSET SHOWS THE PILOT-CUTTER'S ROLLER BOOM REEFING GEER

either side.

We remained here till after the King's birthday, and then, feeling that we ought to get on to our goal, made preparations to start. The steamer which is fitted up as a fresh-water supplier came alongside and filled our tanks with his hose. We had eaten more of the Devonshire cream and cakes than perhaps was good for us, and as soon as the weather looked finer we were ready to get under weigh. We saw the *Orelia*, a big schooner-yacht with auxiliary motor engines, clear from the harbour, but she soon came back, and her skipper told me there was a nasty sea off the Start. But at length we set forth, leaving at ten minutes to one in the afternoon with the turn of the tide.

By one o'clock we had cleared St. Petrox Castle, where, as usual, the wind was fluky. But the Range always has been a nuisance to sailing men. One moment you are becalmed, the next minute a nasty gust comes down from the hills and buries your lee-rail. We were more lucky, however, than one of the ships which set forth in the autumn of 1594 bound for Brazil.

"*Being fully furnished,*" says the chronicler in Hakluyt, "*with all needfull provision, wee departed from Blackwall in October following, keeping our owne coast untill we came into the West countrey, where we met with such gusts and stormes, that the*

A SNUG CREEK OUT OF THE DART

Salomon, spending her mast at the Range of Dartmouth, put into harbour."

But there must have been something very weak in the *Salomon's* rigging, for although

by the earnest care and industry of the generall and others having charge she was shortly againe provided" and put to sea, yet it was not lonor before "the Salomon was returned for England: inforced so to doe, by spending her mast the second time.

As soon as we were outside we found the wind to be about NW. by W., so that as our course was SW. down Start Bay; inside the Skerries we could lay it easily. It was a curious sort of day. The weather seemed uncertain what to do, and occasionally the strength of the puffs from off the land came down on us with some weight in them. We flew along past Slapton Sands, off which we found it advisable to roll in part of the main and stow the foresail, and when the Start Lighthouse bore SW., distant about a quarter of a mile, we steered due S. so as to cut in between the Skerries and the Start Point. We stood right out from the land, having so timed it as to arrive here when the race was slack and the tide just making to the westward. When we had found ourselves well clear of the Start Rocks, nasty jagged pinnacles standing up out of the sea, we opened Prawl Point, but the wind soon headed us, and we could only do a long leg and a short.

The scenery of this coast is rugged and impressive in its lofty grandeur. The pinnacled formation of the land at the extremity of the Start looks most curious silhouetted against the sky, so unreal, in fact, as to seem to have been carved out of cardboard like artificial stage scenery. On the other hand, the general effect conveyed by this Devonshire and Cornish coast is one of extreme awe. Cruel and rockbound, its apparent inhospitable aspect is in wonderful contrast with the characters of the people who live in those delightful little bays and sea-side villages sheltered beneath the hills above. One of the disadvantages of cruising is that one sees so much in an impressionistic kind of way, the imagination is so keenly fired, that one regrets not to have the opportunity and time to linger longer. I have heard yachtsmen bewail the fact that so few chances were offered them of going inland or roaming along the coast. Whenever we were in a snug harbour we used to set out for long walks whenever practicable and scour round the country, but it only whetted our appetite and formed a mental resolve to run down for a few days in the winter or early spring before the yacht was fitted out. But time and resolutions pass on, and somehow these land cruises never seem to come off.

We had thought, when we emerged from Dartmouth, to keep going till we got to Plymouth, but the tide turning against us, and the weather not being too settled, we decided to run into Salcombe. So after tacking into the bay, keeping well over to the western side, we espied an interesting and striking craft brought up outside the bar. She was ketch-rigged, but her sails were a different colour from last year when I had seen and admired this yacht in the Hamble.

We soon saw through the glasses that it was the *Maud*, an 18-ton ketch, well known to sailing men on the south coast as one of the healthiest and ablest types of cruisers; or rather, not a type but an individual, for, with her canoe-stern and her significant characteristics, *Maud* is unique. They tell you that she was built for two men who intended originally to sail round the world alone, but that having left the Clyde and arrived at the Isle of Man there was some mutual misunderstanding, and the partnership was dissolved. I know not whether this is the true story: possibly it is not. But I have heard professional seamen often say in remarking her sea-going qualities, that they would easily trust her in any sea. Yet it surprised us to see *Maud* brought up off Salcombe, when we had supposed she was racing against *Jamie* from the Hamble to Queenstown, and had been discussing almost daily her chances in so sporting a match.

I held been into Salcombe once as a boy, but that was on an excursion steamer, so the experience was valueless from a navigating point of view. With the assistance of the chart and the sailing directions, however, we got in with ease and confidence, using the lead and line now and again in the shallowest parts when we were near the bar.

We hailed *Maud* when abreast and inquired about the result of the race, but could not gather why it was apparently cancelled. In reply they asked us about the depth of water, and, as mentioned, not having taken a craft in here before, we replied with confidence! But the young flood was making, and keeping a cross- shaped beacon in line over a black-and-white patch painted on a stone wall many feet below, in a N. by E. direction, we soon negotiated all difficulties.

As it is easy enough to write this statement, but far more difficult to identify these two marks when entering for the first time, it has been thought well to reproduce them here exactly as they appear from the sea on this bearing; and the cross-shaped beacon, being not easy to locate because not knowing what its appearance is likely to be, has been here also given on a somewhat larger scale in a corner of the sketch. Perhaps these small but essential points usually omitted from charts and pilot books may be of some service to the reader entering here for the first time.

We sailed quietly past the ruined Salcombe Castle, leaving the red buoy that warns you off the Wolf Rock to starboard, and let go our anchor off the town, with *Mooween* and *Lady Moll* for

ENTRANCE TO SALCOMBE HARBOUR, SHOWING LEADING MARKS IN LINE.
INSET SHOWS THE CROSS-SHAPED BEACON

our neighbours.

All that has been said in praise of the beauties of Salcombe is not one whit too much. Its fine natural harbour, its green hills on either side, its deep, clear water enabling you to see right to the bottom, its bluey-brown rocks and pretty gardens coming down to the water's edge, its sandy bathing coves and little fishing craft, are all separate jewels of different kinds that form the whole crown of beauty which enriches this bit of Devon. Ashore, the old-fashioned streets, and inns, and people, and the well-wooded ravines, the musical accent of the Devonians, have an effect that is always soothing to the nerves of the town-bred being. We were very happy as we swung to our anchor, with the local stone pier in easy dinghy distance for fetching supplies.

The food was cheap and good, the air was balmy, and, what is more practical to the sailor-man, the bottom of the harbour was good holding-ground. So we were altogether quite content here, and loath to depart. But two days after we had come the glass began to rise steadily, the sun at last came out in earnest again, and the weather was looking quite summer-like, so some time after *Mooween* and *Lady Moll* had started we decided to cancel a day's dinghy sailing and get farther west while we had a chance. We should perhaps return here again: at any rate we hoped to. So the cable was shortened in, the main was peaked well up, the anchor broken out again, the jib hoisted, and away we went down the harbour.

CHAPTER 9

From Salcombe to Plymouth Sound

We had cleared Salcombe Bar by a quarter to three in the afternoon, and with the wind at south-west made short tacks inshore so as to keep out of the east-going tide. But a big black yawl-yacht, which had come out most of an hour ahead of us, stood right out to sea before going about, and being right out in a foul tide, he made little headway in the light wind. Off this portion of the coast there is usually a biggish swell, and when the wind is strong and against tide it is no pleasant place for small craft. As we had entered we had experienced a little of it, and other small fry that had put out the same day bound west we learned had soon put back.

But today only the pleasantest little waves were about, and if we could have coaxed out a little more wind we should have indeed been happy. Those northeast winds that ought in any normal summer to have favoured us were singularly absent this cruise. We had not really had a consistently fair wind since the sail from Poole to Weymouth, and now the prospects of making a quick passage were not many.

Bolt Head, guarding the entrance to Salcombe, was a wonderful sight, rising majestically into the blue sky. I had set off the previous day late in the afternoon to walk round, finding the distance much greater and more circuitous than appeared at first. The narrow bridle-path which skirts round the rocks with a sheer drop of several hundreds of feet below gave one no feeling of security, hopping over slippery stones, with a few flocks of sheep grazing behind and a startled rabbit darting out among the heather. Then the sun had gone down a glorious red, and I had been able to trace the outline of the land from this height far away into Cornwall, almost to the Lizard.

A nice breeze had sprung up from the west, and a small yacht under the cliffs was hurrying on before it, rolling her boom so much as to be in danger of gybing every moment. It must be a bleak walk for the coastguards along here in the snowy weather. Not a soul was about, and the only sounds were those of the sea hollowing out the rocks below, and the occasional bleating of the sheep. Twilight came, and out of the midst of the sea a flash sparkled, revealing Eddystone Lighthouse in the middle distance.

There was a little hut at the edge of the cliff, evidently for the coastguards, connected up with telephone wires, but there was no one there at present. To find one's way inland again was not easy, but the night was gloriously warm, and the ten mile walk through Devonshire lanes was well rewarded. Past the Bolt Head wireless telegraph station, only recently opened for transmitting messages to liners going up and down Channel, on through Marlborough to the hills overlooking Salcombe Harbour, the road looked down on to a delicious nocturne whose principal colouring was composed of the little yellow riding-lights against the deep, dark blue of the atmosphere and the water, with the loom of the cliffs and hills enframing it—a real bit of Whistleresque nature.

Dinner was very late that night, for the walk had taken longer than one had intended. In the little dark passage leading down to the stone pier a six-foot figure wearing a typical east-coast tanned jumper hove into sight under the yellow gaslight. It was the anxious mate of the *Vivette*, who had feared the worst, but a little sprig of white heather gathered along the cliffs, and a luminous glow-worm captured in the country lane, were the evidential trophies of the hunt, and, as the mate agreed, the glow-worm would come in handy on a night-passage for lighting the binnacle!

Whilst we were in Dartmouth the spare part of the log had been forwarded on, so that now, being in working order, we put it over the side when off the flagstaff east of Mill Bay. This was at 3.45 p.m., the log registering 40.7 knots. We found this little contrivance very useful before the cruise was over. Smaller than those usually supplied to yachts, it consists simply of a dial which hooks on to one of the projecting arms of the stanchions to support the life-line. The dial resembles that of a cyclometer, but being marked to register knots and fractions of a knot. From this extends your log-line, which trails out well astern of the dinghy, the end being in the shape of a propeller-like fan. The passage of the yacht towing this through the water obviously causes the fan to revolve, and so the line attached to the dial, the connection here being made by means of a small cog-wheel.

Half-an-hour later we saw that we were not doing more than four knots an hour through the water, but we were slipping away from the black yawl, and at least two or three miles ahead of her. At 4.20 the wind freshened very slightly, our course being NW. to avoid the Mewstone to starboard. Ten minutes later the tide had turned in our favour, as we knew from the floats of the crab or lobster pots, and by 4.45 the Bolt Tail Coastguard flagstaff was abeam.

And so we went slowly on for another hour, when, just as it had happened in West Bay, the wind went round to NW., so we had to tack. The entry in the log-book here is, "Ship heading SW. by W. Log reads 47.4." It was slow work, for, twenty minutes later, we had only added another knot and a half on the other tack, and the actual distance made good was of course considerably less. Something interesting from a naval point of view, however, was happening in Bigbury Bay as we passed, but what exactly it was we could not discover.

All that we saw was this: a steamer, probably from her appearance having some connection with the Admiralty, hove-to as a smaller steamer, looking more like a steam-trawler, came out

READING THE LOG

from the direction of Plymouth to meet her. A boat was lowered and rowed off to the latter, and presently came back to the Admiralty ship, while the trawler immediately got under weigh again and stood out to sea in roughly a SE. direction, while the other vessel remained as she was. The smaller craft seemed to be making for a spot on the horizon which might have been a battleship, and after a time the Admiralty vessel went off in the same direction also. We concluded that it might have had something to do with the naval manoeuvres.

The signal which the Government ship had made in the first instance was a black and yellow flag. The incident was so interesting that we were not a little curious to know its meaning.

It is not necessary to weary the reader with the dull, slow progress made during the next few hours, tacking in the lightest of winds, and making precious little headway. As the night came on we stood farther out to sea, so as not to get picked up by any of the islets off Yealm Head. At 10.15 p.m. we took a bearing of the light on the west end of Plymouth Breakwater and of the Eddystone Lighthouse, which fixed our position as being about six and a half knots from the latter, which bore a little to the N. of E. Quarter of an hour later we tacked ship again, and stood in for the shore on a NE. by E. course; but seeing a big liner coming along the land and heading for us, we went about again, and tacked seawards once more.

We learned afterwards that this was the big German-American *Kaiser Wilhelm der Grosse*, which had just come out of Plymouth bound on her eastward journey. With her big black hull, studded with innumerable white lights from her port-holes, she made a most impressive sight as she went on her course. The time of her passing us was exactly 10.45, and we learned later that she had left Plymouth Sound at 10.22.

For an hour or more we were hopelessly becalmed, without a vestige of wind, but an uncomfortable swell, which set everything on board rolling, and the boom swinging backwards and forwards across the stars in the most exasperating manner. A swell would come and away would go the spar, doing its best to break loose, only to be brought up suddenly with a jerk by the sheet.

I wonder something didn't carry away. Meanwhile the amount of chafing to the gear, and the slatting of the topping-lift against the sail, went on unceasingly. There was nothing for it except to grin and hope for a breeze. In the meantime, having made sure our lights were burning brightly, the mate went below and had a sleep. Not till half-an-hour after midnight did the longed-for wind make its reappearance, and a nice little draught it was when it really did come. By 2 a.m. we had got on so well as to bring the Eddystone and Plymouth Breakwater lights in line, which meant that we were now getting sufficiently close to the Rame Head to make us anxious. Had there been a light on the latter I should have felt inclined to continue on with this breeze and make a passage to a port down the Cornish coast; but there being no light to clear me off that headland, and the night being very dark over the land, it was impossible to tell how near exactly it was.

We decided therefore to hold on into Plymouth Sound, and having got the two lights already mentioned in line, went about and tacked into the Sound. Finally, after a good "mug-up" of steaming cocoa, espying a nice, cosy-looking bight, the wind being off the shore, we passed through a fleet of Plymouth hookers going out to their fishing grounds, crept into Cawsand Bay in the lightest of winds (now from N. by W.), and at 4.30

THE *KAISER WILHELM DER GROSSE*
WITH PLYMOUTH BREAKWATER LIGHT IN THE DISTANCE

a.m. dropped anchor just inside Pier Cove, lowered sails, and turned in.

Another lovely anchorage was this, rich in scenery, quiet with the wind as it was, though no place to lie in if the wind got to the southeast. Cawsand Bay, bathed in the sunlight, brushed clean of the black night, with its rocks and foliage, and the fine breakwater opposite, made up for a dozen calms.

The bathing was delicious; the bacon could not taste better as we looked out on to the vast expanse of Plymouth Sound. If Dartmouth was suggestive of the great Elizabethan explorers and privateers, Plymouth sent our minds eternally on to that one fact, the chasing of the Armada.

We could picture Howard, with the new and improved type of ships, sailing close-hauled out of the Sound past our anchorage into the Channel, and getting to windward of the Spaniards the other side of Rame Head; or a few years earlier the setting forth of Drake for his famous Cadiz expedition, when, as we learn from the State Papers of the time, after quite enough disheartening incidents in Plymouth, including the desertion of some of his seamen, that extraordinary self-willed female, Elizabeth, exercising the prerogative of her sex, changed her mind, and sent a messenger post-haste to Plymouth to prevent Drake's going. But the fleet had already sailed when the messenger arrived, so a fast-sailing pinnace was quickly got under weigh, the messenger with his despatch put aboard, and with all speed hastened out of the Sound into the Channel. But bad weather had sprung up

PLYMOUTH HOOKERS PUTTING OUT TO SEA JUST BEFORE DAWN

in the meantime, and the spring days were still treacherous, so the messenger never reached the man he was sent to find, and Drake: was able to go to the south, *singe the Spaniard's beard*, and, incidentally, make a very fine blaze in doing so.

Someone had warned us not to be surprised at anything in Plymouth Sound. "If," said our counsellor, "you should find shells whizzing over the top of your mast, destroyers rushing across your bows, and submarines bobbing up under your stern, don't get anxious; it is the Plymouth manner, and you will soon get used to it."

True, the shells did go whizzing through the air, but they were well over the other side of the water. Entering Weymouth, however, the men ashore had kept up a fire at a moving target in tow of a tug until we were too near to feel comfortable, but in Cawsand Bay we could see all the fun that was going. Owing to the manoeuvres this was limited, but the inevitable torpedo-boat, which always seems to be going in or coming out of the Sound, came past often enough to keep the view interesting. Then there was an interesting old training brigantine which came sailing round the Sound, with a crowd of youngsters learning all kinds of seamanship, from setting and stowing sails to heaving the lead, and finally, in the evening, the Admiralty ship we had seen the

CAWSAND BAY

day before came and anchored in Cawsand Bay.

The village of Cawsand, or Kingsand, as they seemed to name it ashore, was ransacked for more cream and fruit and bread. We made friends with the pilots, and a fine lot of nature's gentlemen they were. A number of barrels were strewn about the beach that gave to the little place an appearance of belonging to a smuggling community, and if the dead men in the churchyard could tell some tales, they would, no doubt, be able to fill an encyclopaedia with smuggling yarns. The whole village was seafaring, if not indeed, then, at any rate, in mind and instinct.

For no one ever seemed to venture beyond his doorstep without a long telescope, not merely the men, but the women folk also. We yarned with the inhabitants, posted letters to civilisation, heard the prophecies of the skipper of the pilot-cutter moored just astern of us, and turned in early; a beautiful, starry night, as peaceful as it was lovely, for in the morning we were to get going again. It was bound to be a head wind, but we could not dare to grumble when everything else was conspiring to make us happy and contented. So we dined early, worked out our course for the morrow, calculated the tides, set the aneroid, and went to bed.

WORKED OUT THE COURSE - AND WENT TO BED

CHAPTER 10

From Plymouth Sound to Fowey

On the last day of June we had catted and fished the anchor, and cleared out of Cawsand Bay by eight o'clock. The morning began with a thick fog, and we suspected that there would be little wind again. A flat calm, varied with occasional will-o'-the-wisps, persisted for nearly an hour, and thus, with the assistance of the sweep, we continued till Penlee Point was abeam at nine o'clock. Then a nice little draught springing up from a little S. of W. we put the ship on a course S. by W., with the flood just making into Plymouth Sound, and a few trawlers lazily waiting for more wind to carry them into port. Off Rame Head we put the log overboard, registering 59.7.

We stood out towards the Eddystone on the starboard tack so as to get the advantage of the last of the west-going tide. At 10.10 a.m., when Rame Head bore N. by E., distant three knots, we went about on the other tack, with the ship's head NNW. towards Looe. We had made no leeway on the previous tack standing out from the land in a line with the Eddystone, for the last of the Channel ebb just about counteracted the leeway we should have made. Thus every bit of the distance sailed so far on this tack had been made good.

We met a few trawlers and Plymouth hookers, the latter with their boomless mainsails, running in home with their night's fish. Away seawards were all sorts of interesting craft: a liner or two near the horizon; closer in were a Russian three-masted schooner, a Cornish lugger, a Plymouth barge with her brown sails; whilst scattered about the sea were a few rusty steam tramps and colliers. Another fine, warm, sunny day, but we were to be favoured with more wind this time. We were in Cornish waters now, and bright and beautiful the coast looked as we slipped along through the little waves.

By 11.45 we had got right up to the Knight Errant Buoy, when we went about again, the log registering 69, so that in an hour and a half we had done 6.3 knots through the water, with the tide against us most of the way. We kept her on a S. by W. course again for another two or three knots. A nice little summer breeze had freshened, as it frequently does at mid-day, and we seemed to be making much faster progress than in reality; but there was a little bit of a fuss going' against wind and tide, that we did not get past the land as rapidly as we had imagined would have been the case.

And so we continued, making the best of the unending contrariness of the wind. As we came on past Looe, with its green island lit up by the sun, and kept on a SSW. course, we saw in the far distance, coming out of a thin haze, a mountain of white canvas advancing rapidly towards us, a picture of ghost-like solemnity. We manoeuvred so as to pass to windward of this vision, and close enough to take her photograph, and as we ran under her stern afterwards read her name, the *Cambuskenneth* of Glasgow, a full-rigged ship of about two thousand tons, bound, no doubt, from foreign parts, having called for orders at Falmouth. It was an inspiring sight, and we were fortunate to have had the good luck of being so near.

With her double topsails, double t'gallants, royals, and lower staysails all drawing, and a trysail on her mizzen, she would not be long running up Channel if the wind held. The big sailing-ships are nowadays becoming something of an exception on the sea, so that when one comes across them, not in harbour, but under way, the occasion is so rare as to make a deep impression on one's mind. Things have altered so much since the introduction of steam, and even the spanker on the mizzen is now more frequently merely a trysail, and the old gaff has been pushed higher up the mast, and retained only as the "monkey gaff" for the convenience of signalling. In the accompanying illustration of the *Cambuskenneth* it will be noticed just above the upper topsail.

Presently, when she had passed, a little lugger came running out of a snug entrance to the land. Neither the mate nor I had ever been hereabouts before, so we hailed the lugger to make sure of our position, and ask the name of this very sheltered, exceedingly picturesque haven cleft in the high cliff.

"That be Polperry, sir," shouted the funny old man as we ran up alongside. The wind was more favourable, he told us, close in along the shore; so we reached in as near as we deemed advisable, and found, as he had said, that the breeze was coming so directly off the land that we were able to lay a W. ½ S. course, which was several points better than what we were able to do farther out in the Channel. We should have liked to have had the chance of exploring Polperro, but we had heard that it was a curious place to get into, and left it as one of those haunts to run down to by land before the yacht is fitted out again—another of those expeditions that but rarely seem to come to fulfilment.

At four in the afternoon we noticed in the bay an auxiliary steam-yacht, in appearance looking more like a converted trawler, stop her engines and lower a boat, from which some of

THE *CAMBUSKENNETH* OF GLASGOW

her crew were engaged in clearing something from a foul propeller; so in curiosity we sailed up, and gathered that the owner's fishing-line had got wound up by the screw. As we stood back towards the land again, where the cliffs rise gaunt, cruel, and rock-bound, we heard the moaning of a bell-buoy, which had recently been placed to mark the Udder Rock, though our chart had not contained the addition.

For some time we had had in view a square, horizontally marked tower, standing up above Gribbin Head, and looking very much like a lighthouse, which, indeed, at first we thought it was. But this is the excellent day-mark which has been erected in order to assist the navigator to find the entrance to Fowey, and to distinguish at a distance the Gribbin from St. Anthony or the Dodman. He who cruises down along this coast for the first time will be not a little puzzled to locate Fowey. The line of cliffs seems to run along in one unbroken continuity, so that the harbour you had aimed for and identified on the chart seems to have vanished. But it is this beacon which is of such use to coasters that it, so to speak, heralds the entrance to one of the jolliest and quaintest natural harbours in the British Isles.

At 5.30 p.m. we were abreast of Fowey entrance, but a couple of miles out seaward. Presently we tacked in to the land, took in the log as we got past the Gribbin, and in company of all sorts of little local craft returning from their afternoon's sail, beat into the narrow, rocky entrance with the tide at half ebb, and let go anchor opposite the town in 2 ½ fathoms of water on the Polruan side at six o'clock. In actual distance we had sailed, according to the log, forty-five miles from Rame Head, making an average exactly of five miles an hour.

Neither of us had so much as seen Fowey before, but one had heard much of "Troy Town," and indeed its dark rocks, jagged and time-worn, its high undulating hills which protect it from the winds, its delicious, clean emerald-green water, its interesting old-world town and church, its beautiful river and interesting shipping, would have kept us there weeks had we been able. We found that a good mark to have in mind as to where to bring

ENTRANCE TO FOWEY HARBOUR
SHOWING ST. CATHERINE'S LIGHTHOUSE ON THE LEFT (UNDER THE ARROW) AND SKETCH OF THE GRIBBIN HEAD DAYMARK IN INSET.

up consisted in continuing up the harbour until a prominent whitewashed house on the starboard hand came in line with the light erected on an iron column twenty feet high abreast of Mr. Quiller Couch's ("Q.'s") house, having a white flagstaff in the garden. If one keeps to the eastward a bit, so as to be just inside the eastern arm of the harbour, a moderate-draught yacht will find plenty of water for herself even at low water springs, whilst she will be very fairly protected from all sides. This berth is certainly preferable to continuing farther up the harbour, as is sometimes recommended, and there are landing facilities just adjacent on both the Fowey and Polruan side.

We were glad to have arrived in this haven of rest, so peaceful and English, and the greatest kindness and courtesy were shown us, both by the members of the Royal Fowey Yacht Club and the Foweyans generally.

To wake up in the morning from a real sleep—the kind that is not granted in towns and cities—to come out on deck with the sun dazzling over this old Cornish town, and the sound of the caulking mallet echoing against the hills over in Polruan Pool as some old topsail schooner is having her decks tightened; to bathe in its clear warm waters, and then eat or smoke or row leisurely about in the dinghy, or climb the hill and look over for miles upon miles along the coast, is to live in Arcadia. One was puzzled for a time why Fowey seemed so familiar to one.

It wasn't a case of a previous existence. But the bits of tar and whitewash slabbed on to the houses, ending abruptly with their back-doors on the edge of the harbour; the rickety, weather-worn wooden landing-stages leading up to them; the exact tone of the rocks and water, the seagulls sitting lazily on the boats, and the boys who played about either in or on the pellucid water—all seemed so natural, so complete, and just what we had expected to see. And then suddenly it all came back to one that what was in the mind was a kind of concentrated extract of the Cornish school of painters.

he colours, and people, and boats, and seabirds had we seen scores of times before, not here but in picture-galleries. All over

Fowey one seemed to see, for instance, Napier Hemy written up large in rocks and water; or, to put the proposition more correctly, here were the original details which had gone to compose many a canvas that had depicted nature with such fidelity and spirit.

Half Polruan too, with its steep, narrow stone streets and its sea-folk, seemed to be decorated this morning with flags and bunting. The schooners and other craft afloat and the quays on land were flapping and fluttering with colours. I rowed across to buy something for the dinghy, and learnt that it was a skipper's wedding today. And so if Fowey suggested Napier Hemy, Polruan instantly brought to one's mind Stanhope Forbes' famous picture in the Tate Gallery called "The Health of the Bride," showing with much charm and simplicity the wedding feast of a sailor and his bride in a Cornish fishing village. One could almost see the wedding feast going on, through the artist's eyes, inside one of those old houses by the quay-side.

But we had already spent a day and a half in Fowey; so we rowed across to the whitewashed house at Polruan, round into a dock which, in the palmy days of shipbuilding, used to be kept busier than it is now, and borrowed some cans with which to fill our tanks. One of Nature's gentle men took me in hand, led me into a dark, little cave in the cliff, and from a well drew forth delightfully cold drinking water. A few journeys and the tank was full, and after watching the arrival of H.M.S. Lynx, one of the destroyers stationed at Plymouth, we were on the move again, this time for the final stage on our western voyage.

Fowey Harbour
from the Polruan side. The light on an iron column will be noticed across the water to the left of the picture, to the right of the ivy-clad house.

CHAPTER 11

From Fowey to Falmouth and Back

With a light air from about south, and the atmosphere foggy and overcast, we cleared from Fowey soon after eleven in the morning and set a course SW. ½ W. for the Dodman, and being off the Gribbin Head at a quarter to twelve, put overboard the log, which read 01.9. We soon overhauled another yacht, rather bigger than ourselves, which had come out of harbour half-an-hour earlier, but the wind was such that we could only just lay our course. The first hour's sailing showed that we were doing our five and a half knots and more. Gradually as the day became older the fog and haze disappeared, showing us a most interesting coast-line with tempting little bays and villages. Some of these landmarks we found useful as we amused ourselves in taking cross-bearings every now and again.

Before half-past one we had the Gwineas Rock abeam—"Gwinges," as the local mariners pronounce it—but the wind began to play its tricks again, and of course headed us off as usual. We tacked ship, therefore, and stood off from the rock for about a mile, and then tacked again, being now on a WSW. course, and by 2.30 we had abeam the Dodman—or the "Deadman," as it used to be known among the old sailing men in the days of the sea chanties. A nice little draught was sending *Vivette* through the water, when it gradually grew lighter and lighter, ultimately dying right away. Just previously two small craft bound eastwards with a fair wind came running along, which we spoke.

The first chanced to be *Mooween*, and the second *Lady Moll*, on their return journey from Falmouth; with favourable wind and tide they soon vanished from our gaze. But as *Mooween* passed I saw something black showing above the water. *Mooween's* owner saw it too and tried to hit it with the sweep, but it disappeared. Whether it was one of the sharks or the sun-fish which are found off the Cornish coast in hot weather none of us seemed able to decide.

From three o'clock till after four we spent an uncomfortable time in the flattest of flat calms, rolling about between the headland and the nasty tide-rip, with hard work at the sweep to keep the yacht from either getting too near the shore on the one side, or getting into the unpleasant boil of the broken water on the other. All the time the little vessel was rolling about in the most annoying fashion, and in spite of our labours in the hot sun we drifted back past the headland towards Fowey.

At about the stage when we were quite ready to cry *jam satis* a faint suspicion of an air seemed to come down on our tired sails, and scarcely daring to speak lest it should die away again as rapidly, we trimmed the sails carefully and put her at it. Happily the breeze freshened "some," so we sped on "some," but, as we

ARRIVING AT ST. MAWES

had expected, the wind was going round with the sun, and before we were across Gerran's Bay we were headed right off our course and making tacks.

But we were not unhappy. Here we were at length within sight of Black Head, beyond which was the Lizard, from which it was only across another bay to Land's End. It was a glorious, warm evening, and there is always a joy at seeing new land ahead, and a fresh, unseen harbour to work one's way into. Besides, even if the wind should drop a little it was almost full moon tonight, and the tide, when once we had got into Falmouth Bay, would carry us up where we wished to go.

But the wind held nicely, and we made our tacks in fine style, and rounding past St. Anthony's Lighthouse, standing watch over the fine entrance to one of the grandest natural harbours in the world, kept on till we had passed the village of St. Mawes, and at dead low water springs ran into a snug little bight at the back of St. Anthony, where a number of other craft—pilots, quay-punts, and yachts—were brought up, and let go about nine o'clock in 2½ fathoms, with St. Mawes over to one side and a most picturesque bit of well-wooded scenery on the other, while in between the tide wended its way backwards and forwards from the Channel. Our actual distance sailed today had been but little more than 35 miles according to the log; but we had encountered bad luck in head winds and calms and a foul tide together.

The morning after broke cloudy and misty, and the glass seemed to be a little uncertain as to what it should foretell. But unless the wind should freshen from the westward we were fairly snug where we lay, though we should have found a more sheltered berth round the bend of the river. So, leaving the mate as anchor watch after rowing me across in the dinghy to the stone pier of St. Mawes, I took steamer to Falmouth and spent a morning ashore getting letters, loafing round the town and shipbuilding yards. The harbour there was full of every kind of craft, trader and pleasure, but amid such a crowd there seemed not too much room if a breeze had come up and anchors had begun to drag; so I was not sorry to have brought up on the St. Mawes side, away from a town and civilisation. By the time I had got aboard *Vivette* again the weather began to look threatening, and there was a certain amount of swell coming up the river from outside. Everything seemed to suggest that it was going to blow before the night, so we got up the anchor, set the staysail, and ran farther up the Porthceuil River, bringing up abreast of where a beautiful country lane ended abruptly on to a boat-builder's.

Here we were nicely sheltered by high land on either side of us, amid most delightful scenery, with plenty of jolly creeks and arms of the river to explore in the dinghy in case we should be weather-bound for some days. This part of the world is full of surprises to the yachtsman coming from the east. Where he would naturally expect to find the rivers and creeks shallow and muddy he finds that they are deep right up to the rocky banks. A little astern of us was the strange sight of a farm perched at the very water's edge, with a big topsail schooner moored alongside and afloat.

Before nightfall I landed by the boat-builder's and climbed the road that leads up to the hill overlooking Falmouth and St. Anthony, with St. Mawes nestling in the foreground with its pretty cottages, its fishing boats and fishing folk. From the local butcher's I was lucky enough to be able to purchase the last few pounds of meat, and by the time the little grocer's store had

IN THE PORTCEUIL RIVER

contributed its share, my load of provisions was heavy enough for the climb up the hill again. At the top I turned round and looked back. The darkness had come on now, and St. Mawes was speckled with little yellow splashes of light. Some of the smaller craft which had been riding to moorings off the harbour had followed our example and run round farther inland past the point, as the wind against tide was making sufficient motion to cause uneasy riding.

Down the lane, perfumed with all sorts of beautiful scents—honeysuckle and I know not what else—the way led me back again to the water's edge, and a hail soon brought the mate up from the fo'c'sle, where the evening's dinner was well under weigh.

In the morning there was time to repeat the walk into St. Mawes, while the mate sketched. At an inn I found the landlord had been skipper in earlier days of a full-rigged ship, so the opportunity of adding to one's knowledge was not wasted. We talked of the *Cambuskenneth*, which he knew well, and told me she was skippered by a St. Mawes man. It is not often nowadays that one has the chance of talking with so interesting a deep-sea captain of a sailing ship, and I hope someday to resume the conversation and to listen to some more opinions on the subject of "monkey gaffs "and the comparative merits of barques and ships. Outside, brought up off the St. Anthony Lighthouse, was a number of full-rigged ships, together with a British cruiser that had been engaged in the manoeuvres—about as fine a contrast between the ships of yesterday and today as one could wish to expect.

To the man who really loves ships I suppose that, excepting Queenstown, there is no harbour in Europe so interesting as Falmouth. During our stay here we counted most of a dozen full-rigged ships and barques of different nationalities, and of about two or three thousand tons each. To sail round them as they remained brought up in the roads waiting for orders to proceed, while perhaps their cargo of grain was being sold several times over on the Exchange in the city, and to notice their maze of spars and rigging, was a pleasure that, with the advance of steamships, may not be able to be enjoyed many years longer.

In the afternoon we made an excursion in the dinghy into a creek which almost joins up with the sea; and, leaving the boat tied to a tree, mounted the steep hill and looked over towards the Dodman.

It was this natural advantage of a winding creek that was found so useful by the revenue officers many years ago, when they surprised the smugglers and caught them in the very act of their iniquity. The story goes that the smugglers had become so bold in the neighbour- hood of Falmouth that they actually ran cargoes ashore in daylight, accomplices being stationed on the overlooking hills in order to signal the approach of the revenue men. On this particular occasion the latter adopted a clever ruse.

They allowed themselves to be observed quietly pulling up in their boat along St. Mawes' creek, and the watchers on the hill overlooking the sea presumed that their enemy was going for a

SAILING SHIP COMING TO ANCHOR IN THE RIVER FAL
FALMOUTH QUAY PUNT BY HER SIDE

pleasant row instead of worrying about the smuggling which at that moment was going on by the coast. So, turning their backs on the creek, they failed to notice the advance of the revenue men, who pulled right up to the head of this delightful creek shown in the accompanying illustration, being careful to keep close under the trees, which naturally hid them from any vigilant eyes on the hill above.

The tide happening to be high, the boat was able to float a long way up the narrowing inlet to the point where it bends round and almost, though not quite, touches the sea. At this point, therefore, the boat was pulled out of the water, hauled quietly and stealthily up the grassy slope, and rapidly launched down the hill again the other side where the sea touches the land. Thus utterly unsuspected, the enemy came round the corner of the cove, and the smugglers were captured red-handed.

The time came for us to leave this fair spot, and so on the Sunday afternoon we hoisted main and jib and ran out of the Porthceuil River, past St. Mawes and St. Anthony, into Falmouth Bay. There was a good breeze, and we sailed in company with a number of Falmouth quay-punts across the bay to the entrance of Helford River, and then worked back. We should have been glad to have gone into this anchorage. The reports we had received of its tranquil beauty had been enticing, but we also wished to see St. Just, so we tacked back into Falmouth with a

FALMOUTH SMUGGLERS' CREEK

topsail schooner, and with little difficulty in finding the buoys ran up to the entrance of another quaint little creek—St. Just—a mile or two up the Fal, where, picking up a vacant mooring-buoy, we settled down for another night.

The wind had been strong and squally during the day, but by sunset it had vanished altogether, and from our cabin doors we commanded a vast expanse of shimmering water, bounded on either side by rich scenery, with a few glorious barques in the centre, and the distant forest of masts sheltering in Falmouth harbour beyond. We made friends with a kindly old Cornishman who was guarding the oyster beds, who also brought us fresh water for our tanks.

What a paradise Falmouth must be for the all-year-round cruiser; for, said our friend, they rarely had bad winters, and it was years and years since they had had snow. Across the river was Mylor Creek, looking full of temptation to us to linger, while farther up the Fal we could have explored till we came to Truro. We had a council of war in the cabin, the mate and I, and hesitated which of these trips could be undertaken, and whether we could not even run round the Lizard to Penzance and thence to

A Lych-Gate at St. Just

the Scillies. But considerations of time and the possibility of our treacherous summer weather holding us in some harbour for a week or two and preventing our return to the Solent, determined us to begin to "run our easting down" tomorrow whilst we had a chance.

Nevertheless, in the morning we could not leave before we had seen something of St. Just from the land side, and set off to see the old church, which stands in the hollow where the creek ends. It would be difficult to find many spots in England so unpolluted by the hand of man, so sylvan and beautiful as this. At the higher end is a picturesque lych-gate, which gives entrance to a churchyard that is famous all over Cornwall for its flowers and ferns and well-kept beds and paths.

You are requested to refrain from picking what is there growing, but on applying at the rectory, provided you do not live either in Devonshire or Cornwall, you are most kindly and thoughtfully presented with a plant or fern to take home as a memento of your visit to this wonderful hamlet. Here, where all ranks of sailor-men, from admirals to fishermen, have been laid to rest in the old churchyard at the end of the creek, looking over to the sea, you will find such peacefulness as will live for long in your memory. The postmistress in the village waxed indignant when we talked with her on the comparative charms of life in St. Just and existence in towns. The former was for honest people: the latter was beneath contempt.

We hurried back, yet reluctantly, through an avenue of trees, past a cottage in whose garden fuchsias and sub-tropical plants were growing, down a path to the beach, and pulled off to the yacht. Up go the sails again, overboard flops the mooring-buoy, and away we go till we get abreast of the German *barque*, where the wind dies utterly away. But there is surprisingly little tide about Falmouth, and as we lie motionless alongside one of these grain-carriers come from South America, we are glad of the opportunity of so intimate acquaintance with her. A Falmouth boatman rows by, whom we ask to express his opinion of the wind that we are likely to be favoured with. "Foxey weather—

that's what it is—no good to no one," was the verdict. But just then we got a little puff and ran across to Falmouth, where the yachts were getting under weigh for the first race of the regatta. We were bound east, but we had letters to call for first, so dropping our hook just off the town, the mate jumped into the dinghy and rowed ashore.

We were soon off again, and by 2.45 p.m. under main and jib had St. Anthony's Lighthouse abeam. As we came out the big yachts were making a fine show, and the famous old *Bloodhound* came foaming along with a crew mostly of keen amateurs. As she came round the mark-buoy she made for us a grand picture of speed and strenuousness, with every man at his post busy but not flustering. Setting a course due east so as to pass well outside the Dodman, whose overfalls would be lumpy today, with the wind at due west, and the tide just making in our favour, we began to foot it in splendid style.

The breeze had strengthened rapidly while we lay off Falmouth town, and we should not take as long to get to Fowey as the previous journey had taken us a few days earlier. At three o'clock, when about half a mile to the eastward of St. Anthony, we put the log overboard, reading 37.6.

By four o'clock we had the Gull Rock abeam, the log reading 43.7, so that we had gone through the water over six knots in the hour, to say nothing of the additional good which the tide was doing us. An hour later we were at the Dodman, and

ENTRANCE TO FALMOUTH
SHOWING ST. ANTHONY LIGHTHOUSE AND THE BLACKROCK

standing on the same course until the Gribbin Daymark at the entrance to Fowey harbour was on our port bow, we gybed and set the staysail as a spinnaker, booming it out with the boathook. Each of our three sails was drawing splendidly, and we were making a good little passage. The sea was a bit lumpy, but nothing came aboard; yet had we been punching to windward we should have found all we wanted.

The day was getting on, and the picturesque fishing fleet of luggers came out from the land, apparently from Mevagissey, and with that sight before us came back that same consciousness of a previous acquaintanceship that we had experienced at Fowey. Just as the latter had seemed to suggest to one's mind Stanhope Forbes and other artists of the Cornish school, and, while we had sailed up the Fal by the grain-ships, we had believed we could see again all that Tuke in his pictures had ever intended to show, so here, as these craft dipped to the waves off Mevagissey, was a living reminder of a Napier Hemy.

As you enter Fowey you have need to watch out for the Cannis Rock, a nasty ledge which stands up about a quarter of a mile from the Gribbin Head, and is visible at half-ebb. But now as we entered the tide was almost high water, so we stood well over to the eastern side, ran in between the rocks, lowering staysail as we entered, and brought up in our old berth on the Polruan side, where we found *Mooween* and *Lady Moll* again. We took in the log as we entered, off St. Catherine's Lighthouse at 6.45 p.m., and found it registered exactly 63.6, so that in less than four hours we had done twenty-six knots, or an average of over 6½ knots per hour through the water.

CHAPTER 12

From Fowey to Salcombe

The first time we had entered Fowey we had seen the quays and shipping of Polruan gay with flags and bunting for a wedding. But now, when we returned, the flags everywhere were at half-mast. I rowed over to draw forth some more of the water from the deliciously cool well, and heard of the sad story of a Polruan skipper in command of one of the topsail schooners, who had just died, away from his own port. It appeared that he had been taken ill while on a voyage down Channel, but refused to give in. It chanced, however, that whilst under weigh the forestay carried away, and for that reason alone he was compelled to put in to Portsmouth.

Whilst there his illness became so serious that one of the crew insisted on fetching a doctor, against which the plucky old man fought to the end. Eventually, however, the crew very properly disobeyed their captain's orders, and rowing off to one of His Majesty's ships in the harbour, fetched the ship's doctor aboard, who promptly decided that the case needed instant treatment ashore; but, as it turned out, the man was too far gone, and death soon robbed the ship of her master. Except for the accident to the forestay the vessel would not have put into Portsmouth, and the Cornishman would have breathed his last on the sea and in the ship that he had known so long.

The fine little breeze that had brought us along so merrily from Falmouth freshened during the night, and *Vivette* rolled a little even in the snug anchorage of Polruan. On the western side of the harbour the waves were dashing against the rocks, and doing their best to hollow out the foundations of the houses above. With wind against tide on these occasions there is ever the annoyance of the dinghy trouble to keep you awake. From the warmth of your blankets you hear the ominous sound of a light, gentle tapping against the yacht's side. An hiatus of quiet follows. Then a big bump ensues, and full of uncharitable remarks regarding dinghies as a class and your own in particular, you leap out of your bunk and go out into the dripping rain as the wind cuts into your flesh through your pyjamas.

Then, after being several times nearly thrown overboard by the motion of the yacht, you attach a bucket to the stern of the dinghy, and turn in again. No sooner have you regained a little warmth than the little creature comes alongside with a bigger crash than before. This time you find that, the tide beginning to slacken, the water-bucket is useless, so the only thing to be done is to haul the bow of the dinghy till it is just over the taffrail. With boats other than those of the *pram*-design this is not possible, but in many an anchorage, when the circumstances demanded it, we found that by getting the little nuisance's snout just aboard, so that she could not swing out, and must ride fore and aft in the same direction as the yacht, a peaceful night's rest was assured, and something of an added pleasure was given to us by realising that some of our neighbours were less happily situated.

More or less dirty weather kept us in Fowey for two days, but we found plenty to see, and do, and yarn about. Mildred, whom we had first met when bound west in West Bay, came in, and brought up alongside of us. We found that had we gone on to Torquay that night instead of Dartmouth, we should have been in port a good hour ahead of them.

We cleared from Fowey at nine in the morning. The weather did not look very promising, but we were a long way from home, and there was no telling whether, even in this first week of July, our treacherous English summer had already gone for the year. The glass was uncertain, the wind was squally, and the sky overcast. We got under weigh with the second jib and about a reef and a half rolled into the main. As soon as we were outside the breeze freshened slightly from the NNW., and setting a course ESE. for the Mewstone, we began to rattle off the knots nicely. By the time we had Polperro abeam we calculated our speed to be about five knots an hour. At 10.40 we got the staysail on to her, and the difference in speed was very noticeable.

At midday exactly we had Eddystone and Rame Head abeam, so that in three hours we had covered just seventeen knots, or an average of five and two thirds knots *per* hour. We had intended to have gone into the Yealm River at the eastern entrance to Plymouth Sound, but with so fair a wind it seemed a pity to lose what little luck we had, and thus we held on as the day was yet so young. There was plenty to interest one all round. Luggers and liners, pilots signalling to the station on Rame Head, a long procession of warships seawards standing up black against the horizon, whilst now and again we met a trader or a large yacht bound the other way, and in and out of Plymouth torpedo craft came running unceasingly like restless black retrievers.

Off Plymouth the breeze freshened and a lumpy sea got up. Had we passed here twelve days later we might have got the wind more southerly, in which case we should have had most of the accidents of time and air that were present in 1588 when the Armada came running up Channel past Rame Head—or Ram's Head, as one sees it called on the early charts.

"The very next day," says the old chronicler, "being the 20th of July about high noone, was the Spanish Fleete escried by the English, which with a South-west wind came sailing along, and passed by Plimmouth."

As we sped on across Bigbury Bay we soon realised we were carrying all the sail that we needed, and sometimes the puffs would come down so viciously for a few moments, that I had to run the little ship into the wind until the worst of the squall was passed. As the day declined we thought that the breeze might moderate, but instead of that it only increased, and finally we decided to roll in some more of the main, as we could not carry in any comfort all that we had. For a time we ran along with greater ease, but the nearer we approached to Bolt Tail the worse it became. There is something of a swell off the coast between Bolt Tail and Prawle Point at the best of times, and today we expected to have our full enjoyment of excitement. We got it.

With the wind now in the direction of about north-west, having backed a little, the water off Bolt Tail was considerably disturbed, and the waves with all this open drift were quite awe-inspiring as they rolled up astern and threatened every moment to come aboard us. What a contrast to the day when we had passed here last, bound west, and we lay becalmed in Bigbury Bay with not even a suspicion of an air to give us steerage way! For an hour and more we spent an anxious time.

Once we lowered staysail, but we soon had it up again when the squall passed, as we might as well run on and get it all over. But at last something had to be done, and what we did was so effectual, and, as far as I know, has never been tried before on a small yacht, that the experiment may not be without interest to yachting men. The success is entirely owing to the inventiveness, or rather the adaptability, of the mate. Whilst we were lying in Fowey harbour we had discussed the voyage of the celebrated Captain Slocum, who had sailed single-handed round the world in a small vessel.

RUNNING PAST BOLT TAIL
INSET SHOWS METHODS OF TOWING WARP

In his book, the reader will probably remember, Slocum says that when running across the ocean with a nasty big sea following he used to pay out two thick warps astern from either quarter, and the result was that just when the waves looked their worst, and were about to break over his ship, the warps somehow seemed to prevent the worst from ever happening. We decided, therefore, to see if there was anything in the idea for ourselves, so before leaving the Cornish port we selected a ten-fathom warp of about two inches in diameter, and made it fast to the thwarts of the dinghy, stowing it in the boat in such a manner that by the assistance of a boat-hook we could easily throw the end overboard and let it tow astern.

Although Slocum had two warps for the ocean, we reckoned that one would be adequate for our purpose. Therefore when off Bolt Tail, and the waves were in all reality threatening enough, we concluded that this would be an ideal opportunity for putting our experiment to a test: so overboard the warp went. If the reader will glance at the accompanying illustration he will see *Vivette* running, and in the inset an enlarged picture of the dinghy with the warp trailing astern of the dinghy.

The immediate result of this manoeuvre was twofold. Firstly, it caused the yacht to be more buoyant and "corky," so that she ran, if more slowly, yet more sweetly and with an absence of drag: her motion through the water was cleaner and with less resistance. Secondly, when the waves towered up astern, and seemed about to carry out their threats, the warp bisected and cut deep into the former, so as to take away the power they had amassed. For several miles the mate stood with his face towards the following sea, and watched carefully the interesting manner in which wave after wave would advance, only to be cleft in half and die away astern.

The principal reason which had actuated us in adopting the experiment was, originally, not so much in order to make the yacht more comfortable in a sea-way, as to prevent the dinghy from charging down on us. But in practice the warp out astern succeeded in doing both, and we were not a little pleased.

Punching to windward and crashing through the spray came a Brixham trawler. As she stood on the port tack close inshore we should have to give way presently unless she went about. To gybe in that wind and sea was not a proceeding that we looked forward to, and we began to shorten in the sheet in readiness; but at the last moment, happily, the trawler went about on the other tack. She looked magnificent with her tanned sails against the green waves and the white spray splashing about her bows.

At length we opened up Bolt Head and the entrance to Salcombe Harbour, and got the staysail down in readiness for a beat up between the high land. Although we had as much as three reefs rolled in the mainsail by this time, yet as soon as we came on a wind we found that we could not have set much more than we already had up.

As is usually the case in respect to rivers, especially between high banks, the wind, which outside was nearly parallel to the shore, was now blowing right out of Salcombr, and we had a period of nasty squally tacking, in which the wind would come down from the high hills in weighty puffs and fluke for several points of the compass. Round we would go on the other tack, with the jib sheet thrashing and getting foul of the capstan. A calm would follow, and we made a bit by luffing up, only to have another squall.

Once—and this is the only occasion since I have had *Vivette*—she heeled over to a sudden blast until the water came up to the

ENTERING SALCOMBE HARBOUR

cabin-top, but at last with the young flood just making we got in between the bar and the western shore, and dropped anchor in our old spot abreast of the town. *Stella Maris*, with two of the Gipsies aboard from Dartmouth, was brought up astern bound for their summer cruise to the Scillies, and her crew entertained us again with much hospitality and many yarns. They were kind enough to admire the way our little ship had taken the strong squalls as they watched her making her way in.

It had been one of the most interesting and sportive sails we had in the whole cruise, and in spite of the loss of speed occasioned by the towing warp, we had kept up an average of over five knots an hour for the whole of the distance from Fowey; for by 3.45 in the afternoon we were well inside Salcombe Bay.

The next day the wind backed farther to the southward so as to be at nearly south-west, and of about the same velocity as we had found it. *Lady Moll* with *Mooween* and two or three other yachts came running in, having cleared out of Fowey shortly after us the previous day, but having spent the night in the Yealm River instead of making the whole journey in one passage.

Our experience off Bolt Tail was repeated in their case, and the accounts we heard from them and others showed that if anything with the wind being farther on shore they had rather more to contend with than we, though they were able to run into Salcombe without tacking. During the morning, finding that our present anchorage off Salcombe town was somewhat

SALCOMBE HARBOUR

lively, and that there was every prospect of the weather going from bad to worse, we ran round the point farther up the river, and made fast to a buoy in the snuggest of little bays, locally known as "The Bag," with hills on either side of us, and a glorious panorama of scenery on which to gaze.

Nothing mattered here. We were near to the shore for getting" supplies, and the wind could blow as hard as it willed without inconveniencing us a moment. Presently several other craft, finding the first anchorage not pleasant, ran round also and kept us company.

CHAPTER 13

From Salcombe to Torquay

We were not sorry to be so comfortably protected, for the weather seemed determined to persist in its bad humour. The glass went down lower and lower, and the rain came down in too plentiful a manner to be cheerful; so, realising that to continue our eastward voyage would not be possible just yet awhile, we gave up playing at summer, and, having hired the moorings we were on for a couple of weeks, arranged with a local boat-builder to take charge of *Vivette* until we should return.

It took us some time to collect our gear and to arrange for departure. Halyards and ropes of all kinds had to be slacked off lest the continuous rain should shrink them up till they snapped; loose gear on deck had to be thrust into the cabin. Shore clothes were dragged out unwillingly, and razors began to get busy preparatory to a return to civilisation.

With no feelings of happiness we locked the cabin door, got into the dinghy, rowed alongside the funny little paddle-steamer which plies up and down the river, and bundled ourselves and baggage aboard. Salcombe cannot boast of the doubtful privilege of a railway station. The nearest is at Kingsbridge, a few miles up the river, but the trip is so pretty and interesting, that one regretted the steamboat journey was so short. A few hours later and the crew of *Vivette* disembarked at Paddington as the dawn was breaking over the big city.

For the next few weeks the summer entirely forgot to fulfil its customary duties, but at the end of the month we went back to Devonshire, thankful to get away from town life. Almost at once the weather began to improve, the warmth returned to the air, the sun came out, and the world seemed a happy place once more. The mate was delayed in town, so going down alone I made our home ready for habitation, gave the little ship a good "spring-cleaning," overhauled all gear, got stores aboard, and sailed up in the dinghy to Kingsbridge to meet my friend. Loath to say farewell to this earthly paradise, another day was spent in dinghy cruises exploring creeks and tiny bays, sailing across to the Portlemouth side, where, finding a stream of fresh water which came from the hills above right down to the seashore, we filled our water-carriers and sailed back again with our cargo to the yacht.

At length one morning early, at the top of high water, before the mist had left the hills, we hoisted sail and drifted down past Salcombe town out into the bay, ready to resume our eastward wanderings. But the wind was scanty, the atmosphere for a time foggy, and the Channel tide was making to the westward, so progress was denied us. For a time we lay brought up to our kedge; but with the advent of a light air we got under weigh again, and making a long leg and a short at last rounded Prawle Point, where we were passed by a flotilla of about a score of torpedo craft, belching out so much smoke as to darken the sky for a considerable distance. As they came abreast of us, bound apparently for Plymouth, they changed their formation from "single line ahead" to "column of division," so far as one could judge.

Gradually the wind freed, and as the day wore on adopted its usual practice of going round to the west; so, setting the balloon staysail, we made the best of the little there was. By the time we were off the Start the race was still active. Although the wind was so light, and there was no sea but the gentlest swell in the Channel, yet the water for over two miles away from the shore was disturbed and "floppy." We stood out on an easterly course until Berry Head was well open and we had the Skerries Buoy in line, and were not a little surprised that these overfalls should be so manifest in such fine weather. But under less favourable conditions this is a most unwelcome spot for the sailor-man. A few weeks later a friend informed me that he passed the Start in a small motor-yacht, and found the race so bad that he was bound to go as much as six miles to the southward of it.

About the time we had picked up a fair tide again, and were expecting some more wind, we had a repetition of the old game. The breeze dropped, and the boom began to swing backwards and forwards in the swell. We should not be in Torquay before nightfall at this rate, and we bewailed our continuous bad luck in rarely getting what, under normal conditions, we had a right to expect. Either there was too much or too little wind, even when we hit it off in the right direction. But just when we were getting most annoyed a nice little evening draught came up from the westward, and we had a most delightful sail, passing Dartmouth and the fine lofty cliffs.

From the narrow entrance came out a three-masted Irish schooner, looking singularly picturesque with everything up and the dying sun lighting up her canvas and rigging. The air was so still and peaceful that we could hear those on board talking. The skipper had evidently brought his wife and children "to bear him company," and it was a strange sound to hear a child's voice on the sea. Curiously enough I had seen this vessel the previous winter lying alongside one of the London docks, and had been lost in admiration of her, and it was passing strange now to meet her again at sea.

As we ran on, taking advantage of the breeze, we set the stove to work and cooked dinner. Past the Mewstone and the rocky islets where the Brixham "mumble-bees" had given us so much excitement, past little bays and mighty hills, we kept on. Excursion steamers were run- ning back to port at the end of the day, trawlers were beginning their fishing, and Berry Head flashed out its light just as we came abreast of its precipitous cliff. The last lap was begun as we rounded into Torbay and set a course N. by W., taking in the balloon staysail and setting the working foresail instead, as we came more on to a wind.

But fainter and fainter dropped the latter as we approached

Torquay harbour, and the lights of the town grew more dazzling. So many years had elapsed since I had been here, and the new harbour had not been then completed, that I had hoped to have saved our daylight in. This was not to be however, though we found it quite simple by paying attention to the red and green lights at the entrance. There was just sufficient of a draught to waft us in, and as the band played its last tune ashore we let go anchor, and, running out a line from each quarter to a couple of mooring buoys on the eastern side of the harbour away from the new pier, got up the riding-light and turned in.

However much Torquay may have altered ashore in the course of time, it has lost none of its charms afloat. To wake up in the morning and realise one was actually here aroused a hundred memories of one's youth. Here one had first learnt to handle a sailing-boat. Round the corner at the bathing cove one had first learnt to swim. In the farther harbour was the old man from whom one had hired boats as a boy, and rowed out to see the whole Channel Fleet assembled, and the *Victoria* and *Camperdown* at anchor in the bay before the terrible historic disaster brought them in collision in the Mediterranean.

There was plenty to look at again both in harbour and ashore, dinghy cruises in the harbour and bay, yarns to listen to, and so many things to be done on board, that we could have stopped here for weeks instead of two or three days. *Donah* and her owner came over from Paignton to welcome us, and at midnight, when a glorious full moon was up in the heavens and the sea was like glass, the motor was set going, moorings were slipped, and away we ran round the bay, with Berry Head's light blinking

ENTRANCE TO TORQUAY HARBOUR

to the southward, and a few fishermen hailing us through the night to keep the "compellor" clear of their nets.

But before we could leave Torquay *Vivette* herself needed attention. Lying during those weeks in Salcombe she had become very foul below the water-line, and her speed through the water in the light winds that had brought us here had been considerably lessened by the growth dragging through. So, in order not to have to linger too long in West Bay, we decided to give the ship a good scrub. At high tide in the morning we towed the yacht with the dinghy to the inner harbour, and making fast alongside the quay, with the peak halyards round a bollard ashore, and a boom with fend-offs to prevent the wall chafing the yacht, set to work as soon as the keel touched the ground, and, as the tide left her, scrubbed with mops and brushes until her sides were quite clean again.

In the evening, when the tide returned and floated her, we towed back to our old berth, got aboard fresh water and provisions to make us independent of the shore for the next few days, called for letters for the last time next morning, and we were ready to negotiate the long passage across West Bay.

SCRUBBING IN TORQUAY HARBOUR

CHAPTER 14

From Torquay to Lulworth

We cleared from Torquay harbour in the morning, but we might almost as well have remained where we were. The day was fine, gloriously fine, but no good for sailing. Very hot, with the wind in no certain direction, and of such strength as scarcely to give us steerage way, we gradually crawled out of the bay, using the sweep sometimes to assist us. Another series of calms was to worry us, yet still we were heading in the right direction. During the afternoon some of the sailing craft were picked up by steam yachts and given a tow back to Torquay. A couple of trading schooners came out of Teignmouth as we got almost

OFF BABBACOMBE
ORESTONE AND THATCHER ROCKS ASTERN

abreast of that town, but they were making little or no headway, like ourselves.

So, not wishing to spend another night becalmed at sea—yet making no headway to our port of destination—we decided to run in as near the land as convenient, and, as it was likely to be a quiet night, to anchor until a little breeze might come in the morning.

The two islands, Orestone and Thatcher, standing up from the sea, were astern of us, and a big yawl was evidently about to do the same as we, when an offshore breeze springing up at sunset enabled us to run back into Babbacombe Bay. With the fall of night it was no easy matter to tell exactly how far off we were from the land. There was a fair or some regatta festivity going on ashore, and these lights alone helped one to steer for where one supposed was the spire of St. Marychurch. Below the cliff, on a level with the sea, were a few weak lights, which might have been from a cottage close to the beach, but afterwards, in the morning, we found them to be the riding-lights of craft brought up much closer in.

Not wishing to stand too near in to the bay, lest the wind might shift, and we had to beat out hurriedly, we let go when the Teignmouth lights were in line with Berry Head, and, as we had expected, found we had five fathoms. Notwithstanding that the wind was a little E. of N., and so coming from the Teign-

TORQUAY HARBOUR

mouth shore, we rolled nevertheless in a very lively manner, though, having taken the precaution of riding to the kedge with a good springy rope instead of the cable, we might have been far worse off. All during the night we had a nice breeze, and there were times when we regretted having halted, but the morning would soon be here, when we should be off again. Uncertain as to what the wind might do before dawn, we took it in turn to keep anchor watch. A trawler was hovering about in our vicinity, and we had no desire for him to repeat the experiment one of his brotherhood had made on the yacht which had been sunk the other day outside Torquay pier in spite of a brilliant riding-light showing. The mate took the first watch, and I turned in for a couple of hours till 1 a.m. After that I kept watch alone till about four. From four till six, as the light returned, we both endeavoured to woo sleep, though very tired with watching, and exhausted by the heat of the previous day.

The wind had got up so much that the motion of the ship was exceedingly lively, and the creaking of spars, the rattling of kettles and pans, the slapping of the water against the yacht's sides, the slatting of ropes and halyards, and a medley of other irritating noises made sleep and rest so utterly out of the question, that we tumbled out and gave it up. Instead, we cooked breakfast, and by holding on to our mugs—the drinking vessels, I mean—we were just able to prevent the contents from being distributed all over the cabin.

By the time we had come on deck she was clipping her bowsprit into the sea in a merry fashion, and to stand upright, without being lurched overboard at every roll, long enough to allow us to hoist up sails and get in the anchor, was a very difficult undertaking. Before seven o'clock we were off again, somewhat sleepy-eyed, but gladdened by the realisation that we had a breeze at last. We had intentions of running on to Lyme Regis, but the wind was now NE. by N., and had we arrived off there we should have had drawbacks to contend with; for if we had stopped a night inside the harbour there we should have had little rest, since the tide leaves the place dry, and there would have been the nuisance of having to keep shifting warps. If, again, we had dropped our anchor outside, there was no telling what the wind might suddenly do, nor whence it might come from, and as I had only had about an hour and a half of "shut-eye" the previous night, and the mate but little more, we resolved to push straight on and get to the other side of Portland Bill whilst we had a chance.

Coming west, the reader will recollect, we had passed round the Bill close to the land and inside the race. But now bound eastward, and not knowing whether we should be able, after crossing over forty miles of bay, to hit off our tide exactly, it seemed more reasonable to go outside and well away from the land, lest in the case of a calm we should be carried by the powerful tides into the terrible race and dealt with as it pleased. There are plenty of incidents within one's knowledge to show what Portland Race can do.

One man I know has seen big topsail schooners turned round and round and rendered helpless when the race got hold of them. The year before we passed a yachtsman had lost his life in the race, and I know of a sailing vessel which entered the race and never came out of it. Even 5000-ton steamers find a decided effect is made on their steering.

The course that I had worked out for *Vivette* was to pass the Bill five or six miles to the southward. By the book of tidal streams I knew all the time the direction in which I was being carried off my course, and allowed for it accordingly. Standing out from Babbacombe Bay until we had the Orestone in line with our stern we got on to our course, and by 8.45 a.m. were off Teignmouth, where the log was put overboard. For the next twenty hours we never saw the land again, and the heavy haze which was over the Devonshire coast did not lift until we were too far away to see any land.

But the wind held excellently for a time, and the balloon staysail again did wonderful service: one could positively feel the knots rapidly reeling-off. Till after midday we had ideal sailing conditions—a fine and favourable wind, blue sea with a nice little motion to make it interesting, and a sky of fainter blue above us with powerful, brilliant sunlight. At three in the afternoon the wind moderated, and the little wisps of white vanished from the sea, yet we were still doing well. At four, however, we were doing very little—we had barely steerage way—and then for two or three hours we lay doing nothing at all, with the log hanging almost perpendicular down in the placid sea.

The mate took the helm, and for an hour or less I had a nap. Soon after we cooked dinner and got everything ready for the night. The lamps were trimmed, the direction of the tide for the next few hours verified, and the distance made good reckoned up. From the calculations thus made we fixed our position as being about 10 or 12 knots from Portland Bill, expecting the latter to bear about E. by N. Occasionally a little faint air would come from somewhere, and we could keep on our course; but it was nothing to congratulate ourselves about, and after having come thus far so well, we were not a little disappointed to be bereft still again of any wind.

Soon after seven we spoke two large sailing yachts, the first of which was flying the burgee of the R.Y.S. We asked them as to the course, and they replied that they estimated Portland Bill to bear about E., distant ten knots, so we were not far out of our reckoning. Then all three of us were becalmed again. Over to the southward a fog was coming-on and shutting out a sailing craft which looked like a trawler. We could hear the thrash and thump of a big ship's propeller getting rather too close to be pleasant, and the prospect of spending the night in the vicinity of the Bill, in the track of liners and all manner of craft rushing by in a fog, was not a pleasing thought to dwell on.

A little more wind came up soon after we had hung out the side-lights, but it was never in the same direction long. For a time we stood out to sea, and finally, when at last the breeze returned to its old quarter about NE., and seemed inclined to stay for some time, I altered my course altogether and determined to run back into the middle of West Bay on a NW. course for four hours, from eight till midnight, and then to run back again on the opposite direction SE., so that by 4 a.m., when there would be enough daylight to see, we might be at least in as good a position as we were now, and, possibly better, if the wind freshened I am convinced that, considering the lack of wind, the presence of fog, and the vicinity of the race and traffic, this was the wisest proceeding. In the hollow of West Bay there is rarely any traffic except a few traders, trawlers, yachts, or, by day, excursion steamers.

We knew our position and the direction in which the Bill bore, though we could not see it; so that by making allowance for the set of the tide as well as for leeway we could not get very far wrong by going a definite number of hours one way and then running back the same length of time in exactly the opposite direction. At midnight, then, with a good breeze, which held throughout the night, we hove-to for a little and then came about and began running back along the line we had come. Gradually the warm smell of something like new-mown hay told us we were approaching the land.

We picked up the four flashes of Portland Bill Lighthouse on the port bow, showing up on about the same bearing where we had expected to pick them up. It is so easy to get wrong in one's calculations at this game; and working out compass courses, allowing for leeway and tidal insets and changing wind, in a small cabin without falling into error is sometimes a little difficult, as those who have tried know well. We were therefore not a little pleased to find that after sailing for twenty hours with no land to fix our position by we were none the less where we expected to be.

With the light now to steer by we were able to keep on until we reckoned the latter was distant about five or six knots. This we did by using the method known as the two-point bearing. By observing when the Portland four flashes bore two points on the port bow, *i.e.* ESE., and then when they bore four points, *i.e.* E., noticing by our log the distance run in the interval, we were able to calculate the distance we were from the Bill.

The principle is of course that of the instance where, the two angles of a triangle being equal to one another, then the sides which are opposite to the equal angles are also equal to one another (*Euclid* 1. 6). When we had kept on our SE. course until the Bill bore NE. and we found that we were the five miles off, all that we had to do in order to round the Bill at the required distance and be well clear of the race was to keep the four flashes abeam until just the other side of the Bill.

This we did, and by daylight were the other side of the lighthouse. At last we had got round, and expected soon to pick up the Shambles Lightship and then alter our course for Weymouth. The gorgeous feed we were going to have when we got inside the harbour, the lovely hours of "shut-eye" we were to enjoy, with no worry about anything, and a clear run home when a westerly wind should spring up gladdened our sleepy, hungry bodies by anticipation. *Vivette* had never sailed better than during the last few hours. There was just enough sea on to amuse her, and the way she took the waves was an exhilarating pleasure.

But no sooner had we opened Grove Point on the east side of Portland than the tide turned against us (as of course we had expected), but to make matters worse the wind shifted farther ahead, so as to send me more than a point off my course. As if that was not enough, when the sun got up the wind began to decrease in force. For several hours the tide was so strong and the wind so weak, that, although we were running through the water at a nice pace, we could see by the land that we were slowly going astern, or, at the best, holding our own and nothing more.

At ten o'clock the wind vanished altogether, and until about four in the afternoon we spent the most unpleasant part of the whole of the cruise in a nasty bucking swell and a broiling sun. There was not so much as a faint air, and the yacht drifted anywhere, sometimes stern first, sometimes broadside on. The dinghy of course had to have her little say on the subject, and persistently bumped up alongside.

For a long time we used up part of our remaining energy in

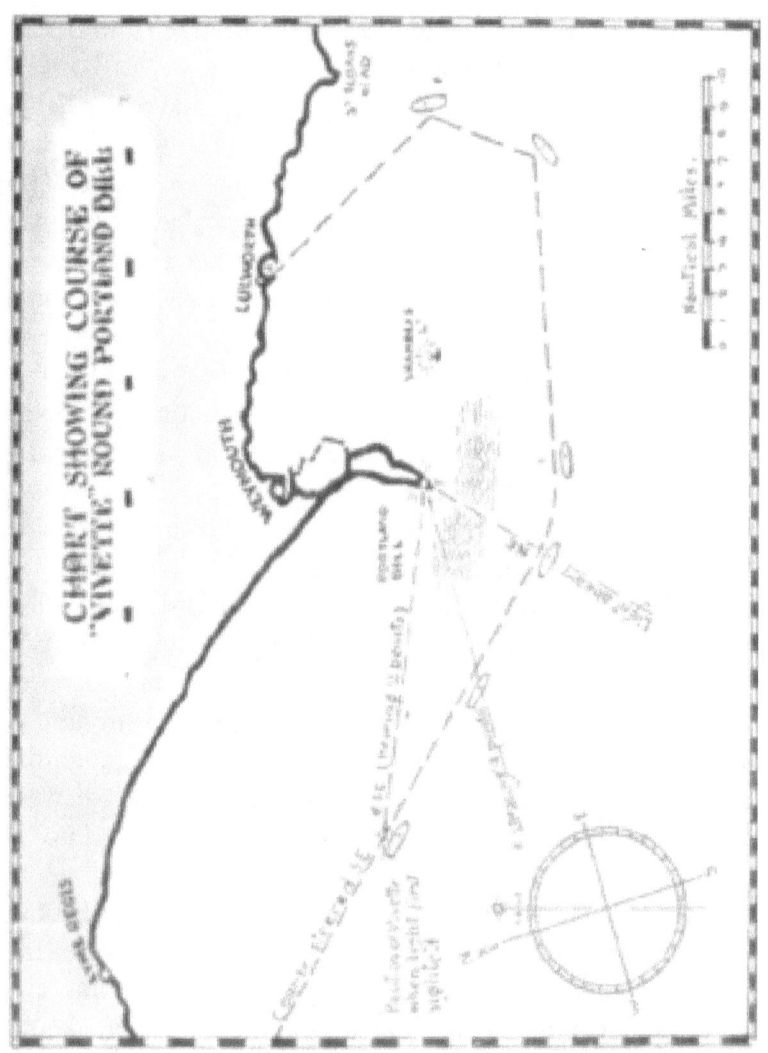

Chart showing Course of Vivette round Portland Bill

fending her off, but finally, being so weak and tired with loss of sleep and food, we lashed the helm amidships, and let both yacht and dinghy do what they pleased. The mate went below and turned in, but the cabin was like an oven. To complete matters, the large can in the fo'c'sle containing the ship's paraffin at last got adrift with the continual motion, and emptied at least half a gallon of its contents into the bilge, whence a pretty odour came into the cabin to intensify the unbearable atmosphere.

Twice, before the calm had quite set in, we had each fallen asleep at the helm with the tiller underneath our arm. If only we could have just a wisp of a wind, we thought it would be bearable. We tried every means we could conceive for refreshing our fatigue.

We tried eating, but the food would not go down somehow. We tried to drink some water from the tanks, but that was nearly as warm as the atmosphere; so we washed in it, but we were

BECALMED OFF PORTLAND BILL

soon as hot again. All the time the boom was thrashing madly from one side to another, and the counter of the yacht would come down with a slam and a bang on to the swell. Fortunately the tide had turned again and was carrying us now to the eastward instead of down Channel. Lucky it was too that we had come well to seaward of the Bill, or we should long since have been in the middle of the race. What we were encountering now was the disturbed water caused by the latter, even though sonic miles off.

Two big trading schooners appeared to the eastward, but when they found the wind was dying down altered their course and stood right out so as to give the race an offing much greater than even we had. Where we lay we were in the very track of the Channel traffic, and the day was getting on. All round, the arc of the sky was cloudless, and not a vestige of wind seemed likely to pipe up from any quarter. We had had two nights out, practically without any sleep, and there seemed every prospect of a third.

The tide would soon change again, and we should drift up and down the Channel, possibly on to the fringe of the race, and no doubt the usual evening foe would come on again. When we were not endeavouring to picture these beautiful possibilities we were lying prone on the deck hanging on to something to avoid being rolled overboard, or dozing in the well, myself over the tiller, the mate with his long stature propped up against the bulkhead. The thrashing of a steamer's propeller, however, at last awoke us to our senses, and a big liner with white gunwales passed us quite close. We must have looked singularly foolish from her lofty decks.

The tide had carried us well up Channel by now, but just as it was about to turn a weak, frail breeze came out from the westward—nothing to get excited over, but better than no wind at all. This gave us barely steerage way. Half-an-hour later and it increased slightly, so that we were doing perhaps two knots through the water. The sun lit up a headland, which I instantly recognised as St. Alban's, so, fearing the breeze might soon die away again, we decided to stand in-shore and get hold of the land before nightfall. The glad news of a little more wind brought the mate out from his couch, and we soon had the balloon staysail on her again. The wind seemed inclined to stay with us, and as we approached St. Alban's and the magnificent coast which stretches right along from Weymouth eastward I was minded to keep on and make a passage through to Poole, but the mate favoured going in to Lulworth Cove for the night to catch up on sleep. Poole seemed to convey nothing to a tired mind: Lulworth by its very name suggested rest and peacefulness. So we altered our course and steered for this.

At six in the evening we had some Bovril, which did us some good, as it was our first food for about twenty-four hours, with the exception of some cocoa which we had during the previous night, and some bread and jam which we had tried to eat off the Bill. But a fine sight was coming towards us in the shape of a four-masted *barque*, with headsails and staysails and jigger let, in tow of a powerful tug.

With her tall spars and white hull she presented a fine sight, and we felt better for having so pleasant a surprise. As we came under her stern we were able to read her name—*L'Avenir*, of Antwerp. *L'Avenir*—"the future"—that was what we had been wondering about for the last few hours. It was amusing to see this in big letters now before our eyes. But our worries were ending, for the tide had turned again and was carrying us on towards Lulworth, and the evening breeze would possibly be gracious enough to hold until we had got in.

If that morning's experience had been something very trying,

L'Avenir FOUR-MASTED BARQUE IN TOW OFF ST. ALBANS' HEAD

the close of the day was one of the most charming bits of the whole voyage. The wind just got us in to this horse-shoe cove, where high cliffs cause it to look even smaller than it really is. A number of summer visitors were rowing about the entrance, and the local fishermen were pulling their boats up the pebbly beach as *Vivette* came in through the narrow, rocky entrance and let go a little distance inside.

Before we had got sails stowed the coastguard had descended from his lofty look-out and come off to us, and in good old clumsy naval fashion bumped into our side as if he were coming along- side a battleship. In return for scraping off some of our white paint he was handed a few candid remarks which we had been accumulating during the last few hours; after which he thrust a book into one's hand to fill up details as to the "name of vessel," "master," "owner," "number of crew," "cargo," "where from"—and more besides.

Later in the evening we dined in such peace and comfort as we had not enjoyed for many a long hour. The air was beautifully warm and balmy. Out away to the south-west Portland Bill was busy with its four flashes again, reminiscent of the previous night. What a contrast to be here in this haven of rest and beauty after being tied up in a small bit of a ship for three days and two nights, with less than three hours' sleep apiece during the whole time! After dinner I got into the dinghy and rowed ashore. I shall

LULWORTH COVE

never forget the delicious stroll up the road which runs along the valley through the hills, past a few houses and pretty cottages. The night was dark but clear, and I remember passing a number of children sitting out in a garden where a luminous pattern had been made in the grass by glow-worms. They were particularly nice children, with musical voices, and singing a patriotic song that was new to one. They were the first sounds of civilisation we had heard since leaving Torquay.

We wanted fruit, and the village store was closed, but the walk had been a great treat, and I rowed back to our home humming some very optimistic tune, as if we were beginning our cruise rather than approaching its end. The riding-light was burning brightly, and the mate was smoking in the well. Like a good friend he had thoughtfully made my bed, and never was royal couch more soft and alluring than were ours tonight. By ten of the clock we were tucked up and asleep, and for ten solid hours they might have fired bombs under the cabin table and we should not have been aroused. Yes, Lulworth was a fine place.

CHAPTER 15

From Lulworth to Swanage, and Hamble

Barely had we sailed out of Lulworth Cove in the morning than the usual calm was waiting for us. Ordinarily we should have felt annoyance, but we were getting used to our bad luck now; besides which we were in soundings all the time now, and could easily let go our anchor instead of drifting. The Dorsetshire coast-line is so singularly impressive and grand, that we would have hesitated to grumble even if all the conditions were not to our liking. At any rate we were just making headway, and the tide was with us.

For companions we had several torpedo-gunboats from Portland, which, moving very slowly, and occasionally bringing up, interested us vastly. A number of small buoys had been dotted up and down the bay between Lulworth and St. Alban's, and we watched His Majesty's ships engaged in the latest Naval fad of sweeping for mines, a lesson which the Russo-Japanese War has instilled into the Admiralty. Two gunboats seemed to tow abreast of each other about a cable's distance apart, each ship having an erection at the stern resembling a thick spar set at an angle of about forty-five degrees, apparently used as a sort of cathead for the sweeping gear. Other manoeuvres followed, including firing at moving targets. There was only another yacht in sight, so we had a sort of private naval review of our own.

By occasional puffs of wind aided by the sweep we at last

reached St. Alban's Head, keeping as before close in to the shore and inside the race, which, like a gigantic ostrich feather, stretched right away for some distance to the south-east. Although the sea was otherwise perfectly smooth, it seemed to make no difference to the existence of the overfalls. As soon as we began to round the headland a nice little westerly breeze sprang up, so booming the balloon foresail out like a spinnaker, we left the other yacht astern, and went along gaily past the exquisitely coloured coast, the brown Tilly Whim caves with Anvil Lighthouse perched above, and rounded Durlstone Head.

We had just been able to get ahead of Peveril Point, and to open Swanage Bay, looking snug and pretty with its green fields and red-tiled roofs, when the tide turned against us strongly; so relinquishing our original plan of making for Poole, we ran into the bay, and picking out the best berth we could find abreast of the pier and out of the way of the passenger steamer traffic, anchored once more. Swanage, in spite of its alluring natural beauty, leaves much to be desired from the yachtsman's point of view. Like other forms of beauty, it is treacherous when it likes. The holding ground, as the sailing directions rightly point out, is indeed indifferent.

As soon as the wind gets easterly it is time to clear out, and we noticed that every one of the yachts at anchor here kept her jib lashed to the bowsprit, with the mainsail all ready for getting under weigh in the shortest possible time. We did the same.

But the glass was high, and the evening was as calm and peaceful as ever. The mate rowed ashore after dinner, replenished his camera, and purchased such stores as Lulworth had not been able to supply us with. In the morning, as soon as decks were washed down and the breakfast cleared away, we peaked the main well up, and after wasting some time off the white cliffs of Bollard Point taking photographs from the dinghy, at half-past nine set our faces in the direction of Christchurch Head.

It was a case of advancing by faith rather than by sight, for another fog had come up, shutting out everything to seaward, and totally obliterating the Hampshire shore. Steering E. by N., and making allowance for the tide which was still coming out of Poole harbour, but would soon change in our favour, and allowing from half to a point for leeway, we began to travel with the wind from about northwest. Our useful and hardworking friend the balloon staysail, which in the light weather had helped us so much during the cruise, was again hoisted, but alas! for the last time, for we were now nearing the end. Gradually the wind backed to the westward and the fog lifted, to the relief, no doubt, of the tug which had come out of Poole "seeking."

Instead of the thick haze we had a rich sunshine again, but still the wind was holding nicely: we could not have wished for fairer conditions. For a time we had hesitated whether to enter the Solent by the North Passage between Hurst and Shingles, as we had come the previous year, or whether to go outside and come up through the Needles Channel for a change. In the fog it would not have been easy to pick up the Christchurch I lead Buoy, but since the atmosphere had cleared we made for the latter, and stood straight on for the prominent white farm, bearing about E. by N. from the buoy.

This is a most useful object when wishing to cross Christchurch Bay and making for the North Passage, and is the mark used by the Bournemouth steamers making for inside the Wight. Then as soon as the red building of Cliff End Fort on the Isle of Wight shore bears SE. by E., all that one has to do is to alter one's course to this, and go straight on. By this means the various traps in the North Passage are avoided, and there is no need for anxiety; but, of course, it would be futile to turn to windward through here with a foul tide.

As we passed Hurst a barge was actually on the Shingles loading pebbles and sand, a big White Star liner was coming out dead slow, followed by a four-funnelled German-American liner. No sooner had the former arrived off Totland Bay than the fog which had left us earlier in the day returned. For a long time we heard a merry quartet continuing from the foghorns of the two liners outward bound, another big steamer coming in, and the Needles Lighthouse making its shrill sound in contrast to the others as a soprano is to a trio of basses. Curiously, though the Needles were shut out from sight no suspicion of a fog came any nearer to us than about Totland, but for a few moments the wind dropped so much that, with the strong tide off Hurst Point, the power of wind and stream was about equal.

Thus, although we were passing the shore at a good speed, the rudder was rendered for a short time inoperative. It is curious, too, what a little bit of a popple is caused off the point where the strong tide rushing up out of the North Passage collides at right angles with the equally powerful stream flooding from the direction of the Needles so as to create a kind of miniature race, which in the event of wind being against tide might cause inconvenience to small craft.

Setting our course E. by N. for the Solent Banks Buoy, we were not long in leaving Yarmouth astern. Never had we seen the coastline on either side looking so beautiful as today. The grandeur of the Dorset cliffs and the cruel majesty of the rocks of Devon had given way to the richly-wooded grass slopes of Hampshire. There was the usual assortment of Solent traffic everywhere to keep us ever interested—more liners, yachts of all kinds, barges, schooners, warships, and I forget what else. Off Beaulieu one of the "County" Class armoured cruisers, H.M.S. *Hampshire*, passed us bound the other way.

Dotted here and there with officers and men at their posts, stuck all over with wireless gear, fire-control stations, and no end of other gadgets, she was every bit as impressive-looking as business-like. Had she come a little earlier, when the other three

H.M.S. HAMPSHIRE

big steamers were passing Hurst and the fog came up, we should have seen an interesting bit of seamanship no doubt with four monsters in none too wide a channel, and each of them drawing about thirty feet of water.

As we came up past the Brambles, and saw again the old, familiar navigation buoys, so well known to all who cruise along here in the summer time, we saw the *Shamrock* and *White Heather* and the others of our crack racing fleets, showing up a fine picture over towards Spithead. Cutting across Calshot Spit, just inside the light-float, past the Castle over to the eastern shore, past the Baldhead Buoy to the entrance of the little opening which leads into the river Hamble, we sailed merrily on. The tide was just coming up as we passed Warsash, pretty as ever, with its water-way just as narrow and congested with craft as the day we had left it. Then, farther up beyond the houseboat *Gitana*, her white hull showing up prominently against the green background of Hamble's trees, we rounded-to, and coming to anchor astern of the training-ship *Mercury,* brought our little voyage to its conclusion.

Before we hauled down our burgee at the end of the cruise we had time to reckon up a few of the lessons that we had learned during the last two summers and our pleasant voyage of over a thousand miles. If we had done nothing wonderful, at least we had an opportunity of forming conclusions which were as interesting as any to be arrived at on shore. The sport

At anchor in the Hamble

of yachting is yet so young that it is barely out of its infancy, and whatever improvements may be forthcoming as to external design and internal economy must result for the most part from actual experience of the kind that we had enjoyed. It is possible to cruise for a year on a bigger vessel with all the seamanship and navigation carried out by paid-hands, without the passengers ever learning more than may be already known of the sea and the ways of ships. But to rely on your own resources, however, and to do every item of the mixed duties of cooking, navigation, seamanship, and catering, you are compelled to keep learning all the time.

Every man will extol his own particular sport to the exclusion of all others, but when all the pros and cons have been weighed, it will still be found that in this yachting game not merely is there relaxation from the ordinary routine which only monotonises life, but there is health to the body and the widest scope for mental and physical activity. Every time you get under weigh there is opportunity for quick but not hasty judgment. Passing other craft, estimating the distance that will clear you, picking up moorings, cheating wind and tide, and a dozen other chances, keep your mind on the alert and quicken your powers of decision. At the same time you are in the open sea air and adding to your health the while; you are arrived right back in the bosom of nature, away from artificialities and shams. In the science and art of the sea game, whether played in big ships or little yachts, it is much the same: there is never any finality, and the more you learn, the more you fathom your own ignorance.

From a more personal point of view the effects on character which instil and deepen a man's physical and moral courage, his spirit of self-reliance, patience, and unselfishness in trying times cannot be lightly disregarded. He learns to be ready for most things and to be surprised at nothing; but all the time whilst playing he is doing something really serious, something which men of all nations have done in earnest for war or for trade from the time of the Egyptians and earlier down to the present day. The professional sailor, the genuine fisherman, even the deep-sea mariner, does not laugh you to scorn though you have come round in your little bit of a ship. In actual experience he respects you the more for relying on your own powers and trusting yourself to the sea. He is willing to yarn with you, and let you into no end of good tips regarding ships and the sea. There are, of course, the customary shore-sharks to be avoided everywhere, but as a rule, when he sees you arrive in port and round-to, the sailor-man is ready to be your friend, whereas had you come ashore from a palatial yacht with a brass-bound crew aboard he would shut down "like a clam."

In port there is always plenty to do on board keeping the "house" clean and making continual improvements in gear and stowage, apart altogether from any attractions of interest ashore. At sea there is not, as many often imagine, a dull moment. Passing craft, a good lookout, watching the changing conditions of wind and tide, calculating distances, working out bearings, and fifty other duties keep your eyes busy all the day and night. You are travelling round the extremities of your mother-land without encumbrance, and with all your luggage and conveniences aboard. You are seeing your country as it can never be seen from the shore, and getting deeper into the heart of things.

Under ordinary circumstances it is unlikely, for instance, that you would ever find yourself one day in St. Just, and a few days later in Lulworth, where no railway can dump its noisy crowd of Philistines to spoil natural peace and beauty. There is of course a little danger now and again, but that only accentuates the excitement, and brings out half-developed virtues to receive their tonic.

Perhaps the present generation, at any rate, will never agree as to the definition of the ideal cruiser. To some extent it will always be modified by personal preferences, questions of size and of accommodation. But with regard to the vexed question as to whether a yacht should carry the whole of her ballast externally or internally, one can only make reply that as in other respects the yacht is a compromise, so here the same principle holds good. The vessel with a lead mine on her keel has undoubtedly certain advantages, but they do not lie in the direction of comfort, if of speed. When the motion of the sea swings the boat from side to side, the fact of the weight being at the lowest extremity must obviously cause her momentum to resemble that of the pendulum. The Bristol Channel pilot craft have part of the ballast on the keel and part inside, so as to make the swing of the pendulum as small as possible.

When *Vivette* was in the motion of the Channel off Portland Bill, for instance, we were glad that we had so much of our ballast inside, for a few hours of balancing yourself on a lively little craft detract from your endurance when you can least afford to allow it. Another compromise that has to be made on behalf of the cruiser as opposed to the racing craft is the relation which speed must bear to comfort. It is impossible to have it both ways, and if your intention is to live as well as sail, to be independent of the shore, going from port to port instead of running out and home for day-sails, you soon decide that comfort is worth sacrificing something of speed. What "coal endurance" is in the mind of the naval man, physical endurance is to the yachtsman. There are limits, and to pass beyond these means encountering unnecessary risk, which is rather folly than bravery.

With regard to the question of rig, there is something to be said for the ketch and something for the yawl; but to split up the area of your canvas and increase the amount of gear on board is hardly necessary, unless the size of your ship exceeds ten tons. Sloops may be all very well for home-sailing, but, for preference, in doing passages I would not exchange for the cutter rig. The convenience of being able to stow the stay-sail when coming to anchor, and the advantage of always having an additional head-sail in case anything carries away forward, cannot be dismissed as of no value.

If it is true that an army "marches on its stomach," so it is equally certain that the remark is applicable in the case of sailing. To neglect the domestic arrangements of cooking is to decrease the efficiency of the crew. We made it a practice of dining on board and cooking every- thing that we wanted. Apart altogether from the increased expense of having meals at an hotel when ashore, there is the added regret of having sacrificed one's independence. At the same time it is essential to insist on regularity of feeding times, and to pay proper attention to cooking. With a good hot meal inside them, your crew will eagerly face an uphill fight, when, fasting, they would have gone about the work with the deepest pessimism.

At least two hot meals a day was our rule, and we kept fit and strong, with the exception of the experience off Portland, where lack of sleep had fatigued us so much as to take away the desire for food. Good, fresh meat taken aboard at every port, plenty of fruit and vegetables, and lime-juice for health's sake, make a sure foundation for the cruising man's wants. The tinned things can be kept for emergencies, and not touched except under those unlooked-for conditions. We cooked dinner usually with the boilerette. The operation was simplicity itself. The meat was cut up into small pieces, and with tomatoes, potatoes, carrots, and turnips was put in together to stew. It required no watching, and could not burn.

And here let it be emphasised, that the simpler the food when cruising the better it is for one's health and the work to be carried out. To live and eat as you would on shore is to make a great mistake. You are out in the hot sun or biting wind, with a keen appetite that needs no tempting. What you want is not so much food that is pleasant to the palate, as substantial sustenance to maintain your strength. As you come down and begin your life aboard after being cooped up in town, the change of life is so sudden, that for a day or two you frequently feel out of sorts. For this reason we usually spent at least a day simply living aboard, until we had become acclimatised to the new surroundings.

We carried for most of the cruise a drogue or sea-anchor on board in case we ever got caught in really bad weather and had to ride it out. Happily, however, we never had occasion to use it except for a different purpose in port, when the yacht was lying to her anchor and the wind was against tide. By allowing the drogue to tow astern, as long as ever the tide was strong enough, the little ship was prevented from careering about the anchorage and from any possibility of tripping her anchor.

When one hears the accounts of Captain Slocum's voyage round the world in a small yacht singlehanded, or of Captain Voss's equally marvellous wanderings in the *Tilikum*, one hesitates so much as to mention the rising of a wave or the puffing of the wind. Whereas we had only cruised up and down the English Channel, these two intrepid mariners had roamed over oceans, doing their navigating and cooking" with as much ease as we in the *Vivette*.

But it is pertinent to draw attention to the fact that whereas in traversing oceans and big seas the waves are long and steady, yet coasting, as we were, round headlands and bays, where the tides are strong and races and overfalls busy, where the nasty short seas cause greater anxiety than the waves farther out, being tossed about instead of feeling the rhythmic swell of the deep sea, was ever a source of some anxiety. If it comes on to blow in the open you can lower everything and ride to your drogue until the weather moderates.

You have everywhere plenty of sea-room, and the amount of drift which the vessel makes from her proper course can be reckoned up near enough. But supposing you find yourself caught in a gale in the Channel when on a coasting trip you are less happily situated. You may ride more or less comfortably to your sea-anchor, but the chances are that the SW. wind is blowing you nearer and nearer to the shore, with the prospect of losing your ship and your life as well. Instead of being able to go below and turn in, knowing that the vessel will be all right without you, it is essential that you keep on the *qui vive* all the time.

The English Channel, being the highway not merely of most of the British commerce, but the road that leads to the Baltic and German Ocean, is full of traffic. At all times of the day and night some ship is coming along, and at night your light might not be easily visible in the trough of the waves to the steamer thrashing ahead determined to be in port punctually at all costs.

There was one other consideration which in the presence

of calms could not help being called attention to during our cruise. Should the ideal cruiser have also fitted an auxiliary motor? There were many times when the wind fell and the tide turned against us that we longed for this luxury, but on the whole I am not sure that we really desired it.

In time it will no doubt be found as the rule rather than the exception on a yacht, but at any rate for small craft three recent and historic tragedies to yachts and life have proved that the danger from fire at sea is far too great to counterbalance the convenience offered. I believe I am right in saying that Lloyd's now decline to insure motor-yachts at any price, so the time for the universal adoption of this assistant means of propulsion would seem to be not yet, though approaching no doubt.

It was still early August, and there were plenty of nice little ports within reach to cruise into, or we could remain at anchor and loaf in the dinghy, as one willed. But the summer would soon be at an end, and already the days were beginning to shorten visibly. Perhaps a few sails outside and back again for the night would suffice before *Vivette* and her crew went into winter quarters, until at the summons of spring and the return of the long warm days the sea would find us coming out to seek once more some of those quaint little anchorages which to have seen is to make you long most ardently to revisit, not once but a thousand times. For, after a time, civilisation on shore begins to pall, and your prehistoric man begins to reassert himself.

Through Holland
in the Vivette

IN THE MIDDLEBURGH CANAL
VIVETTE BEING TOWED ALONGSIDE *JAMALE*.
PHOTOGRAPH TAKEN FROM *JAMALE'S* CROSS-TREES.
VIVETTE IS ON THE RIGHT OF THE PICTURE.

Contents

Preface	167
Introductory	169
A Chapter of Accidents	177
Southampton Water to Ramsgate	190
Ramsgate to Calais	206
Calais to Ostende	217
Ostende to Flushing	229
Through the Island of Walcheren	240
Veere to Numansdorp	257
Numansdorf to Dordrecht	271
Around Dort	285
Dordrecht to Gouwe	298
Gouwe to Amsterdam	311
Amsterdam and Nieuwendam	324
Southwards through Holland	335
To the English Channel and North Sea	348
Appendix	367

Preface

There are two ways of taking a cruise. The first is to sail from one port to another for the sheer delight in reaching a definite place. The joy of seamanship, navigation, and life on board is in itself complete. Shore interests, peoples, and scenery do not come within the scope of the man who elects to adopt this method. He is the counterpart of that other yachtsman, made famous in a certain nautical novel, who regarded the shore usually as a nuisance and convenient only for the purpose of replenishing the ship's stores.

The other plan, however, is to sacrifice none of the pleasures of sailing, but to add to these all the interest which can be derived from the people and the places visited. The shore is to be regarded not solely as a tiresome necessity, but as affording contrasts to the life on board with manifold delights in the customs of the people and the scenery through which one passes.

Each of these methods is capable of being carried out by the keenest of partisans. But for the benefit of those who peruse the following cruise it may be asserted at once that the second of the above methods was followed.

I have again to thank my sailing mate, Mr. Norman S. Carr, for the sketches and practically all the photographs which are included in the present log. For the convenience of those who may not be familiar with *Vivette* it has been deemed well to reproduce her sail- and sheer-plan from *Down Channel in the Vivette*.

E. Keble Chatterton.

CHAPTER 1

Introductory

The kindly reception which greeted *Down Channel in the Vivette*, and the desire both implied and expressed on the part of public and press that a further volume might be issued as a sequel to the former, have encouraged me to present the present log of a cruise to and through Holland and back again to England. How that little voyage was accomplished and with what adventures, the reader will be at liberty to read for himself in the following pages.

It is a little extraordinary that, comparatively speaking, few British yachtsmen visit these interesting waters during their summer vacation, although within the last few years more craft flying the red or blue ensign have been seen in the Low Countries since the introduction of the marine motor. But the fact remains that of the many thousands of tourists who visit Holland annually, quite a minute percentage—so minute, in fact, as almost to be negligible—ever succeed in seeing the Netherlands in the only way in which a correct estimate can be found.

Those who travel by train from one place to another, studying just the towns and places recognised by the tourist-agencies, gain but a limited and far from accurate idea of the country. Those who scour across the flat roads in automobiles certainly are nearer to acquiring a just estimate. But inasmuch as some of the most interesting and instructive portions of Holland are situate in the most unapproachable places, on islands and by the water-side far from trains or high-roads, the ordinary traveller and land-motorist miss these, so that to them they are as if they never existed.

Whatever else Holland is or may become, it always has been, and will ever continue to be, a marine country. Its long and interesting history, with all that it has done in regard to development of canals and inland navigation, with all that it has done in the development of the fore-and-aft rig, the improvements in the science of naval architecture, the art of shipbuilding, and the momentous alterations which that country wrought in vessels' rig, these items alone point to Holland as being essentially a land of mariners.

In addition to this must also be recollected the exceptionally important position which Holland occupied as a great naval power in the seventeenth century, and the spirited contest which was waged in the great three Anglo-Dutch naval wars. Think of Holland, also, as having been a most wealthy nation, as a great colonising country, and a great trading community. Recollect, too, that she produced not merely great portrait-painters but the finest marine artists that the world had ever seen. And finally, call to mind that it was Holland which produced the first yacht that was ever launched, and in whose territory the first English-owned yacht was built.

With these considerations in mind it is impossible to regard the Netherlands as merely one of the Continental countries. And unless one's visit to its confines include facilities for studying primarily its aspects, past and present, as a seafaring country, one returns home with an erroneous idea of values, with a distorted notion of Holland's progress and development. As an example, one may go to Holland exclusively to study the exquisite Franz Hals, and the other great portraitists of the past. But recollect that these portraits are intimately bound up with the marine development of Holland. Patronage of artists is essentially a luxury: it can be bestowed only by the wealthy. Those rich merchants, whose ruddy countenances have been perpetuated for us in their lace collars drinking their wine and beer from milky-white glass or pewter cup, owed their prosperity either directly or indirectly to the part which Holland had played as "wagoners of the sea." Art is dependent on that peace which a navy ensures. The shallow-draughted, square-sterned, wooden warships of seventeenth-century Holland were at once a protection and (indirectly) an encouragement for artists to spring up and devote themselves to the more delicate pursuits of life.

And so the enthusiast who visits Holland only with the intention of studying its paintings is like a person who glues his eyes to one buttress of a Gothic cathedral. He has no idea of perspective: no sense of proportion. He cannot see a cathedral for stones. Therefore it is justifiable to submit that in these two long cruises, which combined ample opportunity of studying carefully all the relics of the past in museums and picture-galleries, at least the right method was attempted to obtain an accurate knowledge of the country, which, in itself, is at once so instructive and so picturesque.

For the rest, the reader must judge for himself to what extent this log exhibits the amount of sport enjoyed. There is always a keen pleasure in seeing new places, especially if those places are foreign. But the greatest delight of all is to get there by your own efforts, and by employing only such forces as wind and tide. This long cruise or cruises must also have some value in refuting that popular but foolish argument, that because a craft is small she cannot go where her bigger sisters are wont to travel. I remember an old sailorman once explaining to me, with great emphasis (re the loss of the five-masted *Preussen*), that it was possible to build sailing ships too big, and that it in nowise followed that the bigger the craft the more seaworthy would she be; and he went on to quote from his own experience.

In a certain gale a 400-ton *barque*, of which he was skipper, and a 2000-ton ship, or *barque* (I forget which), were within short distance of each other; but notwithstanding that the latter was five times the size of the other, it was the *barque* which came out with far less damage, and made much better weather of it than the bigger ship. The smaller ship was, of course, the livelier of the two, but she was lighter, and did not pound into the seas as the other.

Of course there is, to quote a current phrase, "an irreducible minimum" even in the size of seaworthy ships. There are times when it would be more foolish to cross the Thames estuary from, say, Southend to Sheerness, in a sailing canoe than it would be to cross the Atlantic in a vessel the size of *Vivette*. But I believe that, given a well-built, sensibly-designed 5-tonner, suitably rigged and sparred, with adequate freeboard, well-equipped as to her inventory, well- watered, well-provisioned; and, finally, most important of all, well-manned and well-handled, she could endure far more ambitious voyages than most people would suggest.

There were not wanting those, both among the professionals and others, who thought it foolish and risky to attempt such a trip as ours to Holland in so small a craft; and these pessimists, were found croaking both in the English and Dutch ports. And yet what would they have said of the famous voyage of the *Sea Bird*, which crossed on her own bottom in the summer of 1911 from Providence, Rhode Island (U.S. A,), and, after calling elsewhere, reached Rome with her crew of three amateurs well, and the ship in good condition? Now the *Sea Bird* was only 19 ft. on the water-line, whereas *Vivette* is 21 ft.

Mr. Fleming Day, the skipper of the *Sea Bird*, in his log of this voyage, tells a yarn which is characteristic. The *Sea Bird* had arrived at Gibraltar from America, and a Moorish merchant was standing looking down at her from the quay, when he inquired of a Gibraltar yachtsman what was the reason for the *Sea Bird* having made such a voyage.

"Have these men no homes?" inquired the merchant.

"Homes? Yes, of course they have."

"Are there no steamers from Providence with music and dining-rooms and comforts?"

"Yes; plenty of them."

The merchant was perplexed. "Then," he added, "why did they come in that small vessel?"

"They came for sport; they came for amusement," was the instant answer.

Sail and Sheer Plan of *Vivette*

The Moor gave another thoughtful look at the *Sea Bird*, and then shaking his head, "Mad! Mad!" he exclaimed.

There is not much comparison between the magnificent and daring voyage of the *Sea Bird* and the much shorter cruise of the *Vivette*, but that Moor has his counterpart in Amsterdam and other ports, both Dutch and English. It is difficult to explain to such persons as these the depth and extent of the sport and amusement to be obtained by a couple of amateurs in a small craft; and it is useless to waste time trying to instil enthusiasm in utterly irresponsive minds. But that there is to be found the very finest sport in such experiences will be guaranteed by many a sailing man. And if only we had been provided with an auxiliary motor engine for employment in calms, and to help us to beat to windward and to stem tides, we could have done far more.

Those who read Dow Channel in the *Vivette* will remember the detailed description given of her. It is not essential now to repeat this, but it may perhaps add to the reader's interest if I state briefly that *Vivette* is a 4-ton cutter, with the accommodation of many a boat twice her tonnage; that she measures 25 ft. overall, 21 ft. on the water-line, 71 ft. extreme beam, and draws 4 ft. 3 in. She is an excellent sea-boat, and by no means slow. She likes a breeze, and is as stiff as a house. She has a somewhat full-bodied midship section, a cut-away forefoot, with a certain amount of flare for'ard and a short elliptical counter. In most respects she is a small edition of the Bristol Channel pilot cutters, which are perhaps the finest sea-boats of their size and rig to be found anywhere. *Vivette* is fitted with Turner's reefing gear for the mainsail, and is built of yellow pine an inch and a quarter thick. She carries about two tons of lead on her keel, and about another ton of ballast inside. Below she is fitted with every convenience for sleeping three, though I prefer two. She is well-found, with three anchors and one canvas sea-anchor, and all necessary gear for keeping the sea. Sufficient drinking water is carried for two men for four days; but with a little care it could be made to last for a week.

Vivette handles as easily as a small rater, goes well to windward, carries a good deal of weather-helm, and will heave-to most comfortably. Her hull is painted white, with a red anti-fouling composition below the water-line. Her decks are painted a mahogany colour, which is a great convenience. Cooking is done on two primus stoves, one of which can be swung in gimbals for cooking when under way. An 8-foot *pram* dinghy is towed astern, and sometimes on arriving in a strange anchorage it is good fun to sail about in her. The latter carries a brown lugsail, and a dagger centre-plate, which enable her to beat to windward.

Such an introduction, then, may suffice to bring the reader to a perusal of the following log.

TRACK CHART OF THE VIVETTE FROM THE SOLENT TO AMSTERDAM

Chapter 2

A Chapter of Accidents

After her cruise down Channel to Falmouth and back, *Vivette* had wintered at Bursledon, up the River Hamble. During the dark days at the end of the year, when one endeavours to plan out the ideal summer cruise, various schemes presented themselves. Of these one was to go west once more and make for the Scillies. Another idea was to run across the Channel to Fécamp, and cruise along the French coast eastward. I had never taken *Vivette* foreign, and it would be a delightful way of combining a cruise and a continental holiday. Charts were obtained, and the scheme roughed out.

But while this project was maturing it was borne in on me that in any case I should have occasion to visit the Netherlands in connection with a certain matter; and since it would obviously be far pleasanter to sail thither and live aboard one's own floating home during the enforced sojourn in Dutch territory, it was eventually decided to cancel the Fécamp trip and to make for Holland instead. After leaving the English shore it would be entirely fresh sailing ground. The ports, coast, channels, peoples, and places would for the most part be new or half forgotten: there would all the time be more than enough to enthral one's interest; and, finally, we should be sailing to a region whose geographical features would make a delightful contrast to the cliffs and rocks of Devonshire and Cornwall.

That was one aspect that commended itself. But the cruise was also to have its serious side, for I wanted to study at first hand the Dutch shipping of today and the pictorial records of its bygone craft as visualised by the artists of the past. To that end it would be necessary to make for the towns where the best art collections and libraries were located, and since these cities are happily located alongside rivers or canals there was no reason why one should not arrive at the gates of these respective places without the aid of steamboat or railway. That our pleasure did not interfere with research may be gathered from the volume which followed.[1] That our work did not encroach too much on the pleasantness of the cruise will presently become manifest.

I was fortunate enough to find that Mr. Norman S. Carr was able to sign on again as mate, artist, and ship's cook. And as the *Vivette* never carries paid hands, the important matter of crew was at once settled. It only remained, therefore, to urge the ship-wrights to hurry on with their work, and to get the little craft fitted out with the utmost despatch. In the meantime there was plenty to do in getting together the necessary charts and reference books, plotting out courses, working out in great detail the objects of our trip, and generally so arranging matters as to leave no possible loophole for any contretemps other than sheer bad luck. The victualling of the ship for eight weeks or so required a good deal of thought, for we were informed that certain commodities were totally unobtainable in Holland, while others were so much inferior in quality that it were best we should take such articles from England.

On a big yacht it is not quite such a problem to provision for a foreign cruise, but in a little 4-tonner economy of space is of the utmost importance. The various stores certainly did look rather alarming in cubic size before being put aboard, but somehow by the time they had been stowed into the lockers there was no overcrowding and little chance of anything getting adrift. I need not weary the reader with the hundred-and-one details which had to be gone through, and we may pass on to the end of June, when on running down to Bursledon I spent

---

1. *Fore and Aft*: The Story of the Fore and Aft Rig, from the Earliest Times to the Present Day.

a rainy week-end on board at moorings seeing that everything was in order and ready for sea. Numerous minor improvements had been made to the ship, and now with her red-ochred decks, her white-enamelled hull and varnished spars she looked fit and eager for the work she was shortly to attempt. I had no intention of starting until the 9th of July, so before coming down again there was time for a very important addition to be made—an innovation that was found later to be invaluable. This consisted in having a yard- and square-sail made for running before the wind instead of the spinnaker, which is more suitable for racing craft than for genuine cruising. It was adopted experimentally, and the dimensions of the yard and sail were more or less speculative, as we had no very definite data to go upon: in the end neither the idea nor its execution was far wrong, though the mistake was made of having somewhat greater strength, and therefore weight, than was essential. A wire jackstay was fitted forward from the cross-trees and attached to an eye-bolt in the deck by means of a rigging-screw. This was added expressly for the purpose of the square-sail, but incidentally it acted as a further support to the mast. The method of using this sail was as follows:—

Every sailing man knows that with the wind aft a cutter's head-sails are doing little or no good. Therefore the fore-sail, at any rate, can easily be dispensed with. That leaves the fore-halyard available for the square-sail. The sail attached to its yard is laid along the weather deck, and the fore-halyard is bent on to the yard; but in order to control the latter more effectually, and to keep it close to the mast, a shackle is also attached to the spar. This shackle works freely up and down the jackstay, so that in hoisting and lowering the yard can do all that it has to perform, but at the same time cannot blow too far forward.

The fall of the fore-halyard is also bent to the yard to act as a downhaul. Attached to either clew of the square-sail is a sheet of good length, and these sheets lead outside the rigging. Just before hoisting, the man forward hands the sheets to the steersman, who is thus able to belay temporarily, or hold them in his hand till the other man is free to come aft and trim them according to the wind. When running with the wind dead aft or broad on the quarter the square-sail is unquestionably ideal. It cannot gybe, it looks after itself; it is a lifting sail, and is generally so handy that it is surprising the cruising man does not employ it more than he is wont. There is none of the anxiety which pertains to the spinnaker, and there is no necessity to carry a spinnaker-boom.

The square-sail-yard is a shorter, lighter, handier spar. Add to this the fact that practically the whole of the square-sail is in-board, and that it can be carried in almost any weather, and certainly long after the time when a spinnaker would have been stowed. For a little craft to run before, say, a moderate gale in a heavy sea with a spinnaker and its boom hitting the waves every time the ship rolled to that side would be both dangerous and nerve-trying in the extreme; whereas in the case of the square-sail you would merely reef down and then hoist again. So much for theory. How this was put into practice will shortly be seen.

The mate had preceded me by a couple of days when I came down from town with the last batch of luggage. A hail soon brought him off in the dinghy. It was a fine, warm summer's afternoon, and it was delightful to realise that at length we were about to get away cruising, and to lead the free life again. As we pulled off to where *Vivette* was lying in the stream, the old sea-fever seemed to break out afresh in one's body. The grateful breeze, the lap-lap of the water against the bows of the dinghy—so heavily laden that her stern was almost awash—the motion of the different craft as they swayed to the tide, the pure sweet country air, the hills and leafy trees, the very sound of the row-locks—everything that could appeal to the senses seemed to call one out once more to the life that is worth living.

> *I must go down to the seas again, to the vagrant gipsy life,*
> *To the gull's way and the whale's way where the wind's like a whetted knife;*
> *And all I ask is a merry yarn from a laughing fellow-rover,*
> *And quiet sleep and a sweet dream when the long trick's over.*

So we come alongside, bundle aboard, and thankfully change into sea-going clothes, make a final stow of our necessary impedimenta, and then take a look round. The mate had employed the previous day in overhauling the cabin and fok'sle. The bedding had been aired, the lamps trimmed, the stoves examined, and the bos'un's stores attended to. I had sent to Norfolk for the iron fittings of a Norfolk Broad quant, and Moody had made me a pole, for we should need this when we came to the shallow Dutch canals.

There were a couple of boathooks, too, and we should use them often in negotiating locks. The spinnaker-boom, spinnaker, and other unnecessary gear had been sent ashore and nothing superfluous remained. But when we came to hoist the square-sail I found that I had made a mistake, for I had presumed that *Vivette's* old winter main-sail, which was in excellent condition, might be cut into the required shape and thus utilised. The sail-maker had made a good job of it, but being of stout canvas and tanned it was far too heavy—so heavy, in fact, that when it was attached to the yard it was about as much as one man could hoist. This was, then, the first shock to our plans, and it was obvious that either we should have to go without any square-sail at all or else wait till another could be made.

The first alternative commended itself in no way better than the second: for as the whole of our course to Holland was roughly east, and at this time of the year, when the easterly winds have usually ended and the south-westers could almost daily be relied upon, we could expect a fair wind, and that the square-sail would be in use most of the time. At the same time we had a good many miles to cover, and might be delayed along the coast by intervals of bad weather, so the possibility of delay was a displeasing thought. However, on turning out the next morning we speedily realised that in spite of all our well-laid plans, and the meticulous care with which our scheme had been evolved, we had to bow our heads to disappointment.

To begin with, the wind had during the night inconsiderately gone round to N.E., regardless of the fact that the Meteorological Office had distinctly foretold a nice breeze from the N.W. The latter would have meant a smooth-water passage and a fair wind up Channel, but N.E. was not what we either wanted or expected. So we decided to run down as far as the east end of the Isle of Wight at any rate; and if the wind was not then favourable we could run into Bembridge for a while. The jib was shackled on, the crutches stowed away, and the topping-lift tautened, and we had just hoisted the main-sail and were "sweating" it up, when the wire luff-rope of the latter burst at the clew.

What we thought and what we said by way of comment need not be added; but though I saw that we could make a temporary makeshift, and that in fair weather the sail could probably be made to work pretty well, yet the possibility was that it might give elsewhere at a critical moment when we could ill afford to play tricks. The vision of punching to windward in a nasty sea, close-reefed in a tide-rip off Calais, for instance, with a torn main-sail, immediately influenced me to condemn the whole thing and avoid unnecessary risks. I must get a new sail, and at once. Perhaps we might be lucky enough to find one of a size that would fit *Vivette*; otherwise it would take days to make one. It did not take us long to find that there was nothing suitable in Bursledon, so the obvious thing was to search Southampton.

But it was Saturday, and the shipbuilding yards and sail lofts would be closed in a few hours. We consulted Moody, who seeing our plight kindly volunteered to run into that port at once. But, to make matters worse, there were no trains at that time of the day. We were now becoming resigned to this sudden change in affairs when our counsellor again proffered to help us by traversing the distance on bicycle. We waited till the afternoon, but his quest had been unsuccessful. There was nothing in the whole of Southampton that would do. It was now the top of high- water, so we hoisted the main-sail once more, lashed the tack securely, cast off our moorings, sailed out into Southampton Water, and set a course to the south-east.

By the time we had arrived off the entrance to Bembridge it was dead low-water (Springs), so we hove-to and jogged about from 6.30 p.m. until there should be enough flood for us to enter. *Vivette* draws only 4 feet 6 inches, and as dusk was coming on I was anxious to get in without having to feel my way through this very narrow channel in darkness. After a while, therefore, under easy canvas we crept cautiously towards the harbour, sounding with the lead all the time, but our keel touched once or twice without stopping. Running out to sea again to give the tide time to rise, we had another shot for it, for the time was now 8.30 p.m., and the light was rapidly failing.

What puzzled me was that the Drumhead Buoy, which used to mark the entrance, was nowhere to be seen, even with the aid of the binoculars. *Vivette* heaves-to most comfortably under main-sail and jib, but I had no keen desire to do this all night, so again we made for what seemed to be the entrance. But having kept too far to the eastward, we were picked up by a hummock of hard sand, and for three-quarters continued to bump unpleasantly, the north-east wind causing a certain amount of swell. A local boat seeing our predicament came out to us, but as I knew the tide was rapidly rising I declined his assistance.

Presently the vessel floated off and we ran in comfortably under jib as a small steamer's lights showed themselves immediately astern. With a strong tide and a confined harbour crowded with craft, it was no easy matter to pick up moorings in the dark, but a local hand in a boat ahead caught hold of the chain and handed it aboard. The next day we made the acquaintance of Mr. Ricardo, of the Bembridge Sailing Club, who had in former years also done this Dutch trip. He was kind enough to lend us a Dutch dictionary, which came in most useful during the trip. It may seem curious, but I had found it impossible to obtain such an accessory in town. But our intention of remaining in Bembridge was limited entirely by the matter of new sails.

We lost no time in giving out the fact that we wanted a new main-sail, and before long a local waterman suggested that he had just the thing. On examination, however, it was found too small. After some difficulty, when we were just thinking of going on to see what Cowes could provide, we found an excellent

Ratsey and Lapthorn sail in Woodnutt's, and after being altered it was bent on to our spars. In the meanwhile I interviewed Burden, who cut me out a square-sail of nice light stuff, but of sufficient strength. There was no time to wait for the main-sail to be tanned, and at last we were ready for sea, much relieved that at length we could rely on our canvas being sound and certain.

All this had, of course, taken up several more days, but it was just as well that it happened when it did, for during that period the wind had been very light indeed, and what there was of it was easterly or north-easterly, varied by intervals of flat calm, so we should not have got far, and have probably spent an anxious time drifting up and down Channel, repeating our experience of the previous year off Portland Bill. But we found Bembridge beautiful and restful, and these days of dinghy sailing and yarning, varied by periodical visits to see how the sailmakers were progressing, really gave us time to shake down into the life on board.

However, on the Thursday after our setting forth we turned out at 5.30 a.m., cooked breakfast, and started off once more in the direction of Holland. True, the wind was N.W., but it was so light as scarcely to be perceptible. Furthermore, it was foggy, and it was difficult to see more than a few yards ahead. We made short tacks, and had the curious experience of employing the quant to pole us along the shallow water. This, with the aid of the sweep, kept us going on a falling tide. A local ketch had gone out just ahead of us, but she soon lost her way and remained aground till the next tide should float her. The fog was still thick all round. We could not see St. Helen's Fort, or the cliffs at Seaview, or Noman's Fort ahead, and we only espied the buoys just before we were on the top of them.

We could hear the Warner Lightship blowing her fog-trumpet, and by steering about N. by E. we managed to get out into deep water without even touching the ground. After that, as the fog showed no signs of lifting, we kept on a S.E. course, but inside of the Warner, so as to avoid the traffic of liners and other steam craft, until we got within a mile of the Nab Rock Buoy.

VIVETTE AT BEMBRIDGE
THE PHOTOGRAPH SHOWS THE FURLED SQUARE-SAIL WITH ITS SHEETS LEADING AFT

For a time the fog kept clearing and thickening, and we lay becalmed until another draught came, and we went about on the other tack, the tide now setting about S. by E. The atmosphere now seemed like clearing up, the sun burst forth, and with it came more wind. Astern of us came a long procession of variegated traffic dredgers, cargo craft, and a couple of submarines obviously bound for their favourite cruising ground in Sandown Bay. We could not see the Nab Lightship, but we heard her fog-horn and steered for it. For a short while the air cleared, but the moment we came up to the lightship it thickened again into a Scotch mist. We tacked ship again, keeping a firm grip on our position. A big white steam yacht had brought up close by the Nab,[2] and no one could blame her skipper for playing on the cautious side. Fog-horns and steam-sirens seemed to be sounding from several points of the compass, but one especially made us anxious, as from its deep bass note it was evidently coming from a big liner feeling her way from the east to Southampton.

We held on for fifteen minutes east from the Nab so as to be north of the line of traffic, the wind having now gone to a little south of S.E., and at the end of that time went about on the other tack heading S.S.W,, hoping that in another landward tack or so we should be able to sight the Bullock Buoy, and then lay a course for the Looe. But the fog thickened worse than ever, and the whole sea resounded with the fog- horns of the light vessels and the sirens of steamships. It was a pandemonium in which the sopranos of the former were having a discordant duel with the latter.

There was quite a nice sailing breeze, but it was weird and clammy, and the proximity of the big liner, invisible yet audible, made us a little jumpy as every minute we expected her to loom suddenly out of the mist. All at once something dark showed up ahead. It was a pilot boat brought up with main-sail still standing. No doubt he was lying in wait for the liner. We hailed him and asked him how the Bullock Buoy bore, and he gave us

---

2. This was, of course, some months before the Nab was shifted to her present position. The Nab End light-buoy is placed where the lightship was formerly.

an approximate bearing, adding, that he thought the fog might clear. Continuing on our course, straining eyes and ears to locate any approaching vessel, we saw another black mass immediately ahead, but of far greater bulk. Simultaneously the look-out man began ringing his fog-bell. She was a black tramp steamer of about 3000 tons, with a deck load of timber, and she also had let go anchor.

After this we began to feel that it was hardly good enough to continue. We could barely lay the Looe Channel with the wind in that quarter, even if we found the buoys, which was exceedingly remote, and we ran the risk of getting picked up on the Boulder Bank. And if alternatively we decided to go outside, we had a head wind in addition to the fog, and the certainty of finding ourselves amid any amount of steam shipping which ever congregates in the neighbourhood of the Owers Lightship.

The big liner was still growling away not far off, and seemed to have been joined by another big sister somewhere to the southward, and these two had the effect of making us nearly as anxious as a small animal would feel in the knowledge that a couple of bears were likely to pounce down on him at any moment. So we put the helm down, and decided to run back. We soon heard the Nab's horn blowing, and took a bearing, so we knew our position, and with a free wind began to run back on a N.W. course, the wind being as before a little south of S.E. We kept our fog-horn blowing (three blasts to show we were running free), and at 11.15 a.m. had the Nab abeam, distant about a cable. We then set a course west to cross the line of traffic, and then when well over to the Isle of Wight shore altered our direction to W.N.W., so as to make the Warner Lightship, but inside the line of shipping.

About 11.45 a.m. we heard the Warner, bearing in direction a little north of east on our starboard bow. The fog resumed its habit of clearing and thickening. We had thought of anchoring outside Bembridge under Tyne, but it was too thick to approach the shore with any safety. A big liner revealed herself bound to the south-east, groping her way very slowly and cautiously. In the opposite direction came also the tramp timber steamer we had sighted near the Nab. But just as she approached the Warner down came the mist again, and she stopped her engines, and was about to anchor when it cleared once more. And thus the atmosphere continued to change for the rest of the day.

Knowing that it would not be high-water at Bembridge for another five hours, and not being able to see the land in that direction, I decided to take advantage of the fair wind and to run right back to the Hamble. Just as we were sailing between the Noman and Horse Forts, the big two-funnelled Holland-American liner Rotterdam (24,000 tons) showed up dead astern, and as he was coming up straight on to us, and was determined not to alter his course, we bore away a little to the northward. This was evidently the lady who had been growling and for whom the pilot had been waiting, but she had doubtless been at anchor near the Nab for some time.

We had a good steady breeze astern of us, and off the Ryde Middle Buoy decided to use our square-sail for the first time, and found it a great success. Perhaps for ordinary winds we could have done with a foot or two greater depth of canvas, but it carried us along at a fine pace. Someday, if I decide to modify it, I can lace another piece along the foot, just as the Norfolk wherries today lace on the bonnet and the ships of mediaeval times were wont to increase their spread of canvas in fine weather. Before we were up to the Calshot Lightship, the fog had blown away, and the crack American schooner *Westward*, which had so recently come across the Atlantic and was presently to cause such a sensation on the Solent, came running up astern—a fine sight, with a perfect mountain of a spinnaker set and her long white hull dotted with a row of port-holes.

Off the entrance to the Hamble we lowered square-sail, having first experimented to see how near to the wind we could use the same close-hauled, and finally picked up a mooring off Bursledon soon after five in the evening. Whilst we were running up past Portsmouth a curious leak had manifested itself in the bows, apparently somewhere on the water-line, and for a time we had been compelled to keep the pump going continuously. Afterwards it became necessary to pump only once every half-hour, to prevent the water getting over the floor-boards, and by the time we got to the Hamble mouth it was leaking even less. But it worried me to think that there should be a leak at all, and I determined to have it seen to without delay.

So I sought out Moody, and arranged to have *Vivette* put on the hard first thing next morning. But when this was done and we came to examine her, it was found that she had not in the least strained herself when aground at Bembridge, but that the planking had not quite finished taking up after the winter, about an inch or two above the water-line. This had now nearly remedied itself, and a little stopping along the seam soon made her perfectly tight, so that we never had any further trouble with her either that year or the following.

And so here we were back again at the place whence we had set out, but with this difference, that we were now thoroughly ready for sea in every respect. But as if to annoy us beyond endurance, the weather utterly broke up, and for the next four days, when it was not blowing hard from the eastward, there was no wind at all. Then it poured in such torrents as I have never seen it rain before. It thundered and lightened, it blew and it fluked, and the glass went back, so that it was past the wit of man to comprehend what had gone wrong with the weather. Most people will remember this summer of 19 lo as one of the wettest and worst for many a year. And this was the summer we had chosen to go to Holland!

Chapter 3

Southampton Water to Ramsgate

However, even the weather must get tired of being dismal at length, so on the fifth day, after the glass had been having all sorts of romps up and down, but chiefly in the latter direction, to our amazement it began slowly to rise. This was just before midday, so we decided to lose not a moment and to make another attempt. We were lying to our anchor off Hamble, in our old station just below the training-ship *Mercury*, having dropped down from Bursledon the night before. We had filled our tanks with water, so we lacked nothing but an opportunity to get away, and now that at length had come.

At midday exactly we had hoisted sail and were breaking out the anchor, when a friend, in a motor launch, came alongside and courteously offered to tow us out to the mouth; and as the wind was ahead and very light we gladly availed ourselves of the chance. Twenty minutes later we parted company by the buoy at the mouth, dipped our ensign as a farewell, and now at last we really were on our way to Holland.

We left behind the painted buoy
That tosses at the harbour-mouth;
And madly danced our hearts with joy,
As fast we fleeted to the South:

How fresh was every sight and sound
On open main or winding shore!
We knew the merry world was round,

And we might sail for evermore.

It is curious how entirely a gleam of sunshine and a fair wind can change the aspect of things. The Isle of Wight shore was looking so bright and resplendent, the sea was an emerald green, and the atmosphere so clear, that it was hard to realise the variegated weather which had prevailed during the last few days. The easterlies, which had been late this year, had now come to an end, and here at last was a sou'wester, so on we sped down Southampton Water and across the Brambles.

For two hours or more we were becalmed off Portsmouth, but there were warships to look at, and a small new cargo steamer was doing her trials up and down the measured mile. Soon after four the true breeze sprang up from the south, and we trimmed our sheets accordingly. In half-an-hour we had passed the Warner, and after another thirty minutes we were up to the Nab, and the breeze freshening nicely. A fine three-masted steam yacht, with yards on her foremast, passed, bound west, and gave us a friendly hail. At 5.40 p.m. we had the Bullock Patch Buoy alongside, and were soon through the Looe and past Selsey Bill, well on the way to Newhaven. Before night came on we had the sidelights and binnacle lamp going, and the riding light, in the cabin, ready to show to any overtaking vessel.

Setting a course E. by S. ½ S., so as to allow for indraught and keep well clear of the land, we reeled the knots off in splendid style. As the wind had backed against sun earlier in the day, so, true to the old rhyme, back it ran, and gradually, during the night, veered from south to S.W., and even W. Before we lost the light we could see a couple of ships ahead of us and exactly on our course, or slightly shorewards. All through the night we gradually gained on them, until we passed the second, which we found to be a sea-going barge. Worthing was abeam at 9.40 p.m., and the Brighton lights were showing up.

It was a dark night, and though the breeze was good and steady, yet it was banking up to westward, and the improvement in the weather was only to be temporary, so we hurried her along. We had cooked dinner in the boilerette and dined with a

"Dipped our ensign as a farewell, and now at last we really were on our way."

ready appetite when off Bognor, and there was the same rhythmic heave of the ship and the same accompanying orchestra of the wind in the rigging as we had both enjoyed in our cruise to the westward a year before. The mate dines first and then relieves the man at the helm, and presently the cabin light is lowered and the glow from two pipes is the only light in the well, but for the yellow gleam in the binnacle. The glass is tumbling back again, but the breeze is only freshening a little, and every knot is bringing us nearer to our first port.

There is a green light just ahead of us, which keeps us on the alert. There is no masthead light, and her red light is not visible, so she must be a sailing ship on the starboard tack beating down Channel, so we gybe over and give her plenty of room. It is too dark to see more than her light at present, but we're well clear of her now. As we come abreast of her we can just make out her hull, and the dark-tanned sails, and the loom of the hull—seems to be a trawler. Everywhere to the southward of our course the dark waters are speckled with little splashes of yellow light, which indicate the Brighton luggers lying to their nets, and we are careful for our own sakes not to get the rudder caught in their meshes.

Midnight comes and goes, and there are hot drinks in the thermos flask to keep out the cold, which comes over the sea just between night and dawn. The sheets are clacking and creaking, and the blocks are whining to each heave of the waves; the side-lights are burning brightly, and we're well clear of the land.

It makes one feel glad to be afloat on such a night as this. Every moment is worth living, every sense is responsive to the demands of light, and sound, and motion. If I may but slightly modify Mr. Masefield's suggestive poem, the whole idea is exactly summed up in a few lines:—

O, the sea breeze it is steady, and the tall ship's going trim,
And the dark blue skies are paling, and the white stars burning dim;
The long night watch is over, and the long sea-roving done,

And yonder light is Newhaven light, and yonder comes the sun.

By now the breeze has veered from W. to N.W., and we are a mile or more to leeward of our port, but there is the breakwater light, and I intentionally ran her off a little during the night so as not to get too near the land. So we tighten in the sheets, and as soon as she comes on a wind we have an exhilarating sail straight into the harbour. Over to the east Beachy Head is flashing forth its light, but he will soon be quiet, for the sun's greater light is about to eclipse him. It is a curious dawn and none too promising. Low-lying vaporous clouds are blowing seawards from the lofty cliffs as we run inside the breakwater, and there is a suggestion that bad weather is brewing to the westward, so it is comforting to think that here is a good safe port, where we can remain, if really necessary, till the impending storm has passed over.

At 3.45 a.m. we entered Newhaven piers, passing a big sea-going barge outward bound, whose skipper asked us what the wind had been during the night. There was a white yacht also, of about twelve tons, carrying a paid hand and owner's party that was also bound out. We moored in our old berth at No. 9 stage alongside an auxiliary motor yawl, and coiled down. Just astern of us was a Shoreham fishing lugger, *Market Maid*, who sold us three delicious mackerel for sixpence. We breakfasted and turned into our bunks for a few hours, not a little pleased that already we were well on our way to our destination.

And here we were to remain for some time. While we slept the glass went tumbling back, and for several days it rained and blew hard from the S.W. Over the breakwater the sea dashed fiercely, making a fine sight, but there was far too much sea for us to think of making our next port just yet. The fishing luggers were unable to go out, several Lowestoft smacks came running in, and the ss. *Bonahaven* which went out soon put back. There was too much even for her, as she had met seas "like clifts "off the Owers.

So it was no good growling at our bad luck again. The only thing was to wait till it cleared. I know that most sailing men

THE SHEETS ARE CLACKING AND CREAKING, AND THE BLOCKS ARE WHINING TO EACH HEAVE OF THE WAVES.

detest Newhaven, and certainly it is not the finest harbour in the world in some respects. There is so much coming and going of the Dieppe packet-boats at night that it is difficult to get an uninterrupted night's rest. There is nothing worth seeing in the town, and the dirt from the quays does not improve one's decks. But as against all this there is always an interesting assortment of shipping to be studied, including many sailing craft, and ashore there is one of the grandest views obtainable anywhere from the high cliffs which rise up from the beach.

Past that eminence there is always a procession of different types of vessels, and apart altogether from the cross-Channel craft, there are ships to watch making their way into the harbour from outside. But on this occasion our visit happened to be anything but gloomy. Rather it was one long period of laughter, which began from the moment we came alongside our neighbour, and continued till the moment we cast off to go out again.

I don't think that among all the seamen of different kinds and nationalities which it has delighted me to meet, that I ever encountered an old salt who combined in his person so much sound common sense, united with the most original, wholesome wit as the skipper of our next abreast. There is no seafaring man in fiction that is anyway his equal by many a fathom, and my great regret is that there was not concealed some instrument in *Vivette's* cabin that would be able to reproduce some of the dry remarks which this old man handed out to us all day.

The fun began in the early morning when he raised the hatch of his fo'c'sle and addressed remarks to the weather. You might be asleep in your bunk, but you would soon awake on hearing him, and would regret that already you had missed a little of the day's amusement. Some months later, before fitting out again, I went down to Newhaven looking forward to a long chat with my old friend, but he was not there, and I returned disappointed. Still, I hope it will not be long before we meet again.

Our first meeting was at four o'clock that morning, when his head came out in order (I thought) to curse me for disturbing his night's rest. But it was refreshing to find a human being in the best of temper, for not many people are bubbling over with gladness at such an hour. He didn't mind my tramping about his decks making fast my ropes, but what he was a little perturbed about was that "little white yot" that had gone out as we came in. She was bound for Amsterdam, and was far too small for the job. What was more, her owner had taken his wife with him, and he ought to be ashamed of himself for risking the life of a female in a craft of that size.

As *Vivette* was bound for the same port, and was several sizes smaller, we never dared to mention our destination to this old skipper until just before we left. But by that time I'm sure he loved us far too genuinely to hurt our feelings, even had he wanted. Here he was alone on this craft, for her owner did not come down very frequently. But old Dick loved every timber and every bit of stuff in her, for she came from the port where he had been hatched, "and that's God's own country, that is." There was scarcely a port in the whole world but what Dick had been into, chiefly in sailing ships. Frank, open, independent, always ready to see the humorous side of things, full to amazement of interesting yarns of the most exemplary type, with clear convictions on most subjects—convictions which seemed for the most part to be right—willing to lend a hand to anyone who needed assistance, and yet for all that as shrewd and wide-awake as the most experienced man of the world.

There were, of course, many things which he "didn't hold with." One was London, where people spent their lives like rabbits darting down into the earth to catch trains. Nor did he enthuse greatly over steam-ships—"Coal-boxes, that's what I calls them"—for he belonged to the old school of seamanship which is unfortunately now almost dead. He was anything but a fanatic, but he had given up smoking, for it did his eyes no good. But he was a keen "Druid," and nothing he enjoyed more than to go ashore and "enjoy the 'armony of the evening" with his fellow-members.

Of the modern Tommy Atkins he thought less than nothing. "Most of 'em don't 'ardly know which end of the gun the pop comes out of." Incidentally, Dick was quite an artist, and he showed us with becoming humility some of his sea-pieces. He had met in his time some of the most eccentric inhabitants of this earth, as, for instance, the genial gentleman who painted his garden-walk with anti-fouling composition to prevent the weeds from growing.

Dick told us of his own marriage, which had taken place as recently as the beginning of the century, and it happened that the vicar who had performed the ceremony was the father of a former mate of the *Vivette*. According to Dick, this wedding was the first to take place in 1901, so the vicar returned him the marriage fees. That didn't suit Dick, however, who handed them back with a remark that he preferred to pay his own "harbour dues," and a desire that they might be distributed "among the churchwardens and crew."

But all this time the weather showed no signs of easing. The clouds came racing over the Sussex Downs, and the seas still broke over the breakwater. It was pitiable weather for July. "Looks as if an 'orse 'ad kicked it," was Dick's dry comment. But there was another friend, or rather three more, who were weather-bound in Newhaven, though I did not discover it till we had been there some days.

Those who may happen to have read *Down Channel in the Vivette* will remember a mention of the trading ketch *Iris*, which was weather-bound with us the previous year in Dartmouth. She had a crew of two men and a boy, all of whom were of Devonshire. Lying next astern, we had fraternised with them and found them very obliging and nicely dispositioned, and I had often wondered during the winter months how they were faring.

One day, during our *sojourn* in Newhaven, I was walking along the quays when my eyes happened to catch sight of a craft that seemed very familiar. Simultaneously I read the name *Iris* on the stern, and was just wondering whether she had the same crew as before, when there was a movement forward, and the boy (now grown into a youth) looked up, recognised me at a glance, and, without saying anything, walked aft, shouted down the hatchway, and immediately up came the *Iris* skipper, followed close behind by the mate—the identical trio that were aboard her before.

Men and matters change so much in a twelvemonth that one is sometimes apt to be disappointed. But it was not so this time. A little later on, when I was returning from a shopping expedition in the town, I encountered them ashore. They professed they had often talked about the *Vivette*—and I quite believe what they said—and had often wondered to each other how we had got on. And where were we bound to this time? Holland? That little "yot," then, does get about a bit. Yes; the *Iris* had been painted up this year, and had a proper fit out.

Freights were very bad; here they were weather-bound again, but it was just as well, for the skipper had hurt his back and been "chronic." When did they come in? Why, it must have been the same morning as yourselves. They had been at anchor near the Looe during the calm, and that was the other of the two vessels which *Vivette* had followed through the night.

But at last the North cone, which had been flying for some days, was taken down, and the glass began to rise steadily. Only one yacht had come in during our stay, and that was the celebrated *Javotte* of the Royal Clyde Yacht Club, which had arrived before dawn under trystail from Ostend after the racing. She had not encountered bad weather until Beachy Head, and eight hours after her arrival she cleared for the westward again, but as I watched her from the cliff she was putting her bowsprit into the swell of the Channel.

I don't suppose it took her long to get to her port, however, with such a beautiful hull and an able-bodied crew. We were reluctant to say good-bye to old Dick, but we had to be up early and get on. His fatherly interest in us lasted till the end, and he saw to it that we should not miss the tide. We had breakfasted and cleared the harbour by 7 a.m., and the incoming fishermen prophesied a fine day with a moderate breeze. It was a beautiful, bright morning, with the wind in the S.S.W., and the tide just starting to make to the eastward. The conditions were therefore ideal for making a good passage to Ramsgate, seventy odd miles away. It is a long stretch for a crew that carries no relief, but there is no satisfactory harbour in between. Most men will agree that neither Rye nor Folkestone is worth making for, and Dover leaves much to be desired.

Before half-past eight we had Beachy Head abeam, and as the wind was freshening we set the square-sail off Eastbourne. This woke her up as usual, and at 9.35 a.m. we had the *Royal Sovereign* Lightship abeam. We were "boomed out and roaring" up Channel, and gradually but unmistakably the breeze which had begun by being quite light, freshened and increased until we were carrying rather more sail than we could do with. We held on for a time, but the sea was getting up, and it became advisable to roll down a couple of reefs. This was off Hastings. For a time we kept the whole square-sail standing, but by the time we were abreast of Fairlight that also had to be shortened. We were reluctant to stow it altogether, as it was doing yeoman service, so we lowered, reefed it to about half its depth, and then hoisted it again. We had not traversed many more miles before both wind and waves had attained such a degree as to make us very much on the alert, and the mainsail was rolled down to the equivalent of four reefs.

But we were travelling, and it did one good to look up at the bellying of what was, in fact, really an old-fashioned square topsail now. Our rig was exactly that of the old Revenue cutters. Some of the waves, notably off the Stephenson Shoals (Dungeness), were a little alarming, and it was anxious work steering. The dinghy didn't like it at all, and slewed about. But she had long since given up her habit of breaking adrift, and two strong painters kept her always moving. And there was quite a curious incident which occurred in Rye Bay. She was following up on the crest of a wave when she stopped dead for a second, only to be caught by the next wave and turned completely round in a circle, so that the painter was actually found to be twisted.

The nearer we got to Dungeness the worse became the sea

and wind. The sky took on a dismal look as if it had been scattered with coal-dust, and a nasty thick rain commenced to drizzle without in any way abating the breeze. An Atlantic liner and another big steamer came tearing on and left us their wash. Still the wind rose, and still the waves became more threatening. Suddenly all the sailing craft in the neighbourhood, from anything up to about 80 or 100 tons, began running for the shelter of Dungeness Bay till there was quite a large fleet brought up on the lee side.

Off Dungeness, too, there was the usual amount of all sorts of steam traffic, some of which were whistling for pilots, so we had quite enough to keep our eyes busy. Just once I was half-minded to seek the shelter of Dungeness Roads also, but the tide and wind were fair; and if the wind should go round to the S.E. we should be on a lee shore in such an anchorage, so on we kept. Topsail schooners and *barques* turning to windward were sending down some of their upper canvas, and altogether it was an ominous time. Between Folkestone and Dover the crests were so high, and the wave-valleys so deep, that the motion was exactly like that of a switchback.

To make matters worse the wind now came in heavy squalls, which increased the difficulties of handling. Every ten or fifteen minutes the helmsman had to be relieved, as that period was as much as was tolerable. But the climax of the day's sport came off Dover, which was certainly the most exciting period that I have lived in thus far. Very heavy and vicious squalls swept down on to us from the back of Dover town. More than once, but on one particular occasion, I thought it was all over with us, and that we should necessarily broach-to. However, though we were knocked about the cockpit like peas in a bladder, yet, happily, *Vivette* stood up to the full force of those squalls in a manner that was as amazing as it was encouraging.

We never shipped anything but a little spray, and she just kept going hard all the time. There was one thing that would ease her, but it was risky work. If the peak were dropped we might get to the South Foreland all right; and, after that, the wind would

The Squalls of Dover

be slightly off the land, and we should have smoother water. But the little ship was necessarily rolling a fair amount, and it was no safe proposition to go forward on the slippery decks. But the mate was both willing and eager, and he succeeded in slacking away the peak halyard and getting a strain on the topping lift. That was a decided improvement, but I was heartily glad when he had come safely back into the well.

Certainly the worst seas were off the entrance to Dover harbour, where the nasty backwash from the piers came rebounding athwart the east-going tide and wind. It was one mass of broken water, and the weighty squalls in nowise improved matters. By a curious coincidence it was almost exactly this hour of the afternoon, and the tide was in the same direction, when about four months later the German five-masted sailing ship *Preussen* was blown ashore just to the east of Dover harbour. But that was during a very heavy gale; or, as the captain of one of the tugs which was attending her at the time described it to me, of hurricane violence. What we were encountering was quite exciting and sufficiently thrilling, but it was only blowing a moderate gale.

As soon as we had rounded the South Foreland it was like peace after battle. The cliffs took off a little of the wind's force, though some of the squalls were far from light. But it gave us smooth water. Up went the peak again, and we carried our square-sail through the fleet of sailing ships at anchor in the Downs, much to the interest of some of the crews. Just before we got to Ramsgate harbour we lowered it and stowed it neatly to the yard, and then ran with the yard cock-a-billed, deep-sea fashion, feeling not a little elated at our trip, and equally thankful to have got through with our lives. We moored, as usual, in the west gully, and found that everything inside the cabin was wonderfully dry. It had been a nerve-trying day, but full of instruction; and if anything were wanting to give me confidence in my ship, this day had. I am convinced she would go through more weather than one would have the heart to lead her into.

Here was a clear case of being "caught out," not owing to

ignoring the glass or the weather prophets, but in spite of both. At the time of setting forth the storm signal ashore had been taken down. By the time we reached Ramsgate the glass had dropped two-tenths, and it was blowing very hard, as the local men remarked. Bound the other way—from Ramsgate to Newhaven—provided one has a fair wind and can keep up a good speed, it is possible to carry the tide for almost the whole way, and I had done this trip in eleven hours in *Vivette*, but there was nothing like the sea that we had today.

But now—from Newhaven to Ramsgate—owing to our speed, and the strength of the wind keeping the tide going for a slightly longer direction easterly, we had actually carried our stream all the way from Newhaven to Deal, for the ships were only just beginning to swing in the Downs as we came through. The most direct course between the two ports is 73 knots. But owing to being compelled to alter my course a good deal because of the seas, the distance was at least another four knots more.

For instance, we stood well to the southward instead of the nor'ard of the Stephenson Shoals, and off Dungeness stood further out to sea in the hope of getting smoother water. After that we tacked in towards the land, hoping that there might be a tendency for the wind to come off the shore. But this was a mistake, as we only got matters worse. However, altogether we had covered 77 nautical miles, and since we arrived at Ramsgate at 5.50 p.m., we had done this distance in just under eleven hours, which works out at seven knots an hour. And this for a vessel measuring 21 ft. on the water-line is something quite worthy of remembrance.

As it turned out, we got in none too soon, for it came on to blow much worse that night and the following day. The glass went back another four or five-tenths, and the daily papers foretold really bad weather. One yacht was towed into Ramsgate by a Ramsgate trawler the day we arrived, and there was a little matter of salvage for her owners to negotiate. Astern of us had been following Mr. E. B. Tredwen in his barge-yacht *Pearl* (ten tons). He and his crew of four had been much struck by the way our ship had carried her square-sail all day, and he came round presently to inquire into details. The next year, on reading the concluding lines of Mr. Tredwen's published log, I came to the following interesting statement:

> The square-sail was adopted this season after seeing *Vivette's* experience in our run in company up Channel last summer. The spinnaker will not be used again.

CHAPTER 4

Ramsgate to Calais

As we had been delayed several days in New-haven, so again in Ramsgate the fickle weather which made that year so notorious was to hold us up again. Another succession of gales and flat calms seriously interfered with our plans. We were anxious to get away, but our luck seemed to be out. Just astern of us was a yacht which was doing temporary duty as a hospital, for an unfortunate sportsman had fallen ill, and there nurses and doctors were busying themselves to restore him to health. In a few hours Ramsgate would be full of trippers, but before the end of July we got under way one morning at 8.30, and with a light S.W. air we tacked down to the South Goodwin Lightship. We had left Ramsgate at four hours after high water; therefore just as the Channel tide was beginning to go to the west-ward. We were well provisioned with fresh meat, fruit, and vegetables, water and everything else, so we could keep the sea independent of the shore, if necessary, for several days.

We were bound now to Calais or Dunkerque, and in some respects today was to be the most interesting sail of the cruise. Not owing to the facilities of the wind was it so fascinating, but rather in spite of these. It was so delightful to work out one's calculations, and to watch the set of the tidal streams that run up and down the Dover Straits. The traveller who is whisked across in the turbine ferry from Dover to Calais misses the real interest of the crossing. Even the navigation in one of these ships, except in foggy weather, is simple and direct. The vessel is being driven at 21 knots, and so she can afford to ignore the set of the tides. A pilot informed me that the Dover–Calais craft allow only a quarter of a point for the tide, which practically means that the ship is headed straight for Calais as soon as she clears the Dover piers, and *vice versa*. The turbines do the rest.

But it is quite different in the case of a sailing craft at the mercy of wind and tide. It is useless to set a direct course for Calais, for you would never get there, even if you had a fair wind. You would either overshoot your mark or be carried below it, even supposing you were not picked up by some of the treacherous rocky Ridens. If you can rely on a fair and steady wind you can make your calculations to allow for tide and leeway, and knowing roughly the speed of your ship you ought in these circumstances to make a good landfall.

But, as it happened, on the two occasions when *Vivette* crossed the Channel, there was every difficulty except heavy weather to contend with. For part of the time the breeze was ahead, and for the rest it was either very light or a flat calm. Consequently the tide was doing what it might wish with you. If you want to make a quick passage such occasions are annoying; if you want to make an interesting trip, and make some study of the set of tides, and take any pleasure in navigational exercises, here are real opportunities.

As we tacked down through the Downs the morning mist began gradually to disperse and the Kentish coast was bathed in sunshine, with here and there a roof glinting with specks of light. A few Deal boatmen were hovering about, and a steam tramp was running in close to the pier. Over to the left the *Waratah* wreck, on the Goodwins, was still partially visible, and pilots tell you that she is banking up the sand and altering the formation of the Goodwins in that locality. She lies just to the northward of Trinity Bay and slightly to the southward of the Gull Lightship, and from her position she must have mistaken the lights of the Gull Lightship for those of the East Goodwin. In actual fact, she went between the two, and so piled up in the very centre of the sands.

It took us most of four hours, in the light air, to beat down to the South Goodwin Lightship, and here we could see the great force of the tide racing to the westward. Between the lightvessel and the shore a handsome full-rigged ship was brought up, and the strain on her cable must have been terrific. A British battleship was coming up Channel, so we ran our ensign up to the peak and dipped it, which was instantly acknowledged.

From the South Goodwin Lightvessel I had planned to make our departure. Had the wind been fair the intention was to lay a course thence E. by S. ½ S., and assuming *Vivette* maintained an average speed of five knots an hour, this would bring us to the red conical buoy which is just off the entrance to Calais Harbour. The direct course between these two objects is S.E. ¼ S., and the distance 16 knots, but the force of the tide has to be allowed for as indicated—that is to say, to the extent of two and three-quarter points. The tide off Calais would flow to the westward until 3.30 p.m., so that would give us just about three hours to do the sixteen knots, and then immediately the tide would begin to flow N.E. and we should be in the most favourable position for carrying it up the coast to Dunkerque.

So much for theory. But the wind fluked so abominably throughout the entire afternoon that I had to be working out courses all the way across. After leaving the lightship, we put the patent log overboard, so that we should have a rough idea of our speed through the water and be able to tell approximately when we were approaching the French coast, for it was not discernible, and the chances of a fog coming down were none too unlikely. So far had the wind shifted by now, that, instead of being able to lay an E. by S. ½ S. course, the best we could do was S.E.

After sailing twenty-five minutes, we fixed our position by the bearings of the lightship and St. Margaret's, and later on by the lightship and Dover Castle, and marked the position on the chart. All this time the tide was setting us to the westward, and now the wind headed us still more, so that we were another point to the bad—S.E. by S. This was at 1.45 p.m. Again we fixed our position, which showed that we were on a line drawn from

Dover Castle and Cape Blanc Nez, but a good two-thirds of the way across, the log showing that we were doing about 4½ knots through the water.

It was a smooth day, with just a nice swell to prevent matters becoming monotonous, and we were getting along more quickly than was apparent, and without any fuss. It was a curious contrast to the other day, when we had passed up Channel. There was now not much traffic about either. A handful of sailing craft dotted here and there, a Japanese gunboat was steaming down to the westward, a French fishing-cutter engaged in line-fishing, and, of course, the Dover-Calais packet tearing across the silver streak as if she was being chased by an enemy. But the west-going tide was rapidly losing its strength, and we were in an excellent position for the time when the flood should make to carry us towards Calais.

That most useful help to navigation, the *Book of Tidal Streams*, told me exactly what the stream was doing for every hour, so at 3 p.m., when we were about three knots from Cape Blanc Nez's chalk cliffs, we went about on the other tack and continued seawards for twenty minutes, and finally put about again. We were now heading for Sangatte, famous for its Channel Tunnel scheme, and, later, as the starting-point for cross-Channel aviators. But though that was still some distance to the windward of Calais, yet the east-going tide was now beginning and would rapidly gain in strength and carry us towards our port.

We picked up the No. 1 black buoy, but then, seeing that a French fishing craft much nearer in was getting a stronger breeze and straight from the shore, I altered my course, ran into the land, and found there was quite a nice little draught coming off the low country just east of Sangatte. The favourable tide was bowling us along, too. Presently the Casino and bathing-vans showed up, and we could hear the sounds of the people on shore. We luffed up close to the western arm of Calais Harbour to avoid being carried on by the strong tide, and at 6.25 p.m., or ten hours out from Ramsgate, ran in between the two piers with the ensign flying at the masthead. In spite of the calms and

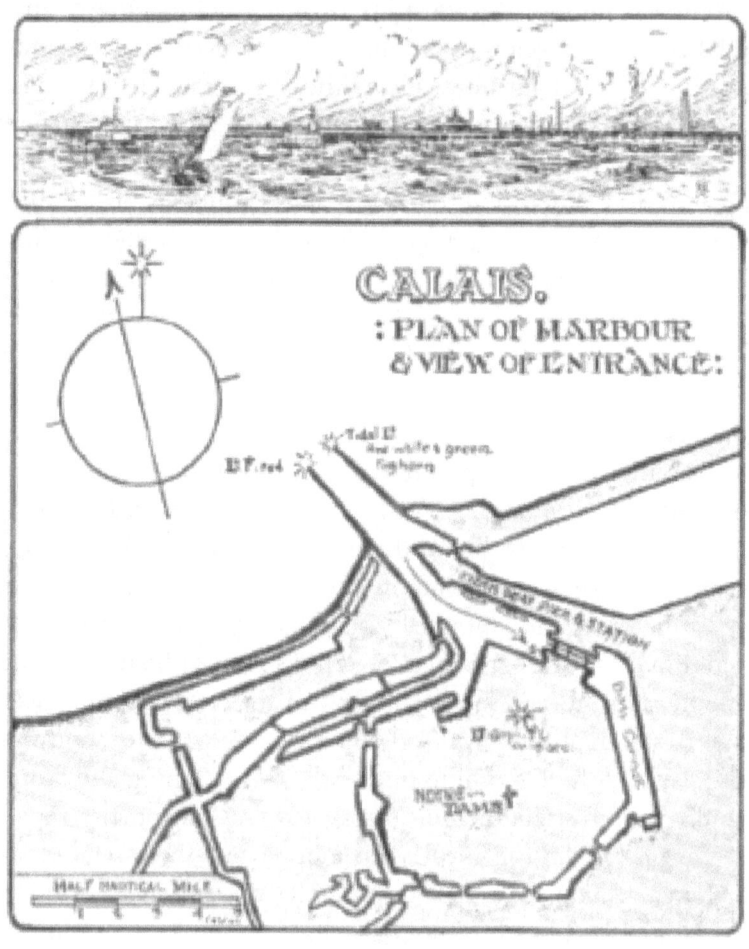

PLAN OF CALAIS HARBOUR

THE UPPER SKETCH SHOWS THE APPROACH TO CALAIS AS SEEN FROM THE SEA. NOTICE THE HIGH CONSPICUOUS LIGHTHOUSE ON THE EXTREME RIGHT OF PICTURE. THE LOWER PORTION SHOWS WHERE TO BRING UP.

flukes, we had made the best use of the tides, and here we were in France.

Captain Marryat, in one of his novels, summed up his opinion of these Continental harbours in language which reads remarkably true to many a sailing man.

> "In France," he wrote, "what are called ports are all alike—nasty narrow holes, only to be entered at certain times of tide and certain winds; made up of basins and backwaters, custom-houses and cabarets; just fit for smugglers to run into, and nothing more; and, therefore, they are used for little else."

Of course things have improved a little since his days, and Calais has been dredged so that a steamer of moderate draught can enter at all stages of the tide. The days of the smuggling cutters and luggers have also long since passed. But otherwise the description is very true of Dunkerque and Gravelines, and largely applicable to Calais. And yet, because these harbours are foreign, because the buildings look different from ours, because the local craft and the language of the people are also different, they exercise a wonderful fascination over one, a fascination which not even the vile stench of the "nasty narrow holes" and the disgracefully kept quays can altogether stifle.

As we sailed slowly inwards the whole populace was busy fishing. Amateur anglers with rods from the piers, and professionals with the aid of their quadrilateral dipnets, which were wound in by means of a windlass either from the quays or from a small floating hut, which could be rowed to different parts of the harbour. We continued on until abreast of the railway station, where the Dover-Calais boats bring up, and then coming alongside the quay opposite, and throwing a line to one of the crew of a French tug which was lying there, got out our fend-offs and stowed sail.

Presently the *douanier*, in uniform and silver buttons, appeared on the quayside above our heads. There was no *escalier* for him to descend just there, so I fetched him aboard in the dinghy, but so precipitous was his leap from the slippery iron ladder that he nearly capsized himself, dinghy and me, whereupon squibs of derisive laughter and much voluble dialogue were let loose by his compatriots on shore.

The "*petit canot*," in fact, was a huge joke, and it vastly amused the junior Calaisiens to see the representative of the Republic being rowed about in a queer little eight-foot tub. He was delightfully good-humoured, but not a little relieved, I fancy, to climb out on to our ship. The usual formalities ensued; there was nothing dutiable, and the health of the crew was good! So he took our tolls, handed us our papers, drank our very good health, and departed. Down fluttered the ensign, up went our burgee, and meantime a delicious odour from the fo'c'sle indicated that the mate would soon have dinner ready.

We had sailed all the wind away, and by the time our meal was finished the light had gone too. I had never been into Calais, and it is always a great pleasure to go ashore at a new port and attempt to size the place up. The tide had risen, so scrambling up the wall I set off to explore, and certainly the first and lasting impression of Calais is "made up of basins and back-waters, custom-houses and cabarets"; but Marryat omitted to add the cobbled streets reeking of bad fish and innocent of even the most elementary efforts towards cleanliness.

It is a wonder that those who inhabit the mean dwellings near the harbour do not die by the dozen of fever in the hot weather. Of course it is an obvious failing on the part of a Britisher that as soon as he finds himself in another country he must instantly commence to criticise it by the standards of his own nation. Even in the poorest of our fishing villages we should have made a cleaner show than this.

And yet over there, looking across the harbour, was something which was done better than we should have attempted. It was a fine piece of statuary to commemorate the lives lost in a local fishing disaster. The composition and execution of the memorial were so delicate and artistic as to surprise us, who are accustomed to the statuary of our London streets. Here was an amusing little study in contrasts. The British mind would not have bothered much about the memorial. It would be enough that it performed its duty as signifying a fact, however crudely, yet the streets would be well-paved and well-drained, and there would be no invitation to fever.

But the Britisher is so practical. When one got to the main thoroughfare of the town things were a little better, and finally the narrow street opened out into a fine large square. And here came a tram, so I jumped in, and we ran along past endless cabarets, across bridges which spanned tidal basins used for scouring out the harbour, and finally we arrived at the sandy beach where the local Casino looks out across to England. Away to the left were the hills of Sangatte, and the night air was warm and balmy now that the harbour was left behind.

But the most characteristic feature of Calais by night is the powerful rays which are cast by the lofty lighthouse, which is so useful to the mariner endeavouring to locate the entrance to the harbour. This building is just under a couple of hundred feet high, and stands at the extreme inner end. On a moderately clear day you can see it for some miles, and it then has exactly the appearance of a white cigarette standing on end. It is invaluable as a landmark, for the locality of Calais is flat, and you cannot easily see the town at first. And when once you are between the piers it will lead you to the proper mooring-place up the harbour. At night, if it is not thick weather, you can see this white light and its four flashes twenty miles away, or practically from Dover. But when in the confines of Calais itself it makes a curious effect on the sky overhead, for the rays shoot out and keep revolving just like so many handspikes for ever turning a ship's capstan.

The next day was Sunday, and the fisherwomen came to the sung Mass in the old church near the quay in their attractive local costumes. So clean and picturesque they looked that they could scarce have come out of those untidy dwellings close by. At the west end of the church there was many a reminder of the cruel coast of the neighbourhood. Here were the lists and lists of the fishing or pilot craft which had perished not far from Calais piers. At the head of the list came the name of each vessel's "*patron*" or skipper; then followed the names of the crew—Antoine, Pierre, Gustave, and so on. And close beside these tablets were little toy models, properly rigged with sails and all, even to the numbers on hull and canvas, representing the craft which once sailed out but have never come back.

I have only seen this coast in fine weather, but even in the flattest of calms the swirls and eddies as one approaches Calais are instantly suggestive of what might be and is for most of the year. The tides are very strong, and it only needs quite a moderate breeze against the tidal stream to raise a vicious sea.

"Whatever you do," said an old English pilot who had taken all sorts of ships up and down that coast, "whatever you do, be careful o' them *Ridens*."

A "*riden*" in France is what we should term a shoal, and the neighbourhood of Boulogne and Calais is especially prolific in these. Exactly opposite to the harbour mouth of the latter, for instance, is the treacherous Ridens de la Rade, and instead of the ten and eleven fathoms you quickly find yourself in two and a half and even three-quarters of a fathom. Close to this comes the Riden de Calais, which varies in depth from about four to ten fathoms, but even here (to quote from the Admiralty *Channel Pilot*)

> "it occasions strong eddies, and during fresh winds from the northward there is a heavy sea on it, and breakers in north-east gales."

And a little further down the coast, between Sangatte and Blanc Nez, you have Les Quenocs and Le Rouge Riden, two ridges of rock and sand concerning which the same authority remarks that

> "the sea runs high on both shoals when a strong wind opposes the tide." "A heavy sea," it adds, referring to the Ridens de la Rade, "runs on them with on-shore winds,"

and I understand that this statement is a long way from being exaggerated.

The more modern fishing-vessels of Calais are very nice little craft, which seemed to average about twenty tons, some being dandy-rigged and some cutters. A few of them, however, have auxiliary motors, and thus they can, with sail-power helping them, run over the strong tide. But, having regard to the nature of the coast and the frequent instances when it is unsafe for sailing vessels of all kinds to enter, and the occasional days when even the steamers cannot make the attempt, the wonder is not that Calais has so limited a fishing fleet, but that she has any sailing craft at all. At springs the tide runs about four knots across the entrance, and even with a beam wind favouring a vessel coming in from the sea it is anxious work to prevent being swept on to pier or shoal.

We lay quite comfortably by the quay from the Saturday night till Sunday afternoon, for unless the wind gets northerly that berth is nice and easy. But should the wind be anywhere from about N.N.E. to N.N.W. the swell rolls in, and makes the place highly uncomfortable. Just to show us that this was a fact, the wind now shifted to that part of the compass, and the swell came in such a manner that *Vivette* began prancing about to such an extent as to risk damaging herself against the quay.

We endured this as long as we could, but when it became intolerable we cast off our warps, hoisted jib, and ran into the Bassin Carnot, which opens from two and a half hours before high-water and closes at two hours after high-water slack. As there are lock gates to keep the water in when the tide drops, we lay here as peacefully as if we had been in a Thames backwater. For companions we had a number of full-rigged ships, steamers and canal barges, for it is possible to get from here by the inland waterways to Paris, and even to Belgium and the Scheldt. Some enterprising motor-yachtsmen have performed these trips, but there are certain drawbacks even for those who prefer inland navigation to the sea.

At night I went ashore again to purchase eggs, fruit, and a yard or two of French bread. From the hotel at the station we obtained fresh water to fill up our tanks, and an English paper gave a most favourable forecast of tomorrow's weather. It was quiet in the Carnot Basin, even to sadness, and everywhere the warehouses were plastered with advertisements concerning the public funeral of the unfortunate victims who had gone down in the *Pluviose* submarine, which the reader will remember was sunk by one of the packet boats just outside the harbour.

But we were visited by a couple of the *gamins* of Calais, who fired off at us, the only English they apparently knew. This consisted of two words, "plom pudin." But what especially interested and amused these youngsters were two stout fend-offs which I had purchased in England, knowing that Holland with its many wharves and canals would be somewhat hard on our paint. It took these boys quite a long time to discover for what purpose these might exist, and then at length they suggested they were just a couple of *"petits ballons."* But here in this port for the first time the ship heard her name pronounced correctly. Poor lady, she had been a little ill-used. In Hampshire the natives insisted that she was *Vivette*, with the accent on the "i." At Ramsgate the postman hailed her in the morning as *Vivettey-'oy*. Now at last, where they speak the *langue des dames*, she became *Veevette*.

CHAPTER 5

Calais to Ostende

It was high-water next morning at 7.21 a.m., so the lock gates would be open till about half-past nine. On turning out we were gratified to find that the weather prophet had not mistaken his calling. The glass had risen, there was every sign of a fine summer's day; and, best of all, the wind had gone round to the S.W. The tide would be making to the eastward in the offing, so we hurried to get away.

But before we could leave there were certain formalities, and we had to get the permission of the *capitaine du port*. They waved me to the office, demanded certain dues for coming into the basin, questioned me as to my next port, handed me another chit of paper; and at last we were free. One of the men threw us a line till we were through the lock, a towering bucket-dredger steaming slowly just astern. Then, hoisting up our sails, we soon ran down the harbour.

The tide was now running strongly, so we got in the sheets and kept as close as possible to the western pier, intending to go between the Riden de Calais and the Ridens de la Rade, for I wanted to be well clear of the shore before getting on to the course. But the tide was carrying me so rapidly on to the Rade, in spite of a spanking breeze, that I had to take a board in the direction of Sangatte for ten or fifteen minutes; and then, having gone about and arrived midway between the two buoys that guard these two Ridens, I wore round, eased sheets, and put her on an easterly course for the Dyck Lightship a dozen miles away.

This was one of these ideal days that stand out in one's memory when many a cruise has been half forgotten. There is usually just one such day as this in the season's sailing, and it is worth waiting for. Every condition was ideal. The tide was fair for some hours yet, the wind was strong and free, the sun had come out bright and brilliant from a blue sky, the sea was a lovely emerald-green tipped with little whisps on the crests of the waves; and stretching away on the starboard hand was a long line of yellow beach, with a verdant country running back inland for many a mile, dotted here and there with a quaint windmill or a solitary church spire.

We soon had the gaskets off the square-sail, and up it went, bellowing beautifully to the bonny breeze. In come the sheets, the jib is eased off a little, and everything is drawing nicely, and doing its duty. In spite of our delay we had cleared Calais piers by a quarter-past seven, and now it was time for breakfast. But it was too handsome a day to spend time in the cabin, so, laying a cloth on the lee side of the cock-pit, the feast was spread in the open.

We had filled the thermos flask the previous night, so the coffee came out all ready smoking hot. The lockers yielded their contents, and then keen appetites are more than ready. There is just a pleasant kick at the helm and a gentle steady pitch to show that you're controlling a real, living thing, and not a mere inanimate log of wood. The gay panorama flies past you, and the good ship's doing six knots good without effort.

The yard is on the jack-stay,
The tiller's kicking strong,
Up a bit, down a bit,
Steady her along!
There's ginger in this sou'west wind,
Hang on, boy, hang on!
Oh, six is on the log-slate,
The wake's a cable long.
Here comes a puff, so mind your luff

"Doing 6 knots good"

Or else you'll get ding-dong.
There's ginger in this sou'west wind,
Hang on, boy, hang on!

And right ahead, dead on our course, is the Dyck Lightship. We have slipped past Gravelines, and have done twelve knots in two hours exactly; and now we enter the West Pass, one of the best buoyed and lighted channels anywhere, but over on the shore side there are several wrecks, as if to remind one that it is not always summer and fine weather. We have altered our course now a point to the southward, and for eight or ten miles we are running parallel near to the shore. Here comes Dunkerque, looking remarkably like Calais, with a tall lighthouse rising aloft far up the harbour, but it is far too fair a breeze to waste. Besides, it is not even midday yet by half-an-hour, and we are now doing between six and seven knots, though the tide will soon be turning against us. I want to have a look at Dunkerque someday—this former haunt of pirates and smugglers—so we must run in on our return journey if we come this way. But as we pass the beach with its *kursaal* and striped bathing huts and people it looks very tempting in the sunshine.

A handful of small fishing craft are going about their business, and a biggish steamer is brought up to her anchor in the roads waiting for a boatload of people putting off from the shore. On the port hand the Channel is bounded by a stretch of shoals which extend right up to the buoys, so we are careful to give them a wide berth. The mate narrowly escaped shipwreck on this Hills Bank a few years back. He had come single-handed from Essex and mistaken the buoy, and got inside instead of outside. For a time it seemed a hopeless case, and that his ship would be lost, for she was badly aground. So desperate was his position, that he had collected his valuables and got into the *Berthon* dinghy, ready to row off, when happily the wind shifted right round, and the yacht freed herself and floated into deep water again. But it was a close shave.

We had carried our square-sail all the way so far, but after leaving Dunkerque the channel bends round a point more northerly, so as to be due east. The wind was slowly going round with the sun—clear sign of fine weather—and was now about due west. But now we came to the entrance of the Zuydcoote Pass, which is a narrow channel that turns away from the shore to the port side. Inasmuch as the tide sets athwart the pass, and there is shoal water on either hand, one has to set a careful course and allow for the drift. But in clear weather it is perfectly simple if you can once get your marks.

At the south-western end—that is, the entrance nearest to Dunkerque—the pass is marked by a light buoy. There are then no more buoys until the other end at the north-eastern end, the one on the starboard hand being lighted and the other not. There is a very good mark which will assist the mariner through the Zuydcoote, and is worth making a note of. On the coast, just opposite to the S.W. entrance, will be noticed a long conspicuous building which cannot possibly be mistaken. Seen through the glasses it appeared to be newly built, and might be a monastery, or perhaps some barracks. Assuming you have a S.W. wind (which is most likely), you will find that by getting the stern of the ship on with this building, and then setting a course N.E. ¼ N., this will take you through the best water; and, unless the wind is exceptionally light, will allow for the drift of the tide also.

As this building is not mentioned in any sailing directions, it has been reproduced in the accompanying sketch. As here shown, it is seen just as it appears on a sunny day, stern on to it on the bearing just given. There is also a wreck on the beach

THE LONG CONSPICUOUS BUILDING
THE LANDMARK FOR THE ZUYDCOOTE PASS

close to, which is of further assistance, but as this might possibly break up during winter gales it should not be relied on. The above building, however, can be seen for a very long way even when there is a haze, and will be a great comfort when coming the other way down this pass, for the buoys are not always easy to locate bound west along the West Deeps.

The square-sail had to be lowered as we came on a wind and headed into the pass, but as soon as we had got through it was up again. It was now 12.40 p.m.; but though we were heading E. by N., and were still travelling along at a fine rate, yet the wind was easing down a little, and, unfortunately, still going round with the sun. It was hardly free enough for the square-sail now, so we set the balloon stay-sail instead, and the ship seemed to like it.

It was such fine weather that the light silky stuff was better suited. Otherwise we had not to touch the sheets for hours. All that was essential was to lie comfortably on deck in the hot sun, keep a steady course, and let *Vivette* reel off the knots. And so gradually we came in with the Belgian coast, and at half-past three in the afternoon Nieuport was abeam, and we could see right down its harbour. A yacht or two and a number of people in rowing-boats were dotted about the entrance, and the colouring of the scene with its blues and bright tones was wonder-fully suggestive of the Mediterranean. Today was the first of August, and the month had begun well.

For some hours we had the tide either against us or athwart our course, and now the wind, still weakening, had veered to N.W., and by the time we were abreast of Middlekerke it had veered still further till it was N.E. by N., which meant that the balloon stay-sail must be handed, working fore-sail hoisted, and the best course we could do was a long leg and short—the former shorewards and the latter out towards the Stroom banks. Most picturesque and foreign looked the shore with its green-shuttered villas stretching away to the east close by the sea. Twilight came, but the breeze freshened, and the tide had now turned in our favour.

Two or three local luggers were already beginning their night's fishing. To anyone but a Frenchman or Belgian this *chasse-maree* rig, with its old-fashioned topsail, its crazy mizzen and ill-fitting canvas, seems a kind of marine freak, and the hulls themselves are frequently mere clumsy boxes, with not a fine line anywhere. But though these are rapidly dying out along the coast, and the cutter and ketch are replacing them, yet historically it is rather a pity, for here is a very old-fashioned rig, and the only one which shows the square-sail in its transition stage before it becomes a real fore-and-after.

We cooked our evening meal and dined happily, as we made excellent progress in spite of the head wind. Here were Ostende and ultra-civilisation, with its prices and luxuries. Through the swatchway came the crack turbine packet from Dover, and swung in between the piers just ahead of us. Our sidelights were burning brightly, and we were keeping a good look-out. There was a hot tide setting across the pier-heads, but the breeze had freshened still more, and we could easily stem the stream. At 8.15 p.m., or exactly thirteen hours out from Calais, we entered our port, and had it not been for the fact that the wind had headed us towards the end of our journey we should have made quite a creditable trip.

As soon as you get between Ostende piers your sails are blanketed, and it is a long distance and slow progress as you come up the harbour. We intended to remain here for a few days, so we were bound for the yacht basin, and our turning was to starboard, just past the fishing harbour, where the local smacks bring up. It was difficult in the half light to see where the turning was, and there were so many trawlers, both steam and sail, alongside that we might easily miss the narrow opening. Espying the familiar lines of a North Sea smack with "LT" painted on her bows, I hailed her skipper and inquired for the turning, which he told me. Then, in good honest Suffolk accent, the Lowestoft skipper turned round to get a better view. He was sitting aft enjoying his evening pipe.

"Come acrawst the sea today, sir?" he inquired.

"No—come from Calais."

"Come from Calais, 'ave yer? Oh, yew've done well, that yew 'ave."

It was a pleasant ending to a grand day thus to be welcomed into a strange port. Matters nowadays are quite peaceful and amicable between our East Coast fishermen and the Belgians, but it was not always so, and I remember hearing from one of the former an account of a particularly desperate affray occurring at Ostende, which concluded by one man being hoisted up into the rigging and shot dead. But all that kind of thing belongs to the past, and the Belgian owes a great deal to the influence of the British North Sea smacks in regard to hull and the adoption of the ketch rig. But this influence is not confined merely to their sailing craft. The Belgian fleet of steam trawlers which use this port are the clearest copies of those which have their home at Grimsby, or Great Yarmouth, or the Humber. In fact, as soon as you begin to examine these Ostende steam trawlers you find that most of them were not built at Antwerp or any of the Dutch yards, but in Yorkshire.

We groped our way through the shadows to the entrance to the lock, and remained near the gates till the sluice-master should condescend to take notice of us. After shouting and clamouring for his attention, an excitable Belgian showed up in the darkness, and performed a kind of silhouette dance for our benefit, at the end of which it occurred to him that we desired to enter his lock. We threw a line ashore, as there was a certain amount of stream leaking through the gates and carrying us astern. One of the men gave us to understand that he had now belayed the line, but when the mate came to look he found that the man had hitched it on to the wheel of a light cart, and it was indeed a wonder we did not pull the vehicle down on to our deck!

We had a merry time with boat-hooks and fend-offs keeping the yacht from crashing into the wall as the lower sluices were opened, and our good-nature was strained to its last strand. Finally one-half of the gate was opened, and the lock-man hailed us to come on. As the whole sewage of Ostende seemed to discharge itself into the identical spot where we lay, it needed no encouragement to get into the lock with the utmost despatch.

There was still a good deal of stream rushing out through the half-opened gate, but I presumed the lock-man knew his business, and that the water would quickly quieten down. Please note that we were lying at right angles to the half-gate that was not opened. Therefore we had, so to speak, to get round a corner before we could head straight for the lock. Someone hauled on our line, and we did our best with fend-offs and boat-hooks as before. But the stream showed little or no signs of diminishing, and though we all used the whole of our strength and a certain amount of language too, it was utterly useless until we could persuade the man at last to open the other half of the gate.

Then and not till then could we get in with the loss of a certain amount of paint, one boat-hook, and much temper. In the midst of this a steam trawler came along also, and nearly ran us down, whilst a couple of officials on the shore were particularly anxious to envelop us with their red tape, demanding details, and handing down bits of printed paper, whilst we were trying to prevent the bowsprit being smashed at one end and the dinghy at the other, as the wash from the trawler's propeller sent us charging against the slimy walls. Officialism seems to flourish in Ostende harbour, and it was not till after the event that I learned the way to circumvent it.

This will be mentioned later on in the book. But for the present let the yachtsman be warned against coming into this part of the harbour. Even for a small craft it will cost him more francs than it is worth, and he will have to pay visits to the sluice-master's office (hard-by) and the official at the pilotage (some distance away) before he can be allowed to pass out. Add to this also the fact that the lock is very busy with steam trawlers, pilot schooners, and other craft, which jostle each other as thickly as at Boulter's in the height of summer, and you will be glad that you did not heed the instructions in some of the books of sailing directions.

But at length the nightmare ended, and we tied up in the large basin alongside a pilot craft. It was so very dark, and the shadows from the high buildings of the town made it so difficult to see, that I did not realise the nature of our neighbour, and it was not long, of course, before we had to shift our berth.

For there are two kinds of craft alongside which it is inadvisable to moor. The first are pilots, and the second steam-tugs; for by reason of their calling they are always coming and going, and repose is not for them. But in the morning a most intelligent Belgian seafaring man, who spoke excellent English, directed us to a pleasant berth round the corner in the canal that runs up to the old-world town of Bruges. Here we were quite comfortable and happy for the rest of our sojourn. Astern of us were a couple of handsome English yachts, one of which we soon recognised as the famous *L'Espérance*, flying the Commodore's flag of the Royal Yorkshire Yacht Club, and presently her owner kindly called on us.

We heard the full account of the exciting collision which had occurred the previous summer at Cowes regatta, when the *L'Espérance's* bowsprit met the hull of the historic old Bloodhound and sent her to the bottom. We listened also to the yarn of the incident when the *L'Espérance* was caught in mid-Channel in a gale, between the French coast and Dover. But as the event has been written up and well illustrated in the press, it need not be mentioned further, though it caused some discussion at the time. We coveted this beautiful creature with her immaculate white decks, her mighty masts, her luxurious saloon and ample state-rooms. She had the look of a real thoroughbred, and she could take you round the world, and do it in good time, provided there were wind.

But coming across the North Sea she, too, had dropped into a "speechless," and she lay lopping about with her wings flapping idly to the motion of the waves. And yet even a vessel like this has her limitations, for with her terrific draught there were plenty of enticing little harbours where she could never float, and a trip on the Zuyder Zee would be out of the question. The ladies of the *L'Espérance* seemed more than a little interested in the *Vivette*, and the amusing difference in proportions which

OSTENDE

THE MINARET ON THE LEFT IS THAT OF THE PILOTAGE.
THE TWIN SPIRES ON THE RIGHT ARE OF THE CATHEDRAL

the two craft suggested. The other *ship* could have carried us about on her deck without very much inconvenience; and yet the freedom of the sea suffers all manner of craft, both great and small, to obey the laws of wind and tide.

Two delightfully idle days did we spend here watching the different types of humanity and shipping. I know not which of the two is the more cosmopolitan in this port, but there is far more beauty and grace to be found in the latter than in the former. In a place where artificiality and insincerity ashore have grown up like weeds summer by summer, there are just two features which, as it seems to me, stand out brightly from the rest. The first is the cathedral, which somehow is reminiscent of Milan. It is, however, quite modern, but you forget that if you genuinely love beautiful things. And in a different manner there is the splendid orchestra at the Kursaal, famous throughout Europe, which sends your mind back to those glorious nights at the Opera, when time and circumstance are momentarily suspended, and your emotions transport you into another sphere. Looking across the basin from where we lay was a most pleasing mixture of varied architecture. As a background for the steam trawlers, with their vivid green hulls and stained smoke-stacks, rose up the Dutch-like gables of the houses, with at one end the curious tower of the pilotage, resembling equally a Chinese pagoda and a mammoth pigeon-roost, while at the other the twin towers of the Cathedral of St. Peter and St. Paul.

Chapter 6

Ostende to Flushing

But on the third morning after our arrival we were ready to depart. We had replenished our victualling department, and splendid fun it was shopping in a foreign port. In the course of my expedition I ventured into one of those typically Continental *patisseries*, where the steward from an English craft was having some difficulty in expressing his wants. The proprietress had no English and the steward spoke no French, but at last the difficulty was overcome, and then, turning round to me in a tone that suggested both self-martyrdom and indignation: "A man's got such a job to make these people understand," he complained in the Essex dialect. The attitude of the steward was distinctly funny and characteristically British. It was not that he regretted his inability to speak the language of the country in which he found himself, but he was annoyed that the natives should show such crass stupidity as not to possess the power of using their tongues after the manner of the inhabitants on the banks of the Colne and Crouch.

There was a goodly squash of craft hanging about for the gates to open, and the first portion of the fleet soon filled up the lock. But after an irritating delay we were at last allowed to enter. I had been to the pilotage to pay my dues and obtain my *exeat*, but even now that we were inside the lock and the gates closed behind us we had not done with red tape.

One of the lock-men beckoned me ashore, and I had to scramble up the wall to interview the sluice-master at his office.

Then back again sliding down the rigging, and at last the gates opened and the flood of shipping let loose. It was just like the sudden rush of traffic which pours across Piccadilly Circus as soon as the policeman lowers his hand. The biggest and strongest craft pushed themselves through the first, and the smaller fry did the best they could to avoid being wedged in against the wall. But I had suspected this would be the case, and therefore had been careful to be the last to enter the lock, and to choose a pleasure craft to lie alongside, for I knew her owner would be as careful of his own paint as I of mine.

She was a long, lean racing craft belonging to Antwerp, and bound up the coast like ourselves. Just ahead was another British yacht, the *Xebec*, whose sails were auxiliary to her motor, and her owner was courteous enough to throw us a line, and give us a pluck down to the harbour mouth. As the wind was very light, and between the piers lighter still, this kindly act saved us time and energy. We cast off as we came to the open sea, our friend setting a course through the Direct Pass, and apparently for England, while we turned to starboard, and continued our voyage along the Belgian coast.

It is fairly shallow water outside. You begin with three and a half fathoms, and you drop down to one and a half very quickly. Therefore it is best, especially if there is much scend to the sea, to work short tacks until you have Ostende Lighthouse in line with the railway station bearing S.W. If you keep your stern on with these two landmarks you will soon find yourself in between three and four fathoms, and then you can lay your course to your port. You will have noticed the station doubtless whilst ashore, and at sea the two loftier spires of the cathedral (shown in the full-page sketch) will help you to locate this.

It was ten o'clock by the time we had reached the open, and the wind was light from the N.E., the sky being overcast. As our course should have been E. by N., we could only head in a direction two points to the southward of that, unless the breeze should go round again with the sun as it had done before. However, we could make a long leg into the land, and then a short hitch out seawards.

We fetched close in to have a look at Blankenberghe, Ostende's young rival as a pleasure place, and sailed steadily along past the endless line of yellow dunes relieved with occasional tufts of coarse yellow grass, with here and there a summer villa, its sun-blinds or its bright green shutters. It is curious how extensive is this sand extremity which fringes the northern coast of the European continent. It begins as soon as you pass Sangatte, west of Calais, and stretches right away along the French, Belgian, and Dutch coasts till you get into Germany. And though there is a natural majesty in a rock-bound coast, yet you only want a little sunlight and a blue sky to make these plain yellow sand-dunes possess a singular charm and beauty of their own.

The tide is with us, but we are not going far today, for we want to have a look in at the new port of Zeebrugge. There right ahead we can see in the haze the great solid breakwater, which curves out from the land for over a mile in distance, and forms a large space of three hundred acres' sheltered water, being only open to winds from N.E. and E. The breeze freshens a little now, and we are not long in getting up to the lighthouse which guards the seaward end of this great arm, and is in almost a direct line south of the Wielingen Lightship.

Great things were expected of this new port, and a vast amount of money has been spent in making the breakwater and in dredging. But though there are cranes in plenty along the quay, where were the ships? There was nothing at all except a small steamer, and her presence only intensified the emptiness of this spacious harbour. Commercially, the port of Zeebrugge must be a veritable white elephant, although the Bruges ship canal comes out here; and that, in fact, caused the port to be made.

But if we omit all consideration of finance from the discussion, Zeebrugge is certainly an asset. For sailing craft unable to save their tide into the Scheldt, or caught in bad weather, it offers a most valuable anchorage, and I happen to know of an instance when this was the means of preventing a yacht from probable shipwreck. But in time of war Zeebrugge would become even more valuable still. Its breakwater could easily screen a large torpedo flotilla, which could dash out on any ships making for the Scheldt.

The Wielingen Channel, which would have to be traversed by the big ships, is little more than a mile in width, and passes closely parallel with the breakwater, and in this narrow mile the depth varies from about thirty to fifty feet. The smallest torpedo craft could lie comfortably protected from the heaviest S.W. gale inside this breakwater, and whilst just in Belgian territory could steam to the mouth of the Scheldt in half-an-hour. In view of the excitement which has recently been aroused over the relations between England and Germany, and the consequent uneasiness felt concerning the fortifying by the Dutch of Flushing to preserve the independence of the Scheldt, Zeebrugge, which scarcely ever gets mentioned, stands for a good deal of importance.

But for such small craft as our own it is best not to bring up in this outer harbour, for the inner 300 yards of the breakwater are open to allow the scour of the tide, and if the wind were from that quarter (west), it would give a little craft an uncomfortable berth. But as you round the pier-head steer S.W., and go between the black can and the conical buoys, which will lead you into the inner harbour. The best place for mooring is immediately before you come to the lock gates which give access to the Bruges canal. You lie between dolphins, but care should be taken to get well out of the fairway, as an occasional pleasure steamer runs towards Bruges. If you have auxiliary power, you may care to enter the lock and run up the canal to that mediaeval city.

But we selected neither of these berths, though I should not repeat the experience intentionally. I had been recommended to take the first turn on the port hand of this inner harbour and to bring up there. A thunderstorm was coming up, and we were anxious to get everything stowed dry. So, having traversed the outer port, we came smartly into the fishing basin, and let go anchor in the centre, where there seemed to be most water. Scarcely had we furled sail when the storm broke, and the rain came down in a deluge. I was a little suspicious of the depth of this basin, and as the tide dropped it began to be doubtful if we should float. It was a dreary hole—the most dismal anchorage I was ever in, enclosed by quays along which man never seemed to have trodden. Newhaven harbour is merry and bright compared to this cheerless spot, and the torrents of almost perpendicular rain in nowise added to its merits.

They were spring tides at that time, and the water was falling at a great rate, till finally we were hard aground, and I was a little nervous lest she should sit on her anchor. Finally, at dead low water, there were only three feet in the middle of the harbour, *Vivette* needing four and a half feet to float her by the stern. The bottom was soft mud, and she took no list but sat quite upright on her keel. So getting into the dinghy, we took advantage of the opportunity, and proceeded to give the hull a good scrub below the water-line. During those two days in Ostende, she had got more dirt on her anti-fouling composition than ever she collected from the rest of two cruises, and it was only with the greatest difficulty that we could get it off.

The tide took an awful time to rise, but in the evening a living man actually appeared on the wooden quay, so rowing off in the dinghy I parleyed with him in doubtful French, and he was good enough to show us a hole alongside the quay where we could lie afloat all the time. If any reader should ever find himself compelled to run into this basin, he may care to know that he will find between four and five feet of water at dead low water springs in the north-east corner alongside the staging, but as there is rather a big rise and fall of tide, he will require to tend his ropes periodically.

We were glad to float into this berth at last, and to settle down for the night, but the depressing influence of the place could not be shaken off. Presently a *gendarme* also came down, so I inquired if fresh water could be had. He consulted with the first man, and presently decided that perhaps I might be able to get some by the lock, so starting off to explore the neighbourhood I came to a handful of small shops in the one and only street. I selected a bakery and stated my wants, but the baker said he would fetch his wife. She was very civil and glad of a chance to speak English, which she had been learning during the winter months. She was sorry that they had no drinking water.

"Then what do you drink in this neighbourhood?" I asked.

"We never drink water."

"How do you make your coffee, then?"

"Oh, we collect a little water when it rains and we boil It."

"Perhaps you could spare me a little."

And this she instantly did, but it was not very pleasant, and I should not have had it, but I believe in keeping the tanks full whenever I get a chance. You never know when you may reach your next port. You might happen to get becalmed, or you might have to anchor some distance from the shore, or have to ride out bad weather in the open, and all the time your water supply would be diminishing. It was satisfactory, therefore, to fill up when we could. Further up the quay where we lay were a few fishing craft, which presently hoisted sail and departed. Strange and antiquated boxes they were, cutter-rigged, with hulls resembling the Scheveningen *pinks*. They draw very little water, and their fishing ground is in the neighbourhood of Wielingen and Wandelaar Lightships. I am told that when the whole fleet are at home this basin is chock-a-block with them, and there is precious little room for manoeuvring, so that is another reason for choosing one of the other berths already indicated.

Zeebrugge had made me restless. I turned in for two or three hours, but I was not happy. The first signs of dawn came about four o'clock, so I got in the dinghy and went for a little voyage of exploration round the several harbours, and then wearying of that, went for a walk to see what the place looked like by daylight. It was nothing more than a small village, such as you might find in any of the United States of America. Everything looked too new, and the engineers who had brought this port into being had not sufficiently covered up their retreat. There were water towers and railway lines, and there had evidently been a vast transformation—development I believe is the customary word. It was all very wonderful, but it was lacking in beauty. There was a cafe or two in the village street, and perhaps someday the tourists will come over from Blankenberghe, Heyst, and Knocke. Whenever Zeebrugge becomes a busy port it will be worth a visit. But at present it is a hamlet that has taken itself too seriously, and tried to attain an importance which it has failed to become possessed of.

It was low water at 5.30 a.m., so we couldn't get across the basin just yet. But by the time breakfast was over, the course laid out on the chart, and the ship ready for sea, the flood had made. It was with no regrets that we soon found ourselves out at sea once more, bound this time for the first of our Dutch ports. The early morning had arrived bright and sunny. There was a light breeze from the S.W., which was fair, if only it would hold. The tide would also be with us to hurry us along. But we had not got far on our journey before the wind dropped, and the sky became about as black as it had been off Dungeness that day. We wondered what was about to come forth, for it looked very stormy, and the lightning and thunder of the previous evening would probably come on again. However, we were ready for any alteration in the wind's force if it should come in a howling squall, and in the meantime rolled becalmed in a short choppy cross sea without steerage way, drifting broadside up the Weilingen Channel.

It looked ominous over to the S.W., and thick rain came on, but yet there was no wind. Then a feeble air came aimlessly along, fluked all round the compass, died away, and the boom began to charge about as if trying to burst the gooseneck and the main-sheet. But eventually, when abreast of Knocke, a light breeze, but with more certainty and fixity of purpose, came up from the west. The tide was due to turn against us off Flushing at 1.50 p.m.; and there is this peculiarity to be noted, that whereas in England the stream at the change of tide is slack, and then gradually attains greater velocity till its maximum is reached in the fourth hour, the Scheldt and Maas are different. As soon as the tide turns from flood to ebb, Its greatest velocity is felt during the first hour of the ebb. After that it will gradually ease down, but it will continue to run strongly for an hour and a half after nominal high-water.

In making calculations, therefore, you cannot reason that should you chance to be a little after high-water the tide would only be slack or slightly against you. On the contrary, you will find it running strongly. Now, as we had lost much valuable time in this calm, it became extremely doubtful if we should save our tide up the Scheldt to Flushing. The stream is very strong here even at neaps, and today it was still spring tides. But if it could be done it should be done; so up went our good friend the square-sail once more, and this made all the difference.

The groaning ahead showed that we were getting up to the whistle buoy, and out of the mist came the Flushing to Queenborough mail-boat and a fine pilot schooner running in from her station. At length we were abreast of the Nieuwe Sluis light, the western sentinel of the Scheldt, and now we could lay our course for Flushing itself. From the Nieuwe Sluis to the entrance of Flushing harbour the course is E. by N., but it is necessary to allow also at least another point to counteract the tide. A Belgian pilot told me that was what they themselves allowed, and it was what I had already reckoned to be about right.

The wind was veering still more, so that it was almost N.W., and our course due E. (having allowed for the tide). But by careful trimming of the sheets we got the square-sail to keep drawing well, even though the breeze was so scanty. It was long after one o'clock, and it became a matter literally of minutes as to whether we should get in before the ebb started roaring down. To be on the safe side, I ran her off another point, which had the double effect of causing the square-sail to set better, and would bring me more than well up to the harbour entrance, in case the ebb should now begin to make. But we accomplished our object, and only just in time, for five minutes later the tide was ripping down past the harbour mouth.

It is advisable to warn yachtsmen in making for Flushing the first time to be careful to verify their position. I have heard of instances where men have actually sailed past the mouth of the river Scheldt (which is nearly four miles wide) and not been able to locate Flushing. This may seem a little extraordinary, and certainly shows somewhat haphazard navigation and a neglect to study the chart. Obedience to elementary prudence would prevent such an incident occurring in clear weather. But having said so much, it is only fair to admit that if the mariner relies on landmarks at the expense of a careful compass course, the formation of the land is not a little confusing.

As you come up the Wielingen Channel you see a long line of high sand hills stretching away to the N.W. nearly at right angles to your course, and you begin to wonder where Flushing lies. But presently the sea seems to take a bold swerve round to starboard. There is land this side, and there is something away over to the eastward; but it is apparently below the sea level, and it is difficult to discriminate. There is a strong tide, and everywhere there are buoys, and you begin to get a little anxious.

That is especially the case if the yachtsman has been accustomed to do most of his cruising: in familiar waters, where every rock and headland, every cleft in the cliff, is familiar to his eyes. His seamanship is excellent, but he knows his home waters so intimately that he never worries about charts nor even carries a compass.

There are plenty of enthusiasts sailing about the Solent and other popular cruising areas to whom this description is applicable, and it is unfortunate not to have acquired what the American would probably describe as the "chart-habit." As soon as ever they find themselves away from their familiar bays and promontories they are lost. I am not saying that this is the largest class of amateur sailing men, but I know it includes a very large number, and I can readily understand that such might easily come to grief and lose their craft on one of the innumerable banks which are scattered about the mouth of the West Schelde.

The simplest advice to anyone who has arrived at the second of the two whistle-buoys (numbered 8) is to leave that well to port, and then, having sailed on till the Nieuwe Sluis is in line with the stern, set a course E. by N., but also allow one point more to the southward or the north, so as to allow for tide. You will then see the town of Flushing gradually beginning to show up. To a stranger the plan of the harbour given on the charts is a little confusing, for he finds at least three apparent entrances marked, designated respectively (reckoning west to east) "Commercial Port," "Marine Port," and "Outer Harbour."

Ignore the first two absolutely, for the first is only for the local *hoogarts*, and the second is apparently closed up. It is not immediately easy to locate the entrance to the Outer Harbour until you are nearly there: but you will notice a dark clump of trees. Steer for these if you lack confidence in your course, and you will soon observe the two arms of the harbour, the easternmost being slightly the longer, and the other consisting of a wooden jetty. You are now inside out of the tide-rip, and will see the lock-gates straight ahead on the port hand. If the latter are closed, you will see a red basket hoisted on a pole.

If the lock is open, this will be down. You will find plenty of room for manoeuvring if you want to luff up, but you must keep an eye lifting for a considerable amount of traffic, especially enormous *Rhine-schifts,* and long lines of *tjalks* towing astern of tugs. If necessary, you can temporarily bring up on the port hand, stow sail, and then head into the gates. The lockmen are very obliging fellows, and will always throw you a line. But you should have your fend-offs out and a long boathook ready. Whilst your ship is in the lock it will be necessary for her skipper to go ashore and interview the *sluis-meester*. He speaks no English, but all that he wants is the name of the ship, her tonnage, your own name, where from, and whither bound. The best plan is to waste no time, but write these particulars down on his slate. It is customary to give the two assistant lockmen a few cents, and when the gates open you find yourself for the first time in a Dutch canal, with an absence of tide.

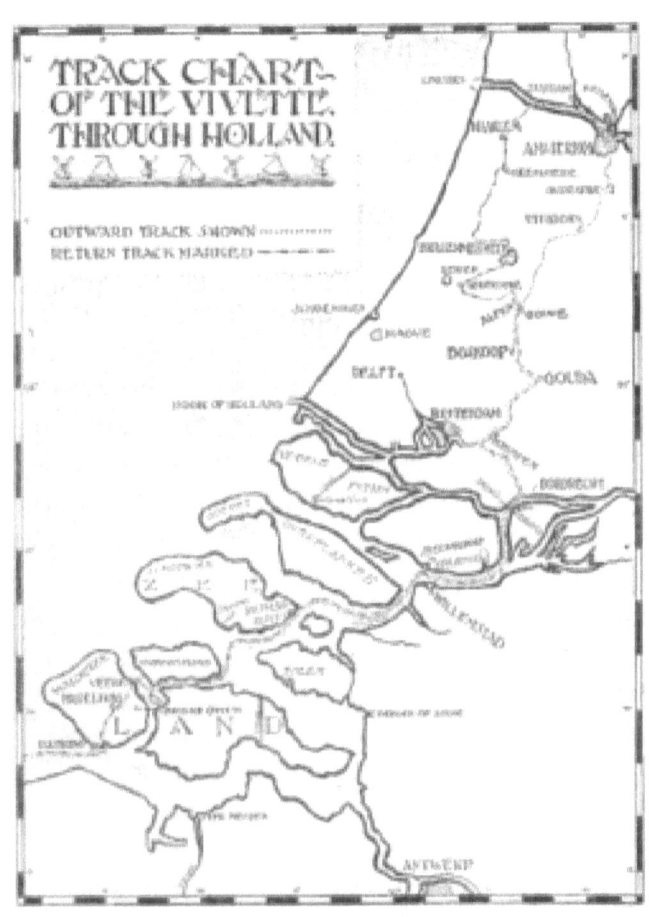

Track chart of the *Vivette* through Holland

CHAPTER 7

Through the Island of Walcheren

Even a small yacht that has come from foreign is visited by the Customs officers when arriving at a French or English port. But though we kept our ensign flying as we first touched Ostende and Flushing, they don't worry about yachts in Belgium and Holland. The gates were closed when we arrived, but as they opened they let loose a perfect museum of Dutch craft. Out came a curious medley of *hoogarts, Rhine-schiffs, klipper-aaks, tjalks, paviljoen poms,* and a clean, well-kept tug. There was something quite dramatic in the way this procession suddenly passed before our interested eyes. Heavy, bluff-bowed, apple-sterned craft with leeboards, massive rudders and weather-vanes, the *poms* and *tjalks* with their short-curved gaffs and well-steeved bowsprits, and the shovel-nosed *hoogarts* with their sprit-sails presented a picture of the sixteenth-century shipping emerging through the lock-gates of the past into the modern twentieth century.

And as if to accentuate this idea the more, so soon as we had got into the lock there followed in a Dutch Admiralty sailing yacht with varnished hull, hatchet rudder and gilded carvings that showed how little had been the alteration since the time when Van der Velde used to paint his pictures of Dutch yachts in Charles the Second's time. I don't know which party was the more interested, those on the Admiralty yacht or ourselves on the *Vivette*. It was a study in contrasts between the old and the new, the historic and the modern. Our dinghy still more amused and interested them. In fact, during our stay at Flushing the youth of the port continually came asking to be allowed to take her for a row.

There were no dues to be paid, and now we were free to moor where we liked. Along the port hand ran the street with houses on the one side. Any number of white-topped mooring posts and wooden stages were here, and as it was Saturday afternoon the vacant spaces were soon filled up by all kinds of sailing craft which had come down through Middelburg. At first we moored here also, but we soon found that it suffered from two drawbacks. There was little privacy, and there was too much risk of being fouled by some of the heavy craft slowing down before entering the lock: so we shifted our berth across to the other side, and tied up in a fine, quiet dock on the starboard hand. It is known as the Number One Inner Harbour.

On each occasion that we lay here there were not half-a-dozen craft of all kinds, yet it is about a quarter of a mile long and over a hundred yards wide. You can easily walk into the town from here, and yet you are not bothered by the curious. But if you are only stopping a night and insist on being in the centre of the town, you can take the first turn on the port hand after leaving the lock, and then bend round to port again. You will find some of the pilot craft being repaired, and there will be plenty of room alongside the quay. The post-office and shops are near at hand; but we preferred our own dock to this.

We remained in Flushing for twenty-four hours, during which there was time to see all that was worth seeing. There are really three portions of Vlissingen (as the Dutch spell it). There is first the port which is used by the mail-packet boats from Queenborough and now from Folkestone. But the passengers are in such a hurry to catch their train to Amsterdam or Germany that they see nothing of the place. That is at the extreme eastern end. At the western side is the newer portion, with a good bathing beach, hotel, sand-dunes and gardens: while in between the two portions is the old town and the little harbour where the *hoogarts* land their catch.

The latter is full of interest, and on this Saturday afternoon

BOTTER CLEARING OUT FROM SCHEVENINGEN HARBOUR

A DUTCH TRADER IN FLUSHING LOCK

it was a strange and entertaining sight to watch a fleet of these sprit-sail craft running in to port up the Galgeput channel before a fair wind. I have elsewhere described the rig of these craft in detail, but the reader who is unfamiliar with their appearance will find one of them sketched on another page.

But for me the choicest spot in Flushing is on the high ground near the old round tower, which was already standing long before the Armada came to Northern Europe. It is now merely a show place, and contains relics of that great Dutch seaman Admiral de Ruyter, who, to our shame, brought his fleet up the Medway and burnt our ships of war. His name to this day is to the Dutchmen what Nelson's is to us, and you cannot get away from this reminder wherever you wander in the Low Country. His statues and portraits are everywhere; he gives his name to streets and tug-boats. But his was the time when Holland was a magnificent sea-power, and he and Tromp and our English Blake were making history.

Come a little way from this tower and you get one of the grandest marine views that you have ever seen. Straight ahead of you there is an uninterrupted view down towards Blankenberghe, to your right is the Walcheren coast stretching away to Westkapelle, whilst away to the left the mighty Scheldt extends to the low, distant shore. At the back of you are the Belgian and Dutch pilot clubs, side by side. They are ever on the lookout for the big liners that here come close in, bound for Antwerp, which every year increases in importance as a great maritime port. I have often watched these men in their straight peaked caps and gold-buttoned uniform go down to the beach below and be rowed off in their well-built, well-manned galley and board the steamship as she slows down. There is much to be learnt from even a short conversation. They know their own job to perfection, and a great deal else besides. They speak very good English, and like all true seamen are singularly modest and humble-minded.

Everyone who has not visited Holland imagines that all the natives dress as you see them depicted on the posters and in musical comedy. This is not so. What is true is that you find these costumes in Flushing, Middelburg, and Veere, but after leaving the Island of Walcheren you scarcely ever find them, except occasionally in villages, until you come to the Zuyder Zee ports. These are the old fashions—*oude modes,* as the Dutch call them—and in the towns the advance of modernity has swept these away. But in Flushing a large part of the population still adhere to the older idea.

Here are the boys dressed up like little men, and the girls like little women. The former have their severe black suits, long trousers and either a round clerical-like hat or a peaked cap. Their fathers are dressed exactly the same, but it gives you quite a shock to see both fathers and small boys smoking cigars. The women-folk have tight sleeves which end several inches above the elbows, and the consequence is that the lower part of their arms becomes as red as raw meat. It is not pleasant. They never seem to hurry, but just saunter slowly along in their white caps and metal head-dress. But the most surprising sight of all is to see a girl thus habited riding along the bank of the canal mounted on a very modern bicycle. It seems too ludicrous to be real.

But even apart from the costumes and the ships, you might know you were in Holland, and not France or Belgium. There is a continual cleansing of their footpaths and houses, and a persistent polishing of every inch of brass. The dogs wearily drag carts jolting along the street with milk-cans that have been polished till they sparkle like silver and gold, and there is something very attractive in the curious, old-world shape in which these great brass milk jugs have been designed. And then as you go down these neat thoroughfares you wonder how it is that every house must have its little mirror outside the window, until you learn that it is not good form for the inhabitants to be seen gazing out, so the mirror reflects what is going on below.

There is a great deal in the history of Flushing that is wrapped up in the nautical history of the world. As you go through the picture galleries in the old Dutch cities, you can see what an amount of shipping used to come to its gates even in the sixteenth century, and how strongly fortified was this place. The old round tower that we just visited is seen with jetties and great galleons where today the pilot galleys lie riding on the short choppy waves. And then you pass beyond the period when Holland shook herself free from Spain, and come to the time of the three great Anglo-Dutch wars, and endeavour to contemplate the excitement that must have obtained on shore when de Ruyter and his ships were seen retreating towards Flushing before the English fleet, who had chased them for a night and a day, until the latter, fearing to trust themselves among the shoals in the neighbourhood of the Wielingen, brought up well to seaward of where today Zeebrugge's breakwater runs out.

They were strenuous times in that seventeenth century, and even when these formal naval wars ended Flushing continued to be a bugbear to us through the eighteenth and nineteenth centuries as the headquarters of the smuggling fraternity, who used to build their 150-ton cutters here, arm them with carriage guns, fill the holds with brandy, tea, and tobacco, and then cross to our eastern and south-coast ports especially.

There was no secret about the Flushing smuggling industry; it was done on a grand scale, employed a good many hands, was well financed, and paid handsome dividends. And even in this twentieth century Dutch North Sea coopers—floating grog shops—have been a source of great anxiety to the Customs authorities, until one of His Majesty's ships has had the good fortune to appear on the scene, and make a capture at the right moment.

But we have no time to think of all that Flushing stands for. There is a pleasant little evening breeze from the S.W., so we cast off our warps and sail up the canal. The bridge just outside the town was closed as we came up, so we had to keep backing and filling until the man in charge was pleased to open it, and then in company with a massively-built *paviljoenpom* we sailed lazily along the canal. The mate was busy sketching our companion, and that pleased the Dutch skipper more than a little. We kept up a running conversation, but how we did it I know not, except that it was wholly concerned with nautical matters, and there was thus a common basis and a live sympathy on that account. Typically Dutch was the scenery, and the extraordinary vividness of the verdure and the distant trees, with the towers and minarets of the approaching town, impressed themselves deeply on one's mind. Down dropped the breeze, and in the calm of the evening here we are through another opened bridge, and arrived at Middelburg, the old Zeeland capital. Here is a genuinely quaint city if you like, with its shady quays and all its streets radiating from the centre. It is a kind of Dutch Bruges, and thus you might lie for days and revel in peacefulness.

But we were not the only yacht. As we came to our berth we noticed a pleasure vessel flying the Belgian ensign, come no doubt from Antwerp, and just ahead of her was a British yacht, *Jamaie* (18 tons), of the Royal Cruising Club, of which I had often heard, and was now glad of an opportunity of going aboard her. She was no stranger to these waters, but she had what every craft navigating Holland should possess—an auxiliary motor. Her crew of four were all amateurs and she was bound our way. The Belgian yacht carried a paid hand, but her owner affirmed that the drawbacks attending the native "*schiffe*" are not less significant than in our own country.

Night dropped, and from one of the towers of Middelburg came the most discordant yet most fascinating jingle of bells, playing an old hymn tune, as they have for centuries. Some of the notes were a bit cracked, but the effect was in keeping with the antiquity of the place, and as soon as they had finished you longed for them to begin again. There is so much to see in Middelburg which appeals to one, that it were impossible to relate everything without writing after the manner of a catalogue, but the contents of its old buildings—its pictures, its tapestries, its carvings, prints, and furniture, fill your heart with joy. And if you are responsive to the beauties of architecture, what could be more glorious than the exquisite Gothic of the sixteenth century *stadhuis*?

The Dutch are a kindly race, especially if they see that you are interested in shipping. They will put themselves to endless trouble if they can be of any service to you. I had seen a rare and instructive print in the *stadhuis*, and desired to get some sort of a copy. The attendant spoke no English, and I only a few words of Dutch; but he understood and led me to where he lived. Then, calling his little girl, he sent me off in her care down the town till we came to an old print shop, where she summoned the old proprietor and introduced me. It was all done with such perfect sincerity and such spontaneous kindness; but I believe that my expressed admiration for a capital little model of a Dutch sailing craft, which the attendant had handled with reverence, may have had something to do with the matter, though perhaps not everything.

But by the time we were ready to depart, there was no wind, except the faintest of airs, and that was ahead. *Jamaie*, too, was starting, so her owner courteously suggested we should lash up alongside and see what the motor could do. And in this manner we proceeded along the canal very leisurely, but we were in no hurry to leave Walcheren. Three or four miles of this easy progress and we came to Veere, one of the sweetest spots in Europe, which so far has successfully resisted all modernising influences. There is happily no railway, so only a few tourists get to know of even its existence, and the rest do not always consider it worth visiting in the funny little steamer which runs up two or three times a day from Flushing. There is not very much to see if you are in quest of thrills, and you could probably conclude your tour of inspection under the hour. Veere is not a town, but just a village, and I only remember one shop. There is no life in the place; and there are some natures to whom Veere might seem very dull.

But if you love colour—bright blues, and greens, and reds; if you love old buildings and pretty cottages, quaint gables, delightful costumes, flaxen haired children, peaceful meadows, an old-world fishing harbour with old-world craft; if you long to smell the good ozone as it mingles with the sweet scents of the country; finally, if you are not too lofty to bring your mind

Dutch Costumes at Flushing

Fishing *Hoogarts* at Veere

Fisherwomen at Veere

down to the intelligence of simple, honest Dutch village folk, who are as sincere as they are slow—then Veere is for you, and is there to be enjoyed. I can hardly believe that Veere has any future, but it has a most interesting past.

You can feel this instinctively, and there is a bewitching sadness in the place which I cannot easily describe. It has seen good times and enjoyed them; this having all long since past, it is not complaining. It is content that it should be, though it does not forget. Time was when Veere was a well-fortified town, a most prosperous port, with a considerable foreign trade, especially to our island. I believe I am right in saying that between Scotland and Veere there was a particularly brisk trade in dried fish and wool.

I have before me as I write a reproduction of an old print, which shows a fleet of big ships sailing about off the town, as it then was. A strong, stubborn wall is seen to encircle the outside of the town, while inside a veritable forest of masts indicates how busy must have been the harbour. In the background rises up the Groote Kerk, which is still standing today. It was first built in 1348, so Veere was already a place of some importance about the time that the battle of Crecy was fought.

The geographical situation is not a little peculiar. It is located on an estuary at the north-eastern end of the island of Walcheren. This estuary comes in from the North Sea, and divides Walcheren from Beveland. It then turns to the right and subdivides the latter into North and South Beveland respectively. At the most northern end they call this estuary Veeregat; but where it flows out to the east into the East Scheldt it goes by the name of

BIRDS EYE VIEW OF VEERE

the Zandkreek, about which we shall speak presently. In olden days, just opposite to Veere, on the North Beveland side, there flourished another town called Kampen.

But a terrible storm overcame it in the seventeenth century and wiped it out. The charts of today give one a good idea of the extent of the devastation, and it is significant that Kampen's successor—Kampens Nieuwland, as it is called—to which the Veere ferry sails every day, is much further inland, up a creek. There is suggestive history even in the very names of the different shoals which make Veeregat so treacherous for the navigator.

In those days when the pilot was simply an expert leadsman or "*lodesman*," who felt his way along not by chart but by sounding, it is easy to imagine that those unhandy ships which came backwards and forwards across the North Sea would sometimes be caught by the 3-knot tide and carried on to the banks. One such shoal, from its position especially likely to cause disaster, is to this day still called the "Schotsman," and it needs no very powerful imagination to believe that some vessel bound to or from that country got ashore at this point.

Into this estuary of Veeregat, then, the small tidal harbour empties itself. But whilst Veere's front door, so to speak, faces a tidal stream., its back door gives out on to the Flushing canal, and thus it becomes doubly a port. We, then, had come to it by the back way, and finding a nicely-kept wooden quay just this side of the lock, came to a halt and tied up. One or two other craft had already arrived, but there was room for us all. A couple

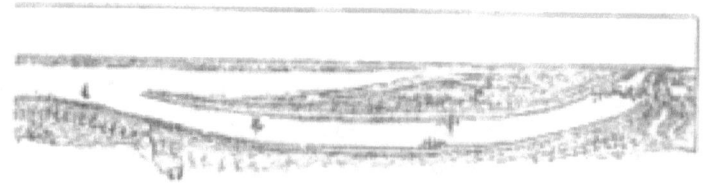

BIRDS EYE VIEW OF VEERE

of Dutch yachts, one of which was a *schokker* but flew the Belgian ensign, were at the further end, and they were to remain some time, for this is the place which artists from all over the European continent know by repute and visit. Some even take houses in the village permanently, for here are peace and rest, with excellent subjects in the costumes and the scenery, and always a rich choice of colours.

The most conspicuous architectural feature of Veere is undoubtedly the Groote Kerk, already alluded to. We have no space to run through the historical incidents with which it has been associated in six centuries. It was burnt down in the seventeenth century and rebuilt, since which time it has been put to such different uses as a military hospital, a workhouse, and barracks. Today it is for the most part in a state of decay. But when you go to Veere, as I hope someday you will, be sure and ascend the tower, and you will have one of the grandest panoramas that you ever saw, consisting of practically the whole of south Holland and all the innumerable rivers, canals, and estuaries running across the flat country as in a map. Windmills and houses, buoys, ships, and people seem to have been dropped indiscriminately into a toy country, with neat avenues of toy trees which as children you used to play with.

Of course, Veere has its *stadhuis* (town hall), with its curious spire, its gables, and bright-coloured shutters to its windows, yet it has not quite the size or wealth of decoration which the one at Middelburg possesses. But if you have any taste for old oak panelling it is worth looking inside for a few minutes.

You can get anything at Veere that you may require in the way of vegetables, milk, fruit, dairy produce, bread, paraffin, and fresh water. You can also lay in a good stock of lager beer from one of the two inns. But that is about all; so you must lay in a good supply of fresh meat before you leave Flushing or Middelburg, for you will get no more till you arrive at Dordrecht. But we were well looked after every morning; and before leaving we were life-friends with at least two of the male inhabitants and one charming little ten-year-old girl, who would come clattering

Loading a cargo of hay in Veere Harbour

along the quay in her wooden *sabots*—"*klumpen*" is the Dutch word—and clad in her neat costume. Of the two men, one kept a little inn down a side street up the village, most picturesquely situated. In that inn we found a perfect treasure in the shape of a large and exceptionally fine model *hoogarts*, properly built to scale, with leeboards, sails, and all. She was no toy, but had been put together by one of the guild of shipwrights. She was rigged just like most of the *hoogarts* lying in Flushing Harbour, and, as seen on another page, with a sprit. The mate asked and received permission to sketch this little craft, and the landlord took it as a great compliment.

A year later the incident was still deeply impressed on his mind, as the reader shall learn later. The second man was the native who used to wait on us every day with the produce of part of his garden. He amused us greatly by his extraordinary good temper and his unemotional voice. But when at length we came to visit Veere again he greeted us as a pair of long-lost brothers, shook hands, and insisted on our knowing his name, which he promptly wrote down for us. So that you may recognise him when we come to speak of him later on, let us introduce Heer Polderman. And what other name could you find to harmonise so perfectly with the Dutch scenery?

I mentioned just now the singular panorama which you can see from the top of Veere church. Let me now call to your attention the companion pictures. From these sketches made by the mate you have something of a bird's-eye view, and they are thus presented because they may assist those who would cruise in these waters. From the extremity of the second picture will be observed the Flushing to Veere canal and the lock. The canal then becomes subject to the rise and drop of the tide, and flows out into the Veeregat, which is seen flowing north and south, eventually turning to the east. That half of the picture which is reproduced on the first sketch shows the continuation of the Veeregat running out towards the North Sea. Everywhere you notice the houses of the village nestling among the trees, and the spire of Veere's *stadhuis* rising up conspicuously. The tidal harbour for the fishing craft is adjacent to this, though it cannot easily be here shown. It chanced that one day I was standing by the lock-gates looking out towards the Veeregat, when I saw a little sloop approaching which seemed somehow curiously familiar. Never before had I seen her, yet my memory told me we were not strangers.

She was manned by a couple of amateurs whom, from their dress, I took to be English, until I noticed their Dutch caps. Still puzzling in my mind, I heard her skipper order his mate to lower sail as they ran into the lock. They were English sure enough, and the craft also. And when they came finally to moor astern of *Jamaie* and ourselves the British fleet at Veere was now raised to three.

"Where are you from, sir?"

"Dordrecht."

"Is that the —?"

"The *Mave Rhoe*."

"That sailed last year from Hammersmith to Havre and back?"

"Yes."

"I took you for a couple of Dutchmen."

"Oh, the caps; these, too, came from Dordrecht. We've had a fine sail."

It was rather strange that the last book I had read before leaving England, that was actually now resting on my shelf in the cabin, was *From the Thames to the Seine*, in which Mr. Charles Pears described so interestingly his adventurous cruise in this *Mave Rhoe* singlehanded along the French coast to Fécamp and beyond. And here by a curious coincidence she had arrived during our sojourn in this out-of-the-way port. The pictures in the book were still fresh to my mind, and that was why she seemed so familiar. But she had changed ownership since her French trip, and this time had come across the North Sea from Harwich, and was now bound down coast to Ramsgate.

As she lay next to *Vivette* we had an interesting study in comparisons. If figures stand for anything, she has many similarities

VEERE HARBOUR
SHOWING THE *STADHUIS* SPIRE ON THE LEFT

to *Vivette*. *Mave Rhoe* has a foot more in length over all, but *Vivette* has a foot more beam. But after this the similarity begins to disappear. Our ship is cutter-rigged, while she is a sloop. The *Mave Rhoe* has a centre-board, which, when lowered, draws six feet. In spite of our length and beam being so similar, there is far more internal accommodation in *Vivette* and more freeboard. *Vivette*, if I may say so, is more of a ship, with better qualities for keeping the sea in bad weather, and nothing would ever persuade me to go cruising outside landlocked waters with a centre-board. And as I looked on our new neighbour I began to marvel even still more at Mr. Pears' daring and to admire his skill in having brought her safe home again through the trying experiences he so well relates.

CHAPTER 8

Veere to Numansdorp

It was difficult to tear ourselves away from Veere, but we had lost nothing during these few days, for the wind had remained at N.E., which was not much good for the next part of our journey. But it meant a fair breeze for the *Mave Rhoe* down the canal to Flushing, and she was in a hurry to get home. *Jamaie*, too, had gone, for with a motor pushing her along she could make good progress to windward.

And so we were left with only the Dutch and Belgian craft now. Frankly, we were glad that the wind was not fair, for it gave us an excuse to remain another day, and this exceptionally fine, bright weather could not last much longer, and the wind would soon get back to the S.W. But at last we cast off our mooring ropes reluctantly, got through the formalities with the *sluismeester* and through the lock itself. Once more we were on tidal waters, and had to pay respect to ebb and flow.

There are two routes open to you after you leave Veere. Either you may turn to port (as in the first sketch seen earlier) and then go by the Roompot Channel along the north shore of Noord Beveland, till you get to Zeriksee. Or, again, you may turn to starboard (as in the second sketch seen earlier) and follow the channel, which changes its name as often as it bends, and so skirt the south shore of Noord Beveland. This will bring you out into the Engelsche Vaarwater, which eventually meets the Roompot off Zeriksee. The first alternative is certainly the easiest and less tricky. There is only one spot in the Roompot to worry you, where the wide channel suddenly narrows. But it is well buoyed, and you have only to watch that the tide does not set you out of your course at that point.

We chose the second of these two alternatives, turned to the right, went by the southern route, and very interesting we found it. You must exercise a little care as you emerge from the tidal portion of the canal into the estuary, for the stream is very strong, and the channel, though well buoyed, is very narrow indeed. Locate the two conical buoys, leave them to starboard, but the two can and one spherical buoys to port. The tide runs like a mill-race hereabouts, and it would be bad for you if you took the ground. After that, by following the devious windings of the channel, and paying the most careful regard to the buoys—conical to starboard, can to port—you may carry on with confidence.

We have a fair tide, a fine breeze, and away we go foaming along. In the Zuidvliet we come up to a couple of *tjalks* which had started half an hour ahead of us, but we soon leave them astern. Besides the buoys to watch there is a good deal of traffic, both steam and sail, and it usually happens that you find it most crowded where the channel suddenly narrows. The extent to which the Dutch in a short space of time have developed the marine motor, and applied it to specially built steel and iron hulls is most noticeable. They are of all sizes, seen everywhere and carry regular cargoes of all sorts.

These are not so bad to meet in confined waters. But the steamers are worse, though not nearly so alarming as the *Rhineschiffs*. The latter form a species of craft which you never encounter in England. Practically they are steamers without steam, as an Irishman might describe them. Imagine a huge, flat-bottomed, steel barge, with plenty of freeboard, and a high bridge and deck-house aft, where the helmsman steers with an enormous wheel set not vertically but horizontally. Nine-tenths of this hull consist of the hold, the remaining portion being for the skipper and his family, their flower-pots and wash-tubs. These craft have no engines of any kind, but have very powerful anchors and cables both forward and aft, those aft leading through holes underneath the counter.

The stern anchors are of the grapnel type, and stockless, being used for checking the *schiff's* way when running into a harbour, or when mooring fore and aft in a channel that would not allow so lengthy a vessel to swing. Two or three short masts, usually flying flags, serve only to accentuate their excessive length in proportion to beam. If the reader will examine the photo on another page he will be able to see one of moderate dimensions.

Now these *schiffs* have no engines of any kind : they are mere dumb cargo-carriers, and are towed by powerful steam tugs for very long distances from as far away as a German town right through Holland and into the heart of Belgium. On one occasion, during exceptionally fine and settled weather, I passed one out at sea. She had just come out through the Bruges canal at Zeebrugge. But these are essentially built for inland navigation, and besides being seen on such rivers as the Rhine, East and West Scheldt, Maas, Ijssel, Amstel, and so on, there is hardly a canal in the Low Countries along which they do not travel, for which reason they are built necessarily shallow and as flat as a box.

In the neighbourhood of Rotterdam and Dordrecht they are being constructed by the score. Some of them are able to carry a load of 2000 tons, which is as much as many a tramp steamer can stow away. And when you meet with a tug slowly dragging this great mass astern, and you happen to be beating to windward in a narrow gut with sandbanks on either side and a strong tide, it is rather anxious work. But it often happens that the enterprising tug-skipper, with a view to making a handsome perquisite, has also arranged to give a few *tjalks*, perhaps a hotter or two, a Dutch yacht and a few other species, a passage. I think I once counted a string of twelve or thirteen assorted craft being towed by one tug, and the procession seemed endless.

But we got along safely through the Zuidvliet, through the Zandkreek, and now we were out into the Engelsche Vaarwater. The wind was northerly, so against us. The tide also opposed us, but if we could just beat up till we got to Zeriksee we should carry a fair stream for the rest of our journey that day, and a fair wind likewise. But the tide was very strong, and the breeze gradually got weaker and weaker, so although we made short boards near the shore to get out of the tide, our advance was slow. This was just an occasion when an auxiliary motor would have made all the difference between success and failure.

All the other sailing craft which had come out astern of us from Veere and the Zandkreek gave it up after beating for some hours, and at length we also decided that as night was coming on and the wind was fast failing we had better find a snug anchorage till the morning. We therefore ran back till we were just inside the Zandkreek, and let go in 4½ fathoms at high-water between numbers 19 and 18 buoys, where there was room for us to swing out of the fairway. We hung out the riding-light and prepared dinner.

There was something very weird and attractive about this anchorage, which I shall always remember: something inexpressibly solitary and primitive. It combined in a curious way some of the features of a Scotch loch, an Essex creek, and a Norwegian fjord; and yet for all that it was unmistakably Dutch, for there were no hills but an occasional lonely farmstead here and there. The sun had gone down with a strange look that was not too hopeful; but if it was going to blow hard this was a snug enough anchorage unless the wind should blow very hard from the east, which was not at all likely.

From S.E. through S. to about N. by E. it was quite sheltered, provided the anchor should hold in the mud. And when we turned out in the morning it was delightful, for once, to be riding to one's anchor and to feel independent of everybody As we breakfasted a number of *hoogarts* were mussel-dredging. As the reader will see from the accompanying picture, these craft, though similar in hull, are slightly differently rigged from the Walcheren craft, by discarding the sprit and employing the more modern gaff and boom, the sail being laced to the mast just as here shown.

NEARING ROTTERDAM

ON THE MAAS. IN THE FOREGROUND IS SEEN A *RHINE-SCHIFF:* THE DISTANT MASTS OF TYWO FULL-RIGGED SHIPS INDICATE THE POSITION OF ROTTERDAM.

A BOTTER FROM THE ISLAND OF URK

With their lee-boards and flat-bottoms these shovel-nosed craft would make nice little singlehanders for any one fond of ditch-crawling; on the east coast of England: and this morning they looked particularly jolly and business-like. They added just the decisive note that distinguished the Zandkreek from Essex or elsewhere.

Our plan was to catch the last of the ebb down the Engelsche Vaarwater, and then to take the first of the flood from Zeriksee up the Keeten Mastgat. Roughly speaking, the general trend of our course was to be N.E.; hence judge of our happiness when we found that the breeze had gone round to S.W., thus giving us a fair wind all the way. The tide off Zeriksee would not make until 12.40 p.m., and if we started at 11.20 a.m. we should have ample time to run so far with the ebb. So at that time we broke out the anchor, and were soon running out from the Zandkreek, down the Engelsche Vaarwater, and into the Keeten Mastgat.

We had arrived off Zeriksee in good time and ahead of our tide, for the flood had not yet commenced to make. The channel is very wide, averaging from half to three-quarters of a mile, and varying from about seven to as much as twenty fathoms deep. It curves about in fine bold sweeps, and, like all these Dutch tidal waterways, it is splendidly buoyed, alterations are continually being made to the charts, and fresh buoys laid down as new swatchways are formed and old passages silted up. This is important to bear in mind, and be careful to get your charts the last thing before you leave town.

The British Admiralty charts are surprisingly good for these parts, being corrected from the latest surveys of the Netherlands Government. Only in one or two instances, of which one happened to be at a particularly tricky position, did the British charts fail to be of the utmost assistance. But the following year I purchased the charts published by the hydrographical department of the Dutch Marine, and I strongly urge all who sail in these waters to do likewise. They are excellent in every respect, are drawn on a large scale, and slightly more up-to-date than ours. A further advantage is that they are printed on a stouter,

AS WE BREAKFASTED A COUPLE OF *HOOGARTS* WERE MUSSEL-DREDGING yellowish paper, and do not become so readily dirtied or injured.

As we ran along before a slashing breeze we were amazed at the heavy traffic which was pouring along. The *Rhine-schiffs*, with their tugs, were there in plenty. There were *ketches* and *tjalks*—a whole fleet of them—turning to windward, and almost every kind of motor and steam craft. Perhaps the funniest of all was a small armoured river gunboat belonging to the Dutch Government. There are altogether five of these little vessels afloat. They are between thirty and forty years old (and look it), steam only seven knots, and are of about 350 tons each. We saw several of them in different parts of Holland, and they amused us because they looked so useless; but perhaps they possess a certain amount of value in patrolling the waterways, though I should be sorry to be aboard if ever they put to sea in a breeze of wind. They are necessarily of very shallow draft, and resemble nothing so much as a flat iron sitting on the water.

The glass was beginning to fall, the wind was piping up, and the sky was glooming over; and by the time we were abreast of the fishing harbour of Bruinesse there was quite a smart breeze. From this point for some miles you have to deal with the trickiest bit of navigation in the whole of Holland, and during the fifteen odd miles between Bruinesse and Hollandsch Diep you have to pass most of a hundred buoys, everyone of which must be identified from the chart, so that you know exactly where you are; for from the main channels there diverge at sharp angles other channels.

It is like wandering in a wood, and as soon as you let go the hold of your position you are lost, and before long will find yourself out of the channel and picked up by one of the myriads of sandbanks in the vicinity of the Krammer. The local men who spend their lives from infancy to old age sailing up and down these channels, and are kept supplied with modern charts, often get aground; so it is still more essential that strangers should be careful, and when I was once yarning to a Dutchman sometime afterwards he was reluctant to believe that we had come through

Holland without a pilot.

But provided you pay great attention, don't cut off corners, and don't let yourself be confused by seeing local vessels using new swatchways known only to local men, you ought not to get astray. From Bruinesse there are no fewer than three channels, all of which ultimately run into the Krammer. Make up your mind to follow that which is the simplest, and stick to this, whether the steamers and *Rhine-schiffs* go by that route or not. Then never fail to tick off each buoy as you pass it, marking it off with a pencil on your chart, so that when you arrive at the parting of the ways, and your attention has to be diverted, or you need both hands to tighten in the sheets, you have your exact position verified, and you can keep looking out for the next batch of buoys.

I am convinced that this is the only way to navigate this treacherous Krammer with any degree of safety. A stranger should not think of attempting this fifteen-mile stretch except in daylight. But if he should find night coming on he can easily run into the little port of Zijpe, just below Bruinesse, and find the snuggest of anchorages for as long as he wants to stop, and sheltered in bad weather from all the winds of heaven. From the chart the least complicated route seemed to be that on the port hand by the Bocht van St. Jacob, though the traffic was all proceeding up the narrow and more direct Vlije van de Noordplaten.

The strong wind developed into a succession of weighty squalls, and we had to roll down some reefs and stow the foresail, but still we flew on with a pace that was most inspiring. With more wind came also the rain, and it became so thick that we could see not more than one pair of buoys ahead at a time. Before long it had developed into just such a day as we had encountered between Newhaven and Ramsgate, but, of course, the sea was smooth, though sloppy. Great, heavy Dutchmen were beating the opposite way, and as they passed astern of us smashing into the pea-green waters with their clumsy bows, while one of the hands was getting some of the reluctant and stiff canvas off her previous to bringing up till the tide should turn, you had exactly a living reproduction of those hundreds of seascapes which the old seventeenth century masters used to paint so well.

We were carrying a smart press of sail, and doing a good six or seven knots, with the tide just flooding. So long as we could see the buoys, and identify the channel, we were all right. But what with the thickness of the atmosphere which obliterated everything beyond thirty yards ahead, and the viciousness of the squalls which compelled me to keep luffing up into the wind, it was a quite a busy time to prevent ourselves being picked up by the banks. Several times we could see nothing ahead except the rain slashing down to the water: once or twice we almost decided to bring up until it should clear, for travelling at this rate we should pile up a long way into any shoal we grounded on. But we never quite lost count of the buoys, though it was puzzling to see which direction the Krammer next took.

Perhaps the channel would suddenly widen out and for a moment you lost the line of the buoys, and still you went rushing on. Then a rapid calculation from the chart for your bearings, a glance at the compass, a slight alteration of the helm and a conical object looking like a gigantic candle-snuffer would wag its head out of the mist, and you could breathe freely for a few more yards.

And so we continued until we got into the Volkerak, when it cleared a little, and the wind ceased to freshen for a few minutes. Astern of us, bringing a strong tide up with them, came the high-pooped sailing barges under easy canvas, and I checked sheets to let one of them get ahead, and indicate by her manoeuvres the winding of the channel, for now we were approaching the most difficult portion of an awkward channel, the nature of which may be described in the fewest words thus. The Volkerak at this point flows precisely at right angles to another mighty estuary known as the Hollandsch Diep. The latter is most of three miles across from shore to shore, but even in the deepest part there is not more than thirty feet of water, and in some of the channels there is still less. But in both the Volkerak and the Hollandsch

Diep there are very strong tides: and since they collide at right angles it is but reasonable to expect that a bar should form just as we are wont to find it where a harbour empties itself and meets the tide setting athwart its mouth.

But though the Volkerak mouth is also from shore to shore about as wide as the Hollandsch Diep, yet practically the whole three miles of the former will be found to consist of a bar of enormous dimensions. On the west side there is a narrow channel, but on the east there is another passage so small that there are only about a hundred yards between the buoys. I had been carefully warned by a Belgian yachtsman whom I met at Veere, that this was a thoroughly treacherous place and wanted watching.

The same informant related the recent incident of one of the Dutch Admiralty yachts which had got hard aground at this spot, and his passengers had to be put ashore in the small boat. It is a notorious place, and the name by which it is known on the charts—Hellegat— exactly suits it. The bar itself dries to the extent of nearly four feet above the water level, and there is little if any slack, for the tides pour through each of these two channels like a torrent. I have not anywhere come across such a current as this. We selected the eastern channel because it was the more direct, and because the barge was making for it.

We kept overhauling her so I sheered about a good deal, and checked sheets still more to deaden our way. Down came the rain so thickly that you could hardly see the buoys. The weather certainly was a little inconsiderate in thickening up always when it was least convenient for us. We were foaming along through the leaden waters with the barge a little way ahead. The mate was at the helm, while I was busy with the chart identifying each buoy. And then a curious thing occurred. It was just possible to find one's way but no more than this, when suddenly the mate called my attention to the barge. We were nearly out of Hellegat now, but there were still shoals on either side.

"Hallo," he exclaimed, "look at that."

The Dutchman suddenly swerved to starboard right from the

channel, and for a moment I began to wonder if I was standing too far to port. But a glance at the chart soon showed that this was not so, and that there could not be more than three or four feet of water where the barge was even allowing for the tide which we had outstripped and was only just rising. "We're in the channel," I answered; "keep on your course."

"They're looking back to see if we're following. I suppose we are right"—this in the mate's most patient but rather doubting voice.

"He'll be aground in a minute, unless this chart is all wrong."

And as I spoke we saw the barge slowing down, seem to hesitate, stop dead, and after a time drag through into six or seven feet of water, and then keep right on. He had saved a good deal by cutting across the shoals, and being practically flat-bottomed it did not matter so much if he touched, though he might have done some damage to his hull from the speed at which he was

"Hallo!" he exclaimed, "Look at that"

travelling. But we wondered at the time, and have often since wondered again, whether the intentions of the barge's skipper were strictly honest, whether he was trying a "Riddle of the Sands" trick, and endeavouring to tempt us where we should have been in an awkward plight. He had watched us for some time coming up astern, and seeing that we were totally unlike most of the Dutch yachts, and were feeling our way carefully, sounding with the lead, and generally proceeding with caution, he may possibly have wearied of acting as forerunner, and determined to get us ashore. The reader may decide for himself, but we have our own opinions on the subject.

It was breezing up quite hard now, and I should have been sorry to have touched. Gybe ho! And over comes the boom. Steady on the helm, and here is the last of the Hellegat buoys. According to the chart, there is a little harbour the other side of Hollandsch Diep, but apparently it has no name given to it. However, it would be better to get inside if we can, for the glass has already tumbled back two-tenths, and there will be more to follow.

The afternoon was ending, and I had no wish to navigate the unlighted channels towards Willemsdorp except in broad daylight. So as the wind was fair for this nameless harbour, which was still invisible in the rain, I laid a careful compass course for where it should be, and in due course picked up the two piers through the glasses. I knew nothing at all about the depth of water inside, nor whether there was a bar at the entrance, but we had had an exciting day, and would be glad to get somewhere before the weather got worse. It was fine to be flying along at this glorious pace, but as we got to the harbour mouth the water suddenly became yellow, and though I fancy we sounded with the lead, I was a little nervous as to whether it would shoal suddenly and we should find ourselves hard aground.

Just for a moment the suspense was keen, but by that time we had rushed in past the two small light-beacons, and with a quick glance had to make a mental map of the harbour to see what space there was. At the end was a wall, and on either side were wooden jetties and quays. We had a furious gybe, luffed up smartly, pulled the unwilling jib down on deck, the halyards stiff and swollen with rain, shortened in the main sheet, let go the anchor, and away rattled out the cable just as a passenger steamer was letting go her warps on the port hand and clearing out. We dragged a little, lowered the rain-stiffened main-sail, and, running out ropes to the starboard shore, made fast.

There was a certain amount of swell, so we kept the anchor to windward, that it might keep us from banging against the wall. It was a bottle-necked sort of a place, where apparently no one lived, and whither no one ever traded. There was no fishing industry—nothing except a railway line and a tiny station alongside which the steamer has lain. There was a steel *klipperaak*, *ketch*-rigged, and of about 80 tons. But otherwise there was nothing at all. But we had had a most sportive day, and here we had arrived safe, sound, and ready to do justice to a most excellent dinner in the cabin.

Chapter 9

Numansdorf to Dordrecht

The reader will learn presently how we discovered the name of this harbour, to which even the Dutch charts give no appellation; but it is permissible to anticipate events by a little, and call the place Numansdorp. The accompanying illustration will enable the reader to gain some idea of its appearance as seen from the Hollandsch Diep. There is in truth plenty of water, and by being lighted, as shown, it can be entered by night or day. To the yachtsman cruising in Holland I can thoroughly recommend this comfortable anchorage, for it is situated most conveniently for negotiating Hellegat, and I afterwards soon found that the Dutch sailing craft use it as a harbour of refuge in bad weather, and for stopping a tide before going south through Hellegat.

The piers are formed of broken stones, and jut out from the grassy shores, but inside you find plenty of room for mooring against wooden piles on the starboard hand. And the moment you step ashore it is delightful. For endless miles stretch acres

Entance to Numansdorf

and acres of bright green prairies, dotted with windmills, and intersected with numerous dykes and ditches. In the distance, now visible because you are standing on the seawall, there are a few farms and a village of some sort, which is Numansdorp proper, and a little cluster of cottages between the harbour and the village.

Night passed, and the next day the wind was blowing at least a moderate gale, and within a very few minutes no fewer than five steel sailing barges and one yawl yacht—the former of about 80 tons, the latter approximately 20 tons—came running for shelter in a hurry. It was very gusty as well, and I noticed they were all close-reefed. As they came into this little port, they dropped their anchors wherever they could to prevent colliding with the walls or each other, and for quite a time the whole entrance was blocked with craft lying athwart.

Some of them only narrowly avoided damaging themselves, and before the last of them was lashed up she had carried away some of her head-gear, and only just saved her bowsprit. It was a terrible muddle, and there was a good deal of time and energy spent in recovering anchors again, shifting berths, running out lines, keeping away from bumping the quays. The Dutchman who combined the office of station-master and harbour-master seemed at his wits' end to straighten us all out. But at length we were all tidy and comfortable. The mate was spending the morning ashore, so I had a busy time alone, and a few more bits of paint were lost from *Vivette*.

We became friendly with most of our new neighbours, and especially with the Dutch gentlemen on the yacht, who courteously showed us better charts than we had, and elucidated several points of importance. Later in the day I set out to walk into the village further inland. A fresh breeze was blowing in from the Hollandsch Diep across the meadows, but it was beginning to fine up, and the sunset was encouraging. The evening was pleasantly warm, and the way was interesting with the sweet smell of the open country to gladden one's soul.

And so I came at length to a village that was typically Dutch with its avenues of trees, neat wooden houses, and well-washed pavements. All at once I found myself in what they would call the High Street if it were England, and I proceeded to search for the shops to lay in stores for our kitchen. The entire population was standing or sitting about under the trees enjoying the calm of the evening. But they so suddenly broke off their conversations and gazed unanimously in my direction, that I was too embarrassed to face the eyes of the whole populace at the first attempt. What they took me for I know not, but every man, woman, and child focussed their eyes so stolidly, that I was compelled to bear away down a shady lane till the first shock had passed. But at the second effort I marched boldly up the street, keeping a good look-out for a fruiterer's.

Before long I became conscious of being followed by a man, who dogged my steps persistently. But espying my goal, I entered and stated my wants. Pears, potatoes, and other commodities were what I wanted, but I had forgotten the right way to pronounce the Dutch words, and the dictionary had been left aboard. Just then an old man with a round hat and a typical Boer face, solemn and unemotional, appeared at the doorway and addressed me in English. He it was who had been tracking my footsteps down the street. With no hesitation he offered his services, and demanded to know what it was that I desired. I informed him half-reluctantly, not quite sure of his sincerity. But I had been needlessly suspicious.

He could get me potatoes and all the other things, so away we went together to a farm. But before we arrived he had told me much about himself and his family. That woman we passed just now was his *vrouw*. Oh, yes, she was a good *vrouw*, he went on, and looked well after his house. The younger woman with her was the *vrouw* of his son, and the latter kept a cafe in the village. (This I took for a hint and made a mental note of.) The farmer sold me quite cheaply all that I required, and then my new acquaintance insisted that I should go and see his own house. He had been in former years cook on a British ship, and was proud of the fact that he was the only man in Numansdorp who could speak English. Had he not been to Cardiff and to the Tyne?

So we arrived at his house, where he presented me with a bag in which to carry my purchases, handed me a cigar, showed me how cleanly his *vrouw* kept the stoves and cooking utensils, introduced me to all the family portraits, told me which was the spouse of which, related in detail how each relative was prospering, pointed to a long framed testimonial on the wall, related some of his sea experiences, and gave me the name of the village.

After having listened to all this, I felt it my duty that we should look in at his son-in-law's café. Having drunk the beer of the country, the old man insisted on showing me round the whole of Numansdorp, and very interesting it was to have so intelligent and informative a guide. Those houses over there were a colony of Russian exiles. Those gardens belonged to himself. "Mine," he said, tapping his breast with the pride of ownership. We swung into the main street once more, and he was determined that everyone of his friends should see that he had an Engelschman in tow. This is a curious and an amusing trait on the part of the Dutchman, and Mr. E. F. Knight found the same experience years ago when he sailed through Holland before writing his *Falcon on the Baltic*.

They like to take possession of you and show you to the other as if to say, "I captured this by my own efforts unaided." And he slowed down so that no one in the whole street should fail to have an opportunity of noting the fact. He was very kind and most anxious to assist me in any way possible, and did me the further honour of escorting me almost down to the harbour. Then with great solemnity tearing a sheet from his notebook, he inscribed his name and address, begging that if ever I found myself again in Numansdorp, I would look him up. With a hearty shake of the hand, he doffed his hat and we parted. In appearance he was exactly like one of the Boer generals who attained great fame in the South African war. He was shrewd, serious, and a man evidently accustomed to wielding authority; and with this he possessed something of the grand manner that one hardly expected to meet in this out-of-the-way village.

By the time I had arrived back at the yacht, the wind, which had been so turbulent, had dropped to a whisper, and the sky was totally unclouded. Without so much as a ripple, the waters of the harbour reflected the yellow riding lights of the little fleet, contrasted with the red and green paths which the beacon-lights were throwing across the entrance. There was a heavy dew which foretold a fine day tomorrow, and the atmosphere was as clear as I have ever seen it; truly a beautiful, idyllic evening. And then from the Dutch yacht next astern came the familiar sounds of "God Save the King" from a gramophone, which seemed strange.

"It is for you," shouted the owner of the yacht, and the compliment was highly appreciated. We were up bright and early the following morning, and had cleared from Numansdorp by about four o'clock. It was a beautiful day, but the wind was N.E. and extraordinarily light, and the conditions were in curious contrast to those which had prevailed when we entered. We should clearly make but little headway today, but we must do our best. Standing over towards Willemstad, prettily situated among the trees, we made a short leg and a long up the Hollandsch Diep. But the tide would soon turn against us strongly, and the sun was killing the wind, so we should clearly have to bring up somewhere for a few hours.

Our book of sailing directions mentioned Strijensas as a small port, but omitted to give any details. The chart, too, was too small to give one an idea as to what we might expect. But here we were off the opening, so it would be interesting to run in and explore. This we did, and found it so narrow that there was just room for us to pass a rowing-boat and no more. It was not unlike one of those dykes that exist on the Norfolk Broads, with reeds lining either side. At the end of this little *gut* we came to a lock, lowered sail, and anchored under the shadow of a wayside inn, where several other craft were moored.

It seemed not half the size of Numansdorp, and it was very shallow. There were sundry little repairs we wanted to make, so

STRIJENSAS

THE PLACE WHERE *VIVETTE* IS SEEN BROUGHT UP IN THE CENTRE OF THE CREEK HAS THE MOST WATER AT LOW TIDE. JUST ASTERN ARE THE LOCK-GATES.

PAVILJOEN POM

SEEN ON THE MIDDLESBURG CANAL

we could easily pass the heat of the day doing these odd jobs and slacking in the glorious sunlight.

With the heat came also great thirst, and there were several journeys to the inn. Quite a crowd collected, and grazed in utter silence and with entire lack of emotion, from the road, wondering who and what we were, and by what strange hazard we had invaded their primitive seclusion. This went on for quite a long time, and it was more than we could do to refrain from laughing right out. Not a soul could speak English; they were content to remain stolidly staring by the hour. Meanwhile the tide dropped more and more, so that finally we could float only in the very centre of the creek. I went off in the dinghy, and made a rough survey of the channel, and if any other sailing men should be compelled to run in here, he may care to have details which are not found elsewhere.

You can easily recognise Strijensas from the outside by the two stone pier-like projections that jut out into the Hollandsch Diep. At the outermost extremity of each a post, with diamond-shaped crosspiece, rises up. A few yards further shorewards, on the port hand, is a six-sided lighthouse, thirty-five feet high. At dead-low water neaps both sides of the creek are very shallow, but by keeping strictly to the centre you will get from six to seven feet of water, and there is the same amount two hours before low water, for the reason that though the tide ebbs there is no appreciable drop after the fifth hour. At the entrance, however, by the diamond-shaped beacons, there is as much as a couple of fathoms. I sounded very carefully in the dinghy all the way, so these depths can be relied upon. Moor by the lock in mid-channel. The sluice-gates are opened at low water for about an hour, which cause a fairly strong stream to flow out, but you can run lines out to either shore.

I mention Strijensas, because it is another of those back-of-the-beyond places which it is a delight to find unexpectedly, and it might be useful to know of in the case of accident. A sailing craft could be laid alongside a *tjalk* and examined below water-line when the tide dropped; or a motor vessel could have her propeller attended to. But in entering, although there is no stream inside, there is a strong tide across the mouth which must be allowed for, or the vessel would quickly find herself on one of the breakwaters. We left there again in the evening, but the tide had barely finished ebbing. We beat to windward till a little past Willemsdorp, and then, as the breeze had died away and darkness had come on, let go anchor in the Kil, a most entrancing spot, with two fathoms almost up to the banks.

This channel turns abruptly out of the Hollandsch Diep, is not unlike the Thames between Teddington and Richmond, and about as wide. There are not too many trees on either side, so it is excellent sailing. It made an ideal anchorage, and is much used by the Dutch trading craft. Indeed I counted a fleet of about thirty sailing craft brought up here to-night, and the number of masts would have made a big clearing in any forest. The tide was very strong, good ground tackle is essential, and if necessary you can sheer in towards the shore where the tide is slightly less.

There is a curious custom in Holland which will immediately strike the British yachtsman. When sailing at night along any of the Dutch waterways, craft do not carry the red and green port and starboard lights, but, instead, hoist a white riding-light at the masthead. The effect is most curious and ghost-like, for below the light the loom of the sail shows up like some weird spectre approaching. In the accompanying sketch there is no exaggeration of the strange phenomenon which is thus presented; and tonight, with the additional shadows of the trees, the idea was intensified as two or three *tjalks* drifted listlessly up with the flood-tide. This white light is doubtless a survival from the older days, but it is difficult to tell which way a vessel is heading, and one cannot but think it is a pity that the usual side-lights as carried on steam craft are not used by the sailing vessels.

Just before dawn I came out from the warmth of the cabin, and watched the thirty different craft get under weigh to catch their tide through the Hollandsch Diep and on to Hellegat. It was an interesting sight to see them one by one clear out from their anchorage and get under way in the darkness. Such a clank-

A Curious Phenomenon

At night the Dutch sailing craft carry only a masthead light, and the general effect, from a distance is to suggest a conical body with a gas-light on top.

clank of windlasses and a clatter-clatter of the loose cables on deck! Such a squeaking and creaking of halyard-blocks! Then a short, sharp sentence from each skipper, up went the head-sails, hard over came each tiller, and down they all went with the tide like so many phantoms flitting silently onwards. At 9.30 a.m. we, too, had broken out anchor and started in the opposite direction, leaving behind a clear space where but a few hours previously you could hardly see the water for shipping.

There was a bonny S.W. breeze again to give us a fair wind, and we bowled along the Kil and Maliegat till we found ourselves in a broad tidal river named the Oude Maas. On the starboard hand were evident signs that the town was busily engaged with its industries, and there was a considerable amount of traffic dodging about—tugs, sailing craft, and tramp steamers alongside quays. With fair wind and tide we had done the five knots in the hour, but we had to keep backing and filling for another half-an-hour.

For this was the famous old port of Dordrecht, and across the Maas is stretched an expansive steel bridge that is a nuisance to all craft except such as can get under the arches without having to lower mast or funnel. In such places as Dordrecht, Rotterdam, and Amsterdam, these great bridges are a source of considerable annoyance to any ship with sails. For they remain closed for most of the day, then suddenly open for ten or fifteen minutes. During that period the glut of traffic accumulated during the preceding hours is enormous, and everything endeavours to rush through at the same time.

We had run backwards and forwards many times up the Oude Maas, when about midday the two narrow openings—one on the east, the other at the west side—swung round. Most of the fleet were heading for the former, so we chose the opening at the extreme left. One craft had gone through quite safely, wind and tide setting straight into the right direction. We were coming along with plenty of way, when suddenly a *hoogarts*, finding he could not squeeze through the opening on the extreme right, came on a wind, rushed towards us across our bows, and

DORDRECHT BRIDGE

THE INSET AT THE TOP INDICATES THE TWO OPENINGS FOR A CRAFT TO GO THROUGH.

narrowly avoided colliding with our bowsprit

We were travelling the faster, so checked sheets to avoid hitting his stern just as he pulled over his helm and squared away for the open arch. Before we could do anything else, the tide had caught hold of *Vivette*, and to our horror carried us on to one of the supports of the bridge, and in spite of all our efforts she hit twice, knocking her bowsprit inboard, where it jammed tightly against the capstan and started the bitts. She swung round, head to wind and tide, and of course, to make matters worse, the dinghy got hitched up the wrong side of one of the projections. Here was a sorry sight and an exciting predicament. I cast the painter adrift, for we were blocking up the passage, and I knew I should soon get her again as she drifted through Dordrecht. The next thing was to clear *Vivette*.

There was a terrible muddle below her forefoot consisting of bobstay, bowsprit shrouds, and jib outhaul. These refused to be gathered in, so I left them. Fortunately she had not injured her hull, for she had hit dead on at the bowsprit end. To our surprise the latter had not broken, and was only badly chafed. We got the main-sail off her and the jib had come inboard of its own accord. It was a thrilling time, for barely had I time to hang on to the lower portion of the bridge with the boathook than a couple more *hoogarts* came running through this opening, and only cleared us by inches.

Meanwhile I had shouted to attract attention on the bridge itself, and a man dressed like a *gendarme*, with a wealth of silver-lace, came down, got into his boat, captured our dinghy, and then closed the bridge. Finally, after making a temporary clearance, we dropped astern, and, under main-sail and stay-sail only, continued our passage.

On either side of the broad river were quays crowded six or seven deep with shipping, and it was no easy matter to locate the narrow entrance to the haven we had intended making for. But for the benefit of other strangers let me say that after you get through the bridge you should then begin to look out for the swimming-baths on the starboard hand. These, as in most

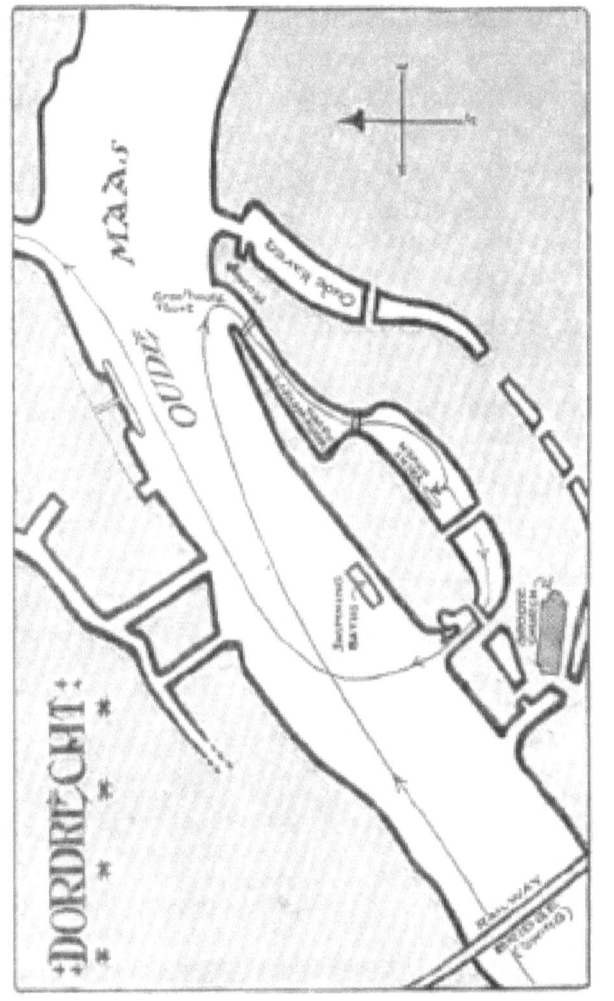

The Arrow and Line indicate the Course to the Yacht Haven after passing through Dordrecht Bridge

continental places, are actually floating on the river a few yards from the quay.

Having found these, carry on till you come to the first turning beyond, also on the starboard side. Run into this, which is called the Wollewevers Haven, and tie up temporarily alongside the quay on the port hand, but be careful that the strong tide setting across the haven entrance does not carry you on to other craft. You can then stow sail at your leisure and tow or sweep into the inner haven, which is reserved for yachts and rowing craft exclusively. All this we had to find out for ourselves, but for convenience it may as well be stated at once.

CHAPTER 10

Around Dort

We luffed up, then, out of the strong tide into the haven where in olden days no doubt the woollen merchants put their goods aboard ship centuries before ever that terrible bridge had been brought into being. We lowered sail again, went under another smaller bridge raised by hand, as the man dangled a wooden *sabot* at the end of a fishing-rod for the toll, and finally brought up alongside one of the quays. It was very shut-in, with quaint old warehouses on one side and old-fashioned residential houses on the other that suggested the palmy days of the eighteenth century.

But the first duty was to find out the exact extent of our damage, and then as speedily as possible to get it repaired. A crowd of interested onlookers had collected on the quay, and one of these, I found, spoke English. I explained our difficulty, and inquired if he knew of a shipwright. Saying he did, he took me along the river front, past most interesting bits of old architecture, and then, turning down a side street, brought up at a workshop, where, according to the sign, Heer Somebody-or-other made masts, blocks, and pumps.

We entered, and after saying something in the native tongue he handed me over to this fair-haired man and departed. The shipwright smiled on me benignly, but for the rest we might have been a couple of deaf-and-dumb people, for neither could speak the language of the other. But putting on his coat, I steered him back to the yacht, introduced him to the bowsprit, which was jammed so tightly that it could not be moved from the capstan, pointed out that the bitts had been knocked a little aft, starting two or three of the deck planks.

I then got the mate to take him into the fo'c'sle, and demonstrate what must be done from inside so as to strengthen the deck from underneath. And while he was beginning to grasp the state of things, and generally to "savvy," I was busy in the cabin turning out phrases from a big English-Dutch dictionary. Such expressions as "make strong," "new oak beam," "brass screws," aided by considerable pantomimic action and the mate's sketching, got us advanced a long way.

It would have made a screamingly funny farce, had I not been feeling a little unhappy after the accident. The fo'c'sle door was open, so I could give directions and keep one finger on the dictionary while the embarrassed man twisted himself into all sorts of contortions in the forepeak, getting very hot, and doing his utmost to understand exactly our wants. This was the sort of thing that went on for some time, until occasionally we would arrive at an *impasse*, and the mate reported that the man could not quite " savvy," so was going ashore to look for someone who could speak English.

I foresaw what that meant, and that we should lose much time thereby, so calling to the mate to keep him there till I could look up sufficient Dutch words to make a sentence, the attack was resumed, and once more the man smiled that he understood. Finally, after a good deal of mutual patience, the man got busy, returned to his workshop, made the beams, got the deck right again, fixed the bitts into their correct position, and made a good job of it for six *guelders* (10s.), which was not excessive. We rigged the bowsprit again, got the bobstay and bowsprit shrouds into position, and she was little worse than before we had hit the bridge. But we might easily have been smashed up, and were not a little thankful for a Providential escape.

On the advice of the harbour-master, who spoke excellent English, and was particularly obliging and courteous, we moved into the yacht basin, where he directed the yacht-harbourmaster to look well after us during our stay. The latter and his family lived on a floating houseboat, so it would be very convenient to leave *Vivette* in his hands when we made our excursions in the neighbouring country. There was also a floating rowing-sailing club in the harbour, and there were all sorts of Hollandish craft which were well deserving of our study.

Thus we abode here six days, in which we saw much that we would not willingly have missed. Dordrecht is full of good things inside and out of its museums. There are fine old models of bygone ships, for long years before Rotterdam sprang up Dordrecht was a considerable port. We had sailed up by the same route that our English Charles II. had traversed in the yacht bound to Rotterdam and so to England *via* the Hague at the time of the Restoration, and we had now come to one of the most famous of all the ports which had flourished during the Middle Ages, let alone the seventeenth and eighteenth centuries. And there were pictures both old and new for us to gaze at, and the South African Museum to wander through as one's blood boiled at the collection of virulent anti-British invectives which almost every continental journal hurled at us during the Boer War.

There is a great deal of utter rubbish stored away in this building, and it is difficult to see even a sentimental value in such articles as the English-made gloves and razor which the late lamented Kruger once deigned to use. Much more profitable and interesting to the mind are the old chests, fireplaces, carvings, and furniture in another museum.

There was one "find" that pleased me more than a little, and was obtained from an old curiosity shop near the Oude Haven. The sailing craft of Holland tow behind them a jolly-boat of a most interesting type, and utterly different from the Norwegian pram or other type. I asked a Dutch shipbuilder how he described them, and he said they were known as Boskoop boats: another man said they were simply called Hollandische boats. But whatever name they go by, they seem to me to be the ideal design for anyone who wants a good all-round dinghy. Judge of

ONE OF THE LIFTING BRIDGES ON THE AMSTEL

DORDRECHT

IN THE BACKGROUND IS THE ENTRANCE TO THE WOLLEWEVERS HAVEN LEADING INTO THE YACHT BASIN. THE BRIDGE SHOWN IS OPENED FOR PASSING CRAFT.

my delight, then, to find in this old shop a perfect built model of one of these, properly constructed, varnished and green-painted at the gunwales, with oars, floorboards, and everything correct to scale and detail as in the full size. I was lucky to strike a good bargain, and some day hope to build an eight- or ten-footer from this little model, which is not more than a yard long.

The main features may be summed up as follows. Such a craft is built of great strength, with a perfectly flat bottom, and a good deal of flare. The greatest beam is forward at the shoulders, after which point she narrows till the minimum width is right aft. Her bows overhang, something after the manner of a *hoogarts*, though not quite so excessively. As the boat will have to endure a good deal of bumping, a powerful rubbing strake is fitted, above which is the gunwale, painted green, and relieved with a white band with black on the top, the rest of the hull being varnished. Inside the thwarts are also painted green, white, and black, with the usual sharp Dutch contrasts.

I cannot but believe that such a design might very profitably be employed in England for yachts' dinghies. They need not be built so strongly nor so heavily. But apart from their other features, they would be found to tow well, to be pulled easily over the mud when the tide dropped, could readily be hauled aboard over the gunwale, and, finally, if fitted with a pair of leeboards or a dagger centre-plate, would be fair sailing craft. As regards seaworthiness they are excellent. The flat floor, the high overhanging bows, and the ample freeboard, will be appreciated on such occasions as running out a kedge when a strong wind is blowing and raising something of a popple.

Delighted at this acquisition, the next thing was to seek out once more the "mast, pump, and block maker," who had repaired the bitts. Entering with this precious burden under my arm, he laid down his tools and beamed graciously. After lavishing a certain amount of admiration on the model, he was made to understand by further pantomime, sketches, and the continual mention of the word "*kase*," that we wanted a strong box made in order that the wee ship might travel in safety to England. All this was done and the package safely despatched *via* Flushing.

The harbour-master of the yacht haven, together with his sons, treated us with characteristic Dutch kindness, took us on board their floating home and brought out all the household gods and effected such little odd jobs for us as soldering the boilerette. We learnt a great deal from them concerning *boiers, botters, klipper-aaks, schokkers, botters, hoogarts*, and all the rest of Dutch types. They were imbued with quite the sportive instinct, and *Vivette's* cruise was a source of great interest to all. One day the younger son came alongside with a bucket full of eels, asking us to accept them as a present, but we had to decline. They gave us a great deal of valuable information as to choice of routes and other data which proved most useful and could only be acquired from local men.

The most fascinating portion of Dordrecht is by the Groot Hoofd Poort, a picturesque gateway down by the "*waterzijde*." As you sit under the trees at one of the little round tables belonging to the cafe, you look out on to what is probably the most interesting aggregation of fore-and-aft sailing ships to be seen in any port of Northern Europe. Not merely for their historical associations, nor for the mighty influence which these types have had in the development of the world's shipping, but for themselves alone and their own striking peculiarities, do they compel you to give them careful study, if in any sense you care for nautical matters. Incidentally, as you look out on to so much tonnage you are amazed that even in Holland so much traffic is carried on by water.

Dordrecht formed an excellent place for visiting two cities which we could not afford to miss, but were a little off the route along which we should presently sail to Amsterdam. Rotterdam and the Hague must both be seen; but it was a physical impossibility to take *Vivette* to the latter, on account of certain fixed bridges which were too low for our mast, and the former should cordially be avoided by any small sailing craft, unless her owner is of the type which could find enjoyment sailing about between the Tower and London Bridge. The tides at Rotterdam

THE YACHT *HAVEN-MEESTER* AT DORT
THE CRAFT IS A DUTCH BOIER YACHT.

are very strong, the traffic is immense, ranging of course from big American liners to mere sailing *tjalks*, and there is another wicked bridge which opens only at rare intervals. True, there is free towage through the latter, but before you have arrived there you will have had quite enough, and it is the tug's ambition to get hold of you, tow you through and cast you off in the minimum time, regardless of your paint, your feelings, or your predilections.

So one morning we set off by paddle-steamer, went down the Noord and the Nieuwe Maas, and spent a busy time exploring the museums and art galleries of Rotterdam. This was a real treat in every sense. There is a great deal that is worth looking at in this city connected with its countless quays and canals, its shipping and shipbuilding yards, its streets and its squares. But otherwise Rotterdam was too commercial, too little supplied with noble architecture, too full of Jews, and too busy making money.

We returned after what had been in journalistic language a "fruity" day, and the trip back to Dort in the evening was far from unwelcome. No one can fail to be struck with the splendid seamanship of the skippers of these craft, and few would envy them the daily anxious work of threading their way through so much traffic. But they have a special method of signalling by a flag from the bridge which side of the *Rhine-schiffs* or other craft they intend to pass. But for all that it needs a wonderfully cool head, quickness of judgment, and strong nerves.

The following day we took train and arrived at the Hague, which some people describe as the smartest capital in Europe. It must certainly be the cleanest. If we except Queen Wilhelmina's palace, which is about as disappointing externally as Buckingham Palace, the Hague is full of pleasant surprises. There is none of the bustle and turmoil to live that you find in Rotterdam: the whole spirit of the place is one of dignity, calm, and refinement. It is rich in art treasures of the greatest historical interest, in beautiful buildings, in fine open squares, in clean streets, in avenues of trees that are incomparably charming. And every

Dutch Buildings

where little shallow canals crossed by innumerable bridges form a spidery network over the whole plan of the city.

But there is a further treat for the lover of ships. He has so often heard of Scheveningen and its fleet of pinks, so often seen them running towards the sandy beach, as depicted in the works of modern artists, that he gladly takes tram from the Plein down the Scheveningensche Weg till he finds himself by the North Sea again. He has come down a wonderful long avenue of leafy trees most of four miles long, and now he arrives at a hybrid sort of spot which contains some of the features of a fishing village combined with the cosmopolitanism of Ostende, the bathing, the basket chairs, the *kursaal*, the bands.

But most of these features can be avoided, and you can turn your attention to a consideration of that fast-disappearing creature, the pink. She is anything but a comely wench, and you who have been accustomed to the fine-lined yachts of the Solent may feel inclined to ridicule, for there is just as much proportionate difference between the modern yacht and the old pink as there is between the hobble-skirt and the crinoline.

But then realise the reason for this difference. Here is a village whose natives in different centuries have been making history, whose men and craft were fishing in the North Sea long years before yachts were invented. The beach, if we are to judge from old pictures, has not altered its shallow, sandy nature during the flight of time, and though the square-sail has changed to the cutter rig, yet the hull still continues to be built to the same formula, which demands that her length be just twice her breadth. She was never built for speed, but primarily to be able to keep the sea, lying to her nets like a glorified barrel in the turbulent, treacherous North Sea, and then, having gathered in her fish, to sail back to the beach and remain bumping on the sand till the tide dried right out, when her flat bottom enabled her to sit upright.

For this kind of work you want the maximum of strength, and there is something even ultra-Dutch in the solidity of the pink's character. A sailing match between a number of pinks would be like a race between a fleet of tortoises. You would not wait for the finish; as already stated, they are not speed boats.

And now walk southwards along the beach, past the little groups of tough old fishermen, looking as aged as the pinks themselves, and after you have passed the Wireless Telegraph station you come to the newly-formed harbour, where pinks, and botters, and Katwijk *poms,* with equally curiously-looking crews to match, will be found. There is so much for you to study in the ships themselves, their gear, the fishing nets, capstans, and a thousand details, that you would have been sorry not to have left the crowd and come down to this practically deserted corner of Scheveningen. There are dozens of unusual little details, which most certainly it will delight you to observe and make note of.

An excellent dinner at one of the many nice restaurants of which the Hague can boast, and then back by train to Dordrecht and *Vivette.* Just one day more can we spend lazing round this old Hanseatic port, and then we must bid farewell. Again the tanks are filled and the ship replenished with fresh stores. I went to make some purchases at a grocer's shop which overlooked the harbour. It was evening, and the proprietor was making up his accounts. He spoke English really well, and was able to supply most of my wants. But butter he had not. Rather than let me go elsewhere, he himself insisted on running out. Did I speak French?

Then his little daughter would entertain me till he returned. So he called to her, and a charming little blonde, perhaps twelve or thirteen, with beautiful blue eyes, came smiling forth. I never heard her name, but then and there I mentally christened her Wilhelmina, as it was the only one I could think of. Wilhelmina conversed most pleasantly for the next quarter of an hour in French. She was such a perfectly natural, bright child, with such fascinating manners, that the delay was most happy. When her father returned, he explained that his little daughter had recently begun to learn English, and he would be much indebted if I would hear her. I professed that nothing would give me more pleasure, so away she tripped for her lesson-books. Then open-

Bok   Boier   Boier   Tjalk   Hoogart
Vivette in the Yacht Haven at Dort

ing at one of the exercises, she began to read very slowly and most solemnly the opening paragraphs of Dickens' *Christmas Carol*.

"Marley was dead, to begin with," she read on with only the smallest deliberation. "There was no doubt whatever about that. ... Old Marley was as dead as a door-nail!"

I shall never forget the funny little way she read out "dead as a door-nail," with a kind of staccato jerks. I congratulated father and daughter, gathered up my butter and, the other parcels, and got aboard. Every time from that moment that I passed along the quay there was Wilhelmina always ready with a bow and a smile, for that had been a big day in her young life, and if ever I came that way again I determined to stop and inquire how her English lessons were getting on.

It was now mid-August, and it was clear that the summer weather was beginning to vanish. The nights were getting colder, and the leaves were already dropping off the trees on to our deck. There was a vigour in the wind which told that the time for summer sailing was nearing the end. So yet again up went the main-sail, with a couple of reefs down, for the wind was coming down even in that sheltered haven with heavy gusts. The sons of the harbour-master took our line and gave us a tow into the stream, for we could not sail till we got outside. We cast off and were out into the Maas with a strong tide running, when I heard a thin shout and saw Wilhelmina running along waving us a farewell until we had faded out of sight. And so away from Dort.

CHAPTER 11

Dordrecht to Gouwe

It was a smart breeze from the S.W. again, and we could have done with shorter canvas. What few craft were under way were reefed very snugly, but it was splendid sport as we went along the Noord, a curious waterway which connects the Nieuwe Maas with the Oude Maas. Here were shipyards galore,' where every kind of vessel, from a *tjalk* to a *Rhine-schiff*, was being built. Over to the left was a kind of large backwater, that was employed for breaking-up purposes. Here come old liners and many of the warships sold out of our own and other navies of the great European powers. In this muddy creek they end their days, and are dismembered limb for limb, so to speak. You might call it a kind of marine shambles; and the collection ashore of accumulated deck-houses which had come off a number of old ships was a curious nautical miscellany.

The Noord is roughly the width of the Kil, and has several shipbuilding villages on its banks, such as Papendrecht and Alblasserdam, and indeed almost the whole of the way from Dort to Rotterdam, and beyond the banks are lined with yards showing vessels in different stages of construction. For the Maas and the Noord are practically the Dutch Clyde. This was Sunday afternoon, so happily the traffic of the steam- and motor-ships was comparatively small; otherwise the Noord is not a pleasant sailing stretch. But we had all the wind we wanted in some of the heavy squalls, and were compelled to reef down snugger still. It was blowing quite half a gale, and we learnt later on that there had been several capsizes today, causing the loss of several professional Dutch watermen.

I had been figuring it out that when we came to the Nieuwe Maas we should have not merely wind against us but tide as well, and the breeze would be fresher still in that broader river. We had a look at it, however, but after beating for a little while against a strong tide and a very fresh, squally breeze close-reefed, it seemed hardly good enough; so we ran back till we were just in the Noord. In passing I had noticed a nice, quiet, clean basin, which seemed likely to form an ideal anchorage, so lowering main we ran quietly in under jib alone, and let go in 2½ fathoms good holding ground at nearly high-water.

It is true that we should shortly have had a fair tide, but that would mean we should have it foul up the Ijsel, so we might just as well be content to wait a little longer; for it is useless and foolish not to work your tides where the current is of such force. We were very pleased with this anchorage, and I recommend it to any others who may come this way. But though I am sure there would be no objection to your making use of this basin, yet it ought to be said at once that it is really part of the shipyard belonging to Messrs. Smit & Co., and used for launching and fitting out new ships.

As soon as the anchor was down, I espied an old man, evidently the caretaker of the yard, ambling along; so, deeming it best to make peace with a potential adversary at once, I rowed off in the dinghy, handed him a few cents, and begged that we might be allowed to remain. The reply was that we certainly might (or Dutch words to that effect), finishing up with a deep apology for not being able to speak English! This was more than kind. Later on the traffic that passed along the Noord was very heavy, including tramp steamers bound out to the North Sea, so we were happy that we were so well placed. There was no current in the basin, and we rode head to wind all the time.

The next morning the breeze was still blowing strongly from the S.W., but it had moderated somewhat; so, starting off at 10 a.m., we tacked down the Nieuwe Maas under two-reefed main,

No. 2 jib, and stay-sail, with the last of the ebb. There were several rain-squalls, but that didn't matter. Here was a fine, broad stretch of water—deep, affording the very best of sport—and we made some smart boards with the aid of the powerful ebb. There were several more shipbuilding villages on the port hand, and at either Ijselmonde or Bolness—I forget which—the decorations and garlands were still up, for there had been a launch just recently, and the new ship, looking very spick-and-span, was moored a little way further on.

Most yachtsmen have read and gloated over *The Falcon on the Baltic*, in which Mr. E. F. Knight related an account of his trip from England to Denmark through Holland in the year 1887. There is a passage in that book to which I think it advisable to call attention. He had come the opposite way to us—that is to say, through Rotterdam, and up this river Maas—but in each case our objective was the same: we were making for the river Ijsel.

> "The Ijsel," he remarks, "joins the Maas about four or five miles above Rotterdam, so, not having the faintest idea as to how large it would prove to be, I kept a sharp lookout for any stream that might appear on the port hand.
> "At last, after running some way up the Maas, we opened out what looked like a rather narrow creek. I hesitated, doubtful as to whether this could be my river. I noticed that though many small traders were ascending and descending the Maas, no craft of any description were to be seen on this tributary. A *schuyt* happened to be sailing close to me. 'Is that the Ijsel?' I cried, pointing to the opening.
> "'Is that the way to Gouda?' I cried again, mumbling the first words of the sentence, but bringing out 'Gouda' very loudly and distinctly.
> "A gleam of intelligence lit up the worthy Hollander's stolid features. '*Yah, yah,* Gouda!' he shouted, as he sailed by."

I quote this because I can entirely endorse all that Mr. Knight says of the difficulty in locating the mouth of the Ijsel; and had I not happened to see it the other day as we passed on the steamer, and made a note of it on the map, I fancy we might have sailed beyond it.

There are several curious spaces in this neighbourhood, whose nature I was never able to make out. I made inquiries but could get no satisfactory answer. They were openings from the river surrounded with low stone walls. They looked so temptingly convenient for use as harbours out of the way of traffic and tide, that I suspected they must be otherwise. There was a big notice by the entrance to another of these enclosures where the Ijsel joins the Maas, but we were past before I had time to make out the meaning of the inscription. As I do not remember ever to have seen any craft brought up within these spaces, I suspect they may be for some other purpose—perhaps as oyster-beds. Otherwise they would be very handy for small craft to lie in.

The tide was still ebbing as we came into the Ijsel, but it mattered little as we now turned to N.E. with the wind at S.W. Simultaneously the rain vanished, the weather brightened, and the wind dropped so light that we had to shake out all reefs. Here were more shipbuilding yards and some mammoth *Rhineschiffs*. Surely if they continue to build at this rate there will be no room for the sailing craft of Holland except in the biggest estuaries. There is always a delight in exploring new waterways, and in following a river towards its source. Ours was just that pleasure now.

Sometimes it would twist and turn in such a strangle manner that it was difficult to see whether we were coming to a terminus or not. But you will find after a while that those odd-shaped, curiously-striped objects ashore at most of these corners mark the bend for you and guide you like shore-beacons. Every mile or so came a fresh village, with its cluster of cottages, its farms, and church spire rising over all; then a few more green fields, marshes, rushes, and another hamlet. In this manner we passed Krimpen, Oudekerk, Gouderak, and smaller places.

Certainly the river narrowed to an alarming width at some

corners, and it amazed us to find quite large steamers navigating these ditches and swinging round the bends with a long trail of assorted craft in tow.

The day kept altering its character, and for the most part became now squally and rainy, the wind fluking considerably from S.W. to N.W. There was many a place where we kept afloat only by acting as the steamers did, and keeping in the very centre of the channel, and making a bold sweep round each curve. But there came one straight reach where the wind had shifted dead ahead, so we must needs begin tacking. It was so narrow, the shallows came so far out, and the breeze was so gusty that it was difficult to keep her handled as she ought to be. You would luff up for a squall and then remain blanketed. Next would come a puff, and before you had time to realise it you were across the river near the bank. But it was only once that we got aground, and that was where a *tjalk* was swinging to her anchor and narrowing the Ijsel still more. But we had got so far ahead of our tide that not yet had the flood began to make. It was soft mud, so we waited half-an-hour, took out a line to the *tjalk*, and, soon floating off, continued our journey.

Several exciting escapes occurred further up at some of the narrow corners where the tide was strong, and the wind momentarily dropped under the protection of the reeds and trees, and, as you may imagine, it was usually at these points that you would be hampered by steamers or a tug with six to a dozen craft tied up astern. And then we came to a pretty village with green gardens running down to the water's edge from the fronts of the houses till windmills and patches of trees and more rushes brought us at last to the outskirts of Gouda in the late afternoon.

At the precise moment that we came up to the great cluster of traffic—steam and sail—waiting for the lock-gates to open, it pleased certain gentlemen to launch into the water a newly built *Rhine-schiff* of considerable tonnage straight across the river. There was little or no warning; the thing just happened. We ourselves only just escaped, but a screw passenger steamer coming the opposite way had the narrowest shave of a collision, and reversed his engines only in the nick of time.

Here, then, was Gouda (pronounced Khooda), and we began to wonder how many hours we should have to wait before all that terrible medley of craft had passed through the lock. At least we might edge up as close to the entrance as possible so as to be in readiness, and then we lashed up alongside of an iron vessel to await events. Just then the gates opened, and, as if impelled by a hydraulic ram, a small fleet of biggish craft were suddenly shot out into the tideway and left to sort themselves out as best they might. It looked like disaster for some of us, but only one came to grief, and that was an iron *klipper-aak,* which took charge, dashed straight across the river, smashing her bowsprit shrouds as she buried her nose in the opposite bank.

A number of waiting vessels then hauled into the lock, after which there was apparently just room for one small ship; so hailing us, the lock-keeper signalled to *Vivette* to come in. Towing in the dinghy, giving her a touch now and again with the sweep, we entered, and then the lock was as full as a tin of sardines, and packed quite as tightly. There was a busy time fending off from walls and preventing a steam tug from getting our bowsprit under his counter. Then as the lower sluices were opened the dinghy began to career madly about trying a bumping match, first with *Vivette* and then with a *tjalk.* In the fewest minutes we were heartily sick of Gouda's lock.

And in the midst of this the *sluis-meester* expected that I would leave my ship, climb the rigging, and jump ashore to proceed to his office for the usual formalities. This I strenuously declined to do, until the gates opened and we had got clear, when tolls were levied and the necessary details given. Let the cruising man be on his guard at Gouda, for a crowd of worthless fellows are always hanging about the lock pestering you for tips. They are the only sharks which I encountered in the whole of Holland, and they have to be dealt with firmly.

But at last we were free to proceed, after wasting valuable time. The next mile or so is a distinct disappointment, and our hearts fell. Picture, if you please, the narrowest of canals, lined with mean dwellings and factories on either side, so that no wind could possibly get in and not too much sunlight. Narrow the space still more with an interminable line of *Rhine-schiffs* and all manner of shipping along both banks, and you have an adequate idea of what we had to contend with. So one of us rowed a head towing in the dinghy, whilst the other steered. A steamer would suddenly come round the next corner and clear you by only a foot or perhaps less. So we were heartily glad when this miserable mile came to an end and we got the other side of a swing bridge.

Here was a bright contrast indeed, and more what we had expected Holland to be. This was bright, open, clean country stretching for endless miles as it seemed, till it touched the horizon. There were more avenues of those toy "Noah's Ark" trees, bright green grass, ditches, and laughing children. It was a warm, soft evening, and we were not sorry to be comfortably moored to a couple of posts by a grassy bank with a fine, clear space for our eyes to gaze upon and Gouda lock well astern and forgotten. Henceforth the rest of our journey was on river and canal with no need to work out tides. During the night there was a considerable amount of steam and motor-ship traffic in a hurry to get their goods down to Rotterdam before morning. The motor craft begin ringing their bells some distance away for the bridges to open, so that the engines need not be eased down and they can go on their way unimpeded, but the whistling of the steamers and this clanging of bells through the night is sometimes apt to get on your nerves.

We had a look round Gouda. Some of the canals which intersect this old town are very quaint, especially when the moon casts eerie shadows through the trees. We filled up again with water and fresh victuals as usual, ready to proceed, for we had still a good distance to cover. After breakfast we became conscious that the male voice which had been shouting for some minutes was aimed at us. And as soon as we paid attention it redoubled its vigour, but what was it all about? We tried to catch

TYPES OF DUTCH CRAFT

a word here and there, but our inability to understand only excited the man by many degrees. What had we done, or what was impending? We looked at him speechless In wonder, but by now he was getting quite angry, until my ears heard a word ending with the letter "k."

"I've got it—he wants to sell us some milk."

So, turning to the man, "*Niet melk*," we shouted back, "*niet melk*,"

But that was like fuel to a furnace, and the next words were utterly incomprehensible, though I suggest that a free translation would read something like this. "Milk be bothered, you couple of idiots, do I look like a milkman? Can't you understand me?"

And there was a slight pause till he began again and I tried hard to identify at least one word and at last recognised two. It was not "*melk*" but "*trek*," and the following word was certainly "*paad*" or I was a Dutchman myself.

"*Ja, ja*," he replied with relief, "*trek-paad*," and as he spoke he pointed to the windless sky. But we had not come to Holland to be towed along by a horse, so we declined all offers of trekking. For a time he persisted, and, seeing he had wasted speech upon us, departed full of annoyance. The people of Gouda may have sterling virtues, but the latter were not apparent during our short sojourn, and with no regrets we forsook the place. It was a flat calm, so setting our sails for the time when a breeze might arise we quanted along the tortuous waterway.

We had to wait till a train passed over an adjacent bridge and the opening was clear, and then, sometimes sailing with a little draught from the S.W., sometimes pushing our way along with the useful quant, we progressed through interesting yet flat country. You lose count of the number of waterside villages through which you pass, but there are plenty of features to keep your eyes busy all the time—windmills, old farm-houses, quaint haystacks, nursery-gardens, countless acres of cattle-grazing pasture on one side of the canal and small shipbuilding yards on the other. Here comes another bridge, but if you blow your fog-horn persistently as you approach, you have no need to wait, and the old man raises it and dangles his wooden sabot for your cents as you sail through.

But always those tugs towing their strings of craft, driving you close to the banks to prevent collision in such narrow confines. We have heard a great deal lately about the suction theory in relation to passing ships in shallow waters. But if you would study the application of this theory you cannot do this better than in some of these Dutch canals, which with their total absence of tide and shallow depth are ideal experimental tanks and in a later page a certain incident will be related to give point to this statement. The canals of Holland, or at least most of them, are centuries old, and designed when there was no idea that ships could be propelled by mechanical power.

Until the steamship and the motor craft were introduced into Holland in such numbers, these canals were good enough for any sailing vessels. But now that they are crowded with *Rhineschiffs* and power-ships all in a hurry to get to their destination and usurping by right of force as well as necessity the greater portion of the waterway, the pure sailing vessel is not fairly handicapped. She has to run the everlasting risk of collision as soon as she gets away from the big estuaries of the Scheldt, Maas, and other broad tidal waters. The fact is that you need to have a motor in your ship and a propeller fixed astern if you want to do Holland in perfect comfort and to hold your own.

It is an ideal country for motor-cruising, and it is only wise that this point should be appreciated and admitted.

It is a curious coincidence that the conditions which we experienced today were identical with those which occurred to the *Falcon* when she started from Gouda to go the same way. It was just the same hot cloudless day twenty-two years ago, so the *Falcon* chartered a tug, whilst we relied on our quant. And then we came to Boskoop, perhaps the largest of these waterside villages we had yet passed. Very neat and clean it looked with its tilled houses glinting in the sunshine and the sparkling water running past the end of its gardens.

Æsthetically, yes, Boskoop is a fair spot. But to a sailing craft it is annoying. The canal widens out, and then suddenly contracts so that it may be spanned by a very short bridge. Now, although there could be no tide, yet whichever way the wind is blowing there is formed quite a strong current, which rushes through this bridge as through a funnel. It happened that just before we were going through a breeze sprang up: it happened, further, that a steamer was blocking up the canal at the opposite side of the bridge waiting to get through, and that a big ketch of about 100 tons plus another steamer were coming on immediately in our wake.

The bridgeman waved to us to come in and held up the steamer that was coming towards us. She was backing and filling and at one time seemed destined to collide with us. But he blew two blasts on his siren, so as he was intending to come to port I steered to pass him on my starboard hand. It was just then that a little puff filled the peak of the main-sail: there were too many buildings to allow the lower portion to be filled, and the current for a few yards was so strong that it was touch-and-go for a little while.

We only just escaped hitting something, but the quant saved us. And then there were the steamer and the ketch to remember, but all too narrow as this ditch of a place was, we scraped through without touching anything till at last the houses vanished, and we were out in the pure country once more. An old-fashioned, shallow-draught, beamy, black yacht with a skipper and three Dutch yachtsmen was also coming along towed by a line and horse till she got to Boskoop, where she remained for the night.

The man ashore in charge of this steed was our old friend whom we took for a milkman, and it pleased him in no wise to find we had now found a little breeze. But, having finished with the black yacht, he espied a motor-barge whose engines had broken down and the crew were quanting her along as best they could towards Gouda. So the "milkman" opened negotiations to tow her to Gouda. For a time the bargaining went on amicably, but his terms were evidently too high for the barge's skipper, and in a short space of time the quarrelsome, excitable trekker was hurling abuse and losing his temper. We sailed past, leaving them at it, but there was a good deal of wrath being expended when we last looked back.

More strings of craft astern of a tug, and we came to a railway bridge, where we were compelled to tie up till it opened, and then we found ourselves in the straight reach which leads into Gouwe. To appreciate fully the possibilities of this spot, you must bear in mind that here is a lock, which is usually open. Consequently there is no need for the motor- or steam- ships to stop. But as soon as you emerge through this sluis, you cross literally at right angles another very busy waterway—that is, in fact, the Old Rhine.

Now it would seem to most people of discernment that a man would be stationed here at this junction to regulate the traffic and to prevent by means of flag or semaphore one line of vessels from Gouda rushing across the bows of others coming along the Rhine. But this is not done, and the small sailing craft have quite a second-rate time. What Clapham Junction is for trains, and the Mansion House is for vehicular traffic, so Gouwe Sluis is for steamers, *Rhine-schiffs*, motor cargo-boats, *tjalks*, *botters*, and all the other kinds of craft that navigate the Dutch waterways. But there are no signalmen or water policemen that seem to keep order, although there are men actually attached to the lock and to a bridge.

If ever *Vivette* was near being run down, it was at Gouwe. A motor-barge came round from the Rhine at too great a speed, nearly hit the walls of the lock in trying to get straight, and then found herself heading into a tug and her string of satellites. Having just avoided these objects, she swept close to us, so close that I thought our Dutch cruise would end right there. There is no need to enlarge upon the subject, but it was a happy, thankful moment when it was all over.

At length, seeing there was a momentary respite in the traffic, we crept on with sails lowered, and the dinghy towing ahead. We came through the lock, crossed the Rhine, the bridge opened to let us pass, and now we were on the beautiful river Aar, where we could remain the night.

Out of the whirl of Gouwe into a paradise! There was scarcely any traffic here, for most of the shipping goes by the other route to Amsterdam, along the Oude Rijn and so through Overtoom or Haarlem.

But because I had learned that the Aar, the Drecht, and the Amstel rivers were quiet and secluded, pretty and interesting, besides affording the most direct route to the city of Amsterdam, I had purposely chosen to come this way, although everyone had advised me to go *via* Haarlem. And I never once regretted my choice.

CHAPTER 12

Gouwe to Amsterdam

We lay where a break in the long line of willow trees left a clearance for the top of our mast; and for all the world we might have been at some such place as Wroxham or Coltishall on the Norfolk Broads. But there was not a suspicion of a hill anywhere. To the right the illimitable green meadows and the black-and-white cattle as you see them in Cassiers' pictures; to the left a shorter green stretch, until the gables of red houses and the spire of a church indicated a distant village. So the mate set off thither, and returned with bottles of that excellent lager beer which you buy in Holland. It was pleasant to dine amid such pastoral peacefulness after the excitement of a windless day.

But during the night the weather completely altered; it rained hard, and by the time we set off in the morning it was blowing very fresh. But the wind was S.W., so it meant we should be able to run before it the whole way to Amsterdam. We knew there were sundry bridges, and at least one more lock to encounter before we should arrive at our goal; so, for ease of handling in these narrow places, and that we might be able to lower sail more quickly at the stopping places, we deemed it better to roll in a couple of reefs. If this was to be our last day's sail, it was certainly one of the most enjoyable.

The fine breeze held, and we went through a rural fairyland full of all manner of pleasant surprises. Now we would seem to be rushing through a well-kept private estate, with its miniature canals and tiny locks all to scale; now we would come to windmills, gardens, farms, pretty cottages, rustic bridges, parks, and houses as old as time itself. Here were grassy banks, and reeds, and weeping willows, and then all of a sudden the river would wend round a corner and widen out into a majestic thoroughfare, with jolly waterside cafés and happy people enjoying the sweet air.

We had been warned how shallow were the Aar, the Drecht, and the Amstel, but we barely touched, only twice. The first time was when we hove-to till a barge had come through a bridge; the second was when we were trying to cut off a corner. By keeping our foghorn blowing in the approach to a bridge, it was always open for us in readiness. But the day was not to pass without one excitement. According to the map, we should soon come to the Huis ten Drecht lock, but it was difficult to see in which direction the river turned.

At first it looked like a *cul-de-sac*, then it appeared to turn to the left. We were carrying a smart breeze with us, and travelling at least six knots, when we suddenly found that though there was one turning to the left, another also bore to the right. The latter was certainly our course, so we suddenly altered the helm, and before we could see round the sharp corner we were actually at Huis ten Drecht lock. There was no room to luff or gybe; either alternative was now impossible. The only course was to act as we did. Fortunately the gates were opened this end, or we should have been smashed up.

As it was, we dashed into the lock with main-sail and jib full. The mate rushed forward, let go halyards, pulled the gaff down, muzzled the jib; whilst I endeavoured to steer with the helm between my legs, haul in the main-sheet with my hands, throw a line ashore to the *sluis-meester*, who happily chanced to be there waiting, got fend-offs out, by which time the mate was busy with boathook, and we brought up only just before our bowsprit began to try conclusions with the further gates, that were of course shut. But it was another of the many "near-things" which helped to enliven our cruise.

For mile upon mile we had the river to ourselves. Only once

we met anything out of the ordinary, and that consisted of a tug towing a great bucket-dredger and three or four mud-barges. There was an occasional passenger steamer, and also a motor-barge or two, whose modern advent must have made a great increase to the incomes of some of the small vegetable-growers. The latter have their front doors looking out on to the river.

At the back of the houses are the kitchen gardens, where cabbages and other produce are grown. In a neighbouring meadow graze the *milch*-cows. Roads are few, and Amsterdam is not very close. But here comes the motor-barge every afternoon and finds the churns of milk, the sacks of cabbages, beans, peas, potatoes, and so on, all piled by the waterside in readiness to be taken to the Amsterdam market or some other town. The barge scarcely stops her engines, before she has bundled the produce aboard and is off for the next farm. It is a cheap, reliable, and rapid method of getting the goods to market, and tends to encourage the farmer no less than the owner of the barge.

Village succeeded village, bridge after bridge flew past, and at length we found ourselves on the broad reaches of the Amstel. As the afternoon wore on, we could see the distant roofs of a great city, and now that locks were done with and the breeze had dropped, we shook out our reefs and sailed delightfully onward. A local *boier* yacht was cruising about, now running back home for the night.

Here came one or two yacht-builders' yards, and here at last was a magnificent broad stretch of the river which led right into the heart of Amsterdam. It reminded me of nothing so much as the Seine at Paris, though wider, with fine opulent houses on either side, but it was difficult to get accustomed to the utter absence of any current. Here were the club-houses of the leading rowing associations, and nice clean streets and mansions of the wealthy overlooking the Amstel. On either hand small canals branched out of the river, for here we had arrived at the northern Venice, and it would not have surprised us to see gondolas flitting about.

Right straight ahead was a noble stone bridge, such as one sees spanning the Seine; but how on earth should we get through it? Immovable it seemed as the stone of which it was built. Eagerly we looked at the arches, but not one of them had the appearance of being capable of being raised.

Furthermore, all the steam craft lowered their funnels to come under. We blew the fog-horn till we were almost up to the arches, but never a sign of opening. And then the thought came that perhaps we had come into Amsterdam by a route that was useless to a vessel with a fixed mast, and we should have to retrace our steps perhaps as far back as Gouwe, and then come to Amsterdam through Haarlem. But just as I was sorrowfully meditating on this, the mate of a pleasure steamer coming by signalled to me to keep blowing, as the bridge would open. But there were electric trams running across, and nearly as much traffic as passes on Westminster Bridge, and I could not see how a stone arch could be moved.

So, as we had to go somewhere, espying a quiet canal on the port hand, I luffed into that, lowering sail at the same time and tied up to some railings outside somebody's front door! It was indeed the most extraordinary stopping-place *Vivette* ever enjoyed. But how about that bridge? It was coming on dark and we could not hang on to these railings all night. A crowd quickly collected in the street to view the strange sight, so I began to parley with them. We desired to get through yonder bridge. How could it be done?

All seemed to shout different directions, but there were two men to whom nature had given a certain measure of intelligence. Of these two one was obviously an Amsterdam shark and a typical city ruffian, so he was to be avoided at all costs. The other spoke a little English but was so nervous and blushed crimson every time he gave expression to his thoughts, that conversation was carried on only with difficulty. We pointed to the top of the mast, pointed to the bridge, made a very fine histrionic display with *Vivette's* deck as a stage, but all to no purpose.

So at length, getting into the dinghy, I rowed off to explore. Having got the other side of the bridge, I saw a building labelled

THE RIVER AMSTEL AT AMSTERDAM

THE CENTRAL ARCH INDICATED BY AN ARROW IS OPENED
FOR SAILING CRAFT TO GO THROUGH

VIVETTE LYING IN THE YACHT HARBOUR ON THE IJ AT AMSTERDAM

TYING UP FOR THE NIGHT JUST ABOVE GOUWE SLUIS

"*kantoor*," to which the nervous man pointed. "*Kantoor*," I knew, meant office of some sort, and by it was another lock. Clearly this was some sort of toll-house. I therefore tied up the dinghy, interviewed an official in uniform, who immediately understood. The bridge should be opened forthwith. By the time I had got back to the railings and towed *Vivette* into the centre of the bridge, the trams, motor cars, and crowd were held up, and a small arch, made not of stone but of steel, raised itself into the air, after the manner of our Tower Bridge, and at last we were through. But I could not get used to the absence of tide. It seemed so strange there should not be a current of some sort.

We paid thirty cents (sixpence) for this, then one more bridge, a lock, and yet another bridge—more cents again—and we brought up alongside a quay for the night. It was very public, but that could not be helped, for it was dark and raining. A crowd of inquisitive gazers rapidly collected, and for the next hour we were visited and kept cross-examined by all who could speak English. The mate who had hailed us near the bridge had come ashore from the passenger steamer, and was very sensible and helpful. The rest of the crowd insisted on knowing from where we had come, what port in England, what ports we had touched on the way, how many men were we, what was the speed of the vessel, how much provisions we carried, &c., &c. Some, I fear, took us for liars, but there were some business men who had lived in England and had now just come out of their offices in Amsterdam after their day's work.

"I also am a sport-man," said one, as he pressed cigars on us and threatened to call on us later. Another gazer was very anxious to show me the way to the Post Office, but after going part of the way I dismissed him and preferred to proceed without an escort, only to find him hanging about the quay by the time I returned. True, we had made a wonderful impression, but we wanted to dine in peace, and a Dutchman cannot take a hint. We could get no peace until we went below and ate our meal with the cabin doors closed. And then over our cigars there was an accumulated English mail to read. So ended that day.

No one worried us during the night and no one had laid dishonest hands on anything lying about the deck, and the dinghy was still tied up astern. But we had not quite got to our destination, for we had in mind the yacht *steiger* on the Ij (pronounced Eye); so after breakfasting we arranged with the officials to have various bridges opened in consideration of numerous cents, and, towing and quanting through a narrow but pretty canal which ran through the streets, shot through still one more lock and found ourselves in the Oosterlijk Dok with training ships and war vessels in the vicinity.

This was beginning to look more like a port. But a railway bridge spans the extremity of this spacious basin, and as the bridge did not open till midday there was nothing for it but to tie up alongside a tug and wait. The skipper was very friendly and offered to give us a pluck through if we made fast astern of the dredger which he was presently to tow through. It was only a matter of about fifty yards, but it would save us a lot of trouble, as the wind was ahead through the bridge and there was no room to tack.

At twelve o'clock, then, the bridge swung open, the tug tooted his siren, and away we started. And here happened an exceedingly awkward but highly interesting incident, which I think is well worth relating. You must understand that there were two openings, so that after the bridge had swung, it remained disconnected on the central pillar. The tug chose the right-hand opening, which was very narrow and no deeper than you would expect. The dredger was not self-propelled, but placed on a kind of lighter of the clumsiest lines, whose beam was not much inferior to her length.

We swung out, then, and straightened for this opening—first the tug, then the dredger, finally the yacht. But as soon as we began to go through this narrow opening, I found that the rudder, just as happened some time after in the case of the *Hawke* when she struck the *Olympic*, ceased to have the slightest effect on *Vivette*, and it was all that I could do to prevent her hitting the pillar supporting the bridge. But no sooner was this over than she forged quickly ahead, overtook the dredger, and put her bowsprit on to the latter's deck, resting her full weight on the bobstay. I called to the two men on the dredger to cast off, but though that was done we were still dragged on. Then I got my companion to walk to the end of *Vivette*'s counter, so as to depress the stern and raise the bows; but that had no effect. And it was not till the two men on the dredger had been pushing for some time with all their might that we began to drop astern. There was no damage done except for a little chafing of the wire bobstay.

My own opinion is that the tug and the dredger caused very considerable suction in a comparatively shallow water, and thus a fine-lined craft such as a yacht would be influenced as a piece of steel affects a compass. At any rate the rudder refused to act, and later we were dragged on with the tow rope perfectly slack. Some months after I happened to be in the experimental tank of one of the greatest shipbuilding yards in the world. I submitted these details to one whose life is spent making experiments with models, and obtaining data regarding such interesting problems as resistance, wave-making, suction, and the rest.

And he entirely agreed that the phenomena already mentioned undoubtedly arose owing to the dredger's suction. Of course I am aware that in the *Hawke-Olympic* case the former was on the latter's quarter, whilst we were dead astern. Incidentally I might also add that so narrow was the opening and so wide the dredger, that the latter seemed to fill the space as closely as a hand fits a glove. I mention this instance, as there are plenty of seamen who decline to believe in the suction theory, whereas this occurrence happened more than a year before ever the *Olympic* had been put into commission.

Having cast off, then, and hoisted sail, we found ourselves in the Ij, a fine, bold waterway, with wharves and all manner of big ships. Here were liners running to all parts of the world, especially to the Dutch colonies. Here were British colliers and tramps. Here were fussy motor tugs and steam ferry-boats, many-decked passenger steamships running backwards and forwards to

Zaandam, where Peter the Great studied the art of shipbuilding. And besides all these items were the usual fleets of Dutch *tjalks, botters, schokkers, Rhine-schiffs, klippers,* with a small sprinkling of yachts and small motor launches. And as you sail through all this your eyes are kept most busily employed.

We tacked up this Ij, sailed on to have a good look round, and then finally brought up at the yacht harbour which is specially reserved for such craft as ourselves, another British yacht of about twenty tons arriving about the same time from Ymuiden, having come across the North Sea. And here, having at last got to our destination, we celebrated the occasion by cooking an excellent plum-pudding, which we had brought all the way from Bursedon. And the ingenuity of the mate in making white sauce out of barley, and the wonderful "gadgets" which he rigged up in the fo'c'sle for extra special culinary efforts at the end of that day would have put all the sea-cooks of Amsterdam to shame.

Here we were brought up by the two principal yacht clubs of the Netherlands, with every conceivable kind of interesting ships going by our cabin doors throughout the day. There was more than enough to look at, and there were charming Dutch skippers with whom to talk. I remember especially one who spoke very good English and was in charge of a fine iron auxiliary motor ketch-yacht named the *Quo Vadis* belonging to Haarlem. He

Tacking up the Ij

himself was a native of Friesland, had many a time sailed across to Billingsgate in those eel-*schuyts* which you can see riding to a buoy any day of the week as you look over London Bridge.

He had an affection for English yachtsmen, one of whom in a bygone year had dined him very well at a well-known London restaurant, and it will take several decades for the incident to vanish from memory. It was this skipper who had also brought a certain Dutch yacht across the North Sea through the London bridges as far as Richmond, where I had seen her lying. And there was another professional yacht's skipper, who also took a great interest in *Vivette*.

He was in charge of a fine fifty-ton Fife-built cutter belonging to a Dutchman, and he spoke in the highest possible terms of British building and design. She was a very pretty model, and her owner evidently was a keen sportsman; for one summer he took her from Amsterdam down west as far as Salcombe, and another year he sailed her as far east as St. Petersburg. Next year perhaps they might go south to the "Middle Sea" (Mediterranean) said the skipper, for he did not care for the Russians one met up the Gulf of Finland. It was this same man who told me of a strange experience that occurred to him one winter. It was bitterly cold, and, as everyone knows, the Zuyder Zee is quite shallow. They were sailing along and gradually the ice froze round them more and more until the yacht was hemmed in as tightly as an Arctic ship. They were not more than two or three miles from the shore, so leaving her immovable they walked across the frozen surface to the land.

We spent about a week in Amsterdam, using *Vivette* as a house-boat and making daily expeditions to the different parts of this interesting city, but especially to the Rijks Museum, full of unspeakable delights to all who love pictures and ship-models. There were theatres, too, and restaurants, and the usual attractions of a country's capital. There were miles and miles of canals running through the city, docks, wharves, and all the features of a busy port.

Most entertaining it is to see the swift motor craft with full loads of milk-cans dodging in and out of the small, intricate canals, shooting under bridges which had never been accustomed to have engine-driven boats coming under their arches. We were constrained to remain until after the last day of August, which is the birthday of Queen Wilhelmina, and it is a day that I shall remember for a long time. It began with a long regatta held by the two yacht clubs, and we dressed ship in honour of the occasion. From our berth we had a front view of the racing, being close to the starting and finishing line.

The previous few days the racing had been on the Zuyder Zee, but today it was on tideless waters. There were races for almost every kind of craft down to Thames skiffs setting small handkerchiefs of sails. The *boiers* struck me as very slow craft, but some of the seven—or eight—metres (I forget which) did very well. It was a fine, hot, sunny day, and everyone was bright and merry, and the many unusual types of craft were to none more interesting than ourselves.

In another volume I have shown In detail how much we owe to the Dutch for having introduced the yacht into England. Today we are returning the compliment by reintroducing the sport of yachting into the Low Countries, and the Dutchmen are becoming wonderfully keen. Perhaps they have still a good deal to learn in racing tactics: in starting they seemed always to be a long time after the gunfire. And as one sails through Holland it certainly is surprising that there are so few yachts and yachtsmen who avail themselves of such hundreds of miles of ideal sailing waters. But there is no lack of enthusiasm just now, and the results will follow in time.

There was a very charming lady, the wife of a distinguished professor, whose yacht was lying close to us, who, hearing from one of the paid hands concerning the nature of *Vivette's* voyage, waxed most eloquent in praise of English ideals, and yachting especially. The difficulty, she continued, was to find suitable sport for sons instead of the mere attractions of the cafés. Yachting supplied just that sport, and she was anxious beyond words that her own son should excel in this sphere.

The royal birthday ended as it had begun. There were a few fireworks across on the other shore, but it was in the city that a sort of "Mafeking night" was being celebrated. Everyone was in the best of humour, the cafés were crowded, and in the Kalverstraat and other prominent thoroughfares there was high carnival being kept, but I only saw one case of drunkenness.

Everybody was at the full pitch of enjoyment, for the Dutch are very loyal and dearly love their queen. There was dancing on the pavement everywhere to the sound of an organ and kettledrum. I have never seen so hilarious a number of people behaving with so much decorum. I went into one of the principal cafés, and found the great hall so crowded that not a seat was vacant. But there was a little group of ladies and gentlemen over to the left, who, seeing me somewhat bashfully hesitating whether to remain or clear out, sent their chairman to request me to join their table. In any other city but Amsterdam, and certainly any other country but Holland, I should have declined instantly. But I had not sailed from one end to the other in their land without learning that the Dutch dispense with all ceremony and waive all suggestions of etiquette.

As illustrative of this, if I may digress for a moment, I remember being introduced to a certain Dutch artist whom one could describe in every way as a man of refinement and good manners. But we had not known each other three minutes before he turned to me, and asked whether I was married, and if I had a profession. As already stated, the Dutch are too direct in their methods to care for a hint or a suggestion. They mean no offence, but they do not conceal their curiosity.

And so on this royal night I reluctantly yielded to persuasion, and, expressing profuse thanks, joined this happy circle. And had I been one of the Court of the Queen herself, I could not have been treated with greater hospitality. There were speeches from the chairman and others of the party, felicitous remarks about England and the English. I was toasted and presented with flowers, and by the time I had returned thanks, apologised for having to speak in English, and had drunk to the health of her

Majesty and her loving subjects amid many a "*hoch! hoch!*" you might have supposed that England and Holland ten years ago had fought as allies in South Africa against a common foe. It was a memorable evening, and this, I am told, is the one day in the year when the Dutch forget their unemotional character, and lay aside all care.

Chapter 13

Amsterdam and Nieuwendam

It was September now. Most of the yachts had gone to their homes, the weather had broken utterly, and a steady drizzling rain and the long cold evenings began to suggest that it was time to put away our summer toy and get back home to the more serious things of life. I had intended making a short cruise through the Zuyder Zee, but for the next week it blew very hard indeed. For part of this there continued one of the heaviest gales I ever remember, and of this I shall speak again presently. The shallow waters of the Zuyder Zee soon become dangerous to a little craft in such weather, so to our disappointment that trip had to be abandoned. And as the summer had apparently gone, and we were in a hurry to return to England, I had arranged with a firm of shipbuilders, whom a Dutch yachtsman casually met at Veere had recommended, to dismantle *Vivette* and lay her up for the winter.

So we sailed down the Ij through Amsterdam for the last time, and taking the second turn on the port hand after you pass the Juliana floating dock, found ourselves in a nice clean village, away from smoke and noise. Up a little dyke, and here was a pleasant basin with sheds, and all the familiar features of these places where they build the yachts we love so well. But there were other craft, too. One of the Amsterdam steamboats had been in collision and had to lay up awhile till she could be repaired. And there was a Zuyder Zee hotter for us to go aboard and examine in detail, and a handful of yachts, as well as other craft.

An enthusiastic yachtsman from Amsterdam was doing odd jobs to his craft, and thus we made the acquaintance of Heer Hoist, to whom I owe more than I can say for considerable courtesy and kindness. He it was who gave me many a valuable hint, assisted me in getting the yacht insured in Amsterdam for the winter, arranged with his man Arij Kowenoord to look after the sails, the cooking utensils, blankets, ropes, and all the thousand and one articles which make up a yacht's inventory, till we should come back the year following. It was Heer Hoist who used to translate my letters to Messrs. De Vries Lentsch when I wrote from England giving instructions for fitting out; so I cannot think of Nieuwendam without remembering one who was a very good friend to *Vivette* and her crew.

Twice before had English yachtsmen had business with the De Vries Lentschs, and it was they who had built the hotter yacht *Coo-ee* which I had seen on the Norfolk Broads ten years ago, after she had arrived safely from across the North Sea. The other visitor was a well-known member of the Humber Yawl Club, who sometimes puts his wee ship on board a steamer, and then sails about Holland.

But whilst we were lying in this snug berth under the shadow of Nieuwendam church, with Amsterdam's towers in the background, and the liners showing up in the middle distance, we had time to walk down the leafy avenue to see the famous Orange Locks which give access from the Ij into the Zuyder Zee, crowded with *botters* bound back from the North Sea to the Islands of Urk and Marken in the Zuyder Zee. Here you have the *oude mode* of dress once more—the baggy breeches, the *sabots* and all, as you have seen in many a poster and in many a musical comedy.

But these much-patched clothes are the costumes of a magnificent race of seamen. I have watched them at it, so I know. And if faces are any guide to character you can trust these *botter*-men as you would your own kith and kin. Then, on another day, we took train to Monnikendam, that curious shallow port by the Zuyder Zee, with the Isle of Marken just rising up in the near

Dutch Costumes

distance. But the tourists have spoilt the Monnikendammers, so I prefer to forget them and remember only the place itself.

And at last came the time when *Vivette* went under the tripod to have her mast hauled out. Two or three strenuous days were spent getting everything out of her—spars, and fittings, and even her ballast—till she was a mere hollow wooden shell floating on the top of the water. At length she was taken up a narrow dyke that just fitted her, put into a cradle, and, a horse having been attached to a windlass on shore, she was hauled out of Dutch water and into the shed. But even yet we had not done with her. There she remained, mute and still, taken from her wonted element.

We were not quite ready, as the steamer we had intended taking from Amsterdam to London, which would have given us a longer look at the sea, was full, so we had to remain one more day. Therefore that night we went up to bed by a ladder, but there was not overmuch comfort in the ship now. Such a packing there was after our two months' cruise; such a hardship to get accustomed once more to shore-going clothes! We had been good customers at the little Nieuwendam café during those muggy few days when we would keep running across the road to refresh our thirsty bodies after toiling to dismantle and lay things away.

Many a time had *mijn-heer* refreshed us with delicious Pilsener. But now there was no more "Pilz" left—not a bottle. It was clearly time that we went.

So bidding farewell to Heer Hoist, and entrusting *Vivette* to

En Route for England

De Vries Lentsch and his sons, we set off for the village quay, and, preceded by half the firm's staff carrying our miscellaneous baggage, we boarded the little steamer that runs across to Amsterdam, took train thence to Rotterdam, and in a few hours found ourselves in one of the cabins of the *Batavier V*.

The Rotterdam river was as busy as when we had first seen it, but it was fascinating to watch the water-traffic from the decks of the *Batavier*, now that we had no longer any responsibility. She was a fine little ship, and we thoroughly enjoyed our steam down the Dutch coast, across the North Sea, and up the Thames to London Bridge. As we sat at dinner in the *Batavier* saloon soon after leaving Rotterdam, I overheard scraps of a conversation between an English vicar and another gentleman which made me prick my ears. When the latter had left the table to go on deck, my neighbour turned to me with a remark: "Our friend seems to have had a very trying time. He was shipwrecked the other day off Ymuiden."

A few minutes later I found myself talking to the owner of the barge-yacht *Gwalia*, which I remembered to have seen on Queen Wilhelmina's birthday getting under way, and sailing down the Ij towards Ymuiden. The story as related by her owner was as follows: They had got out into the North Sea intending to cross to England, but bad weather had come on, and they had been compelled to run back for shelter near the piers. A shift of wind followed, so that they found themselves on a lee shore, and before long the strong breeze developed into that heavy gale, whose force I marvelled at even though we were so snugly sheltered in Nieuwendam.

A wicked sea got up, he told me, and a terribly anxious night was spent, during which they expected the heavy sprit to carry away, and come crashing down through the barge. She was an exceptionally strong ship, having been a converted typical Medway craft such as you see in the London river any moment of your life. They were in a most perilous position, and after burning flares during the night for assistance, she drifted so close to the piers that the owner and at least one of the crew were able to jump off. But eventually the crew stood by her for a while until she was driven ashore. She was considerably damaged, and was, I understood, abandoned. Her owner was expecting his men to join the *Batavier* at the Hook of Holland, but they were not there when we stopped. The rest of the story I never learnt, but a few days later I read the following notice in a London paper under the heading of "Wrecks and Casualties."

"*Gwalia* (British yacht), before reported ashore near South Pier, Ymuiden, has been assisted afloat by salvage steamers, and towed into Ymuiden. Leaks slightly. Amsterdam."

So I hope that after all she was not destined to end her days in an alien land. But I fancy this experience impressed the *Gwalia's* owner that the barge rig for open sea work leaves a great deal to be desired, and that from the advantages of a sprit must be subtracted many highly important drawbacks.

It had been a holiday full of sport, of excitement, of Instruction and unending interest, notwithstanding the many delays with which it had been begun. Considering all the locks and quays and narrow places we had frequented, it was surprising how little *Vivette's* paint was damaged, and how clean and smart she looked. There was many an opportunity during the ensuing winter to think over the good times we had spent, and some of the friends we had made in Holland did not forget to write. *Kaptein* Brouwer of the *Quo Vadis* remembered us when Christmas came round, and I heard also from Heer Hoist that *Vivette* was being well looked after. All sorts of plans were worked out to be attempted in the following summer.

With such a favourable starting-place as Amsterdam, I was minded to push still further north, cross the Zuyder Zee, then go by canal as far as Delfzyl, then through "The Riddle of the Sands" locality past Norderney to Wilhelmshaven, and thence through the Kiel Canal to Denmark, after which if weather and time permitted to Sweden.

But everyone will remember that suddenly a match started a mighty conflagration: or, to change the simile, that a virulent attack of spy-fever broke out in Germany following the arrest

Zuyder Zee *Botter*

In the North Sea Canal, bound for the fishing grounds

of two Englishmen and subsequent imprisonment. Several other British yachtsmen cruising in German waters were also arrested but released. And that being the general atmosphere, and it being essential that we should have to touch German ports on the way, it seemed more prudent to postpone that trip indefinitely. When matters became even more acute by the time we were due to start, my one aim was to hurry *Vivette* home to her native land as fast as we could go, for I had no wish to be kept tied up in some continental port, unable to sail the seas, while wars ashore and afloat were being waged. How nearly that war occurred about this time is now a matter of past history.

I had been down twice to the Solent in the early summer to get my hand in again and to return again to the things of the sea. The second time was for the Coronation Review, and in the evening I happened to find myself going round the fleet on a steamer. Just as we left Ryde my eyes fell on a white craft whose general appearance was familiar, and then I recognised the Dutch ensign flying at the stern.

She was evidently a stranger to the place, and had brought up too near the fairway. This annoyed the skipper of the steamer, who hailed the yacht with vehement remarks. What he said practically amounted to a translation of the yacht's name. "Where are you going?" he shouted to *Kaptein* Brouwer busy forward. And just then I read under the yacht's stern these letters—*Quo Vadis?*

A few short weeks ashore amid bricks and mortar, and the eternal longing to be afloat again in one's own craft became almost an obsession.

> *O to sail in a ship*
> *To leave this sturdy unendurable land,*
> *To leave the tiresome sameness of the streets, the sidewalks and the houses,*
> *To leave you, O you solid motionless land, and entering a ship*
> *To sail and sail and sail.*

There had been delays, and at one time it looked as if *Vivette's* former mate would not be able to accompany me this year. But at length one warm summer evening at the middle of July both of us and our gear were standing in Liverpool Street station, and at half-past eight we were off once more to leave civilisation behind. At ten o'clock we were at Harwich, and going aboard the fine ship *St. Petersburg*, as striking and handsome as a young Atlantic liner; and before long we had cleared the harbour, and left the bell-buoy moaning astern.

It was a fine night with a flukey wind sometimes off the shore sometimes blowing in from the sea with a slight fog. Between the Cork light and the Shipwash there were several interesting square-sail craft with everything set, and a stern light showing over the rail to warn us off. Like ghosts creeping through the night they faded away, and every few minutes came a man's voice rising up from the lookout. "Light on the starboard bow, sir ... light on the port bow." It was good to smell the bonny sea air again and to feel that the turbines were humming as fast as they could go to bring us back to Holland.

Then, so soon as the Shipwash lightship was passed and we began to edge off from the English coast, it was time to go below and turn into our bunks for a few short hours. During the night a change came in the weather, and by the time we arrived at the Hook a fleet of small sailing craft were running in with the early dawn, for it certainly looked ominous. There was a good hour to wait before the Amsterdam train started, so I employed it profitably exploring Berghaven, a useful little harbour on the port hand as you come up from the sea.

Cruising men compelled to put into the Hook of Holland might find this haven more comfortable than lying in the river. There seemed to be a minimum of at least six feet, judging by the kind of craft that kept afloat, but the mariner should be warned that this little harbour is exceedingly crowded with small tugs and other vessels: and because a strong tide runs past its mouth it should be entered only at slack water or collision would almost certainly occur. There are good warping posts at the entrance, which will be found of assistance.

We breakfasted as the train ran along through the pleasant flat pastures, and before long we were at Amsterdam. Then getting aboard the little steamer which starts from the canal hard-by, we arrived in another thirty minutes at Nieuwendam. At the end of the dyke was *Vivette* unmistakably, looking very proud and prim in her new paint. The workmen were gone to breakfast, but I found the dinghy and rowed back to the steamer wharf to bring the mate and the baggage aboard.

The yacht had been well looked after, and all the improvements and alterations had been carried out in the most satisfactory manner and very reasonably. And here came De Vries Lentsch, with his smoking-cap and long clay pipe, and here were his sons, fine big fellows, healthy in mind and limb. In a few minutes appeared Arij Kowenoord with all the lamps, stoves, saucepans, kettles and the rest polished with typical Dutch brightness as I warrant they never sparkled before. I had sent instructions for the deck forward and the bitts to be overhauled thoroughly, so that the bridge incident at Dordrecht might by no possible means have weakened the ship. The De Vries Lentschs had made a most excellent job, and both deck and bitts were now stronger than they had been even from the very first. No big alterations had been essential this year, but in a dozen minor details the shipwrights and carpenters had added to our comfort and improved the general convenience of the ship.

But there was a good deal of work to be done before *Vivette* was ready for sea, in overhauling blocks, reeving halyards and sheets, stowing the thousand and one articles in their proper lockers and making sure that not a thing was wanting. We took off our coats the moment we got aboard, and we toiled incessantly for two days, stopping only for food and sleep. By five o'clock in the evening of the second day, with stores and water, oil and all, on board we had come to the end. So, having settled the shipbuilders' account and bade farewell once more, we hoisted sail and ran out into the Ij.

Heer Hoist had come over from Amsterdam to speed us on our way. Exciting events were taking place ashore, he told us, and two men had been shot down in the Amsterdam streets the night before. We ourselves had noticed on arrival that the thoroughfares were being patrolled by mounted infantry and cavalry. For this, you will remember, was the beginning of that period of unrest which spread to Liverpool, London, and elsewhere, reaching its alarming climax sometime later. The seamen in the port of Amsterdam had struck, and we saw liners and big ocean-going steamships—whole fleets of them—lying idle without steam or men.

That also affected the local sailing and power craft, the *tjalks*, and the motor cargo carriers to a great extent. Perhaps the only people who benefited by all this were ourselves, for it meant that we were to have the canals through Holland almost to ourselves, and thus be free from that eternal risk of collision which is the one drawback to cruising in the Netherlands. Such a chance might never happen again, and we certainly began our cruise this year with a stroke of luck.

I think it is only fair to those who contemplate visiting Holland in their own craft that this ever-present danger of collision should be emphasised. I remember the owner of the *Gwalia* mentioning to me that he had brought a nice little motor launch out with him to tow his barge through some of the narrow canals. It was while she was lashed up alongside somewhere near Gouda that a trading craft ran into her, crushed her to pieces, and promptly sank her. He could get no compensation, for it was found that she ought to have been towing ahead and not alongside.

Another amateur on a different occasion related to me the narrow escapes he had in his craft, and in particular graphically described a terrible experience when the thick steel hawser of a *Rhine-schiff* swept across his craft and nearly caused a fatality. If you want comparative quietness, the best time for sailing in Holland is on Sundays; the worst time is Mondays.

CHAPTER 14

Southwards through Holland

We were bound home this time, not by the Amstel, but along the broad North Sea Canal, and then turning off to the left *via* the Spaarndam Canal, through Haarlem, Brassemer Meer; and eventually joining the Oude Rijn, having made a bold sweep round to the westward parallel to the sea, joining our former course at Gouwe Sluis. This route would give us a wider knowledge of Holland, and would also avoid those numerous bridges through the heart of Amsterdam. As our course was mostly south or south-west practically all the way back to England, it was more than likely that we should have head-winds for the most part. As to that we must trust to luck, but if the breeze were not favourable in the canals, where it was too narrow to tack, we should be awkwardly placed.

Having cleared from Nieuwendam, we tacked up the North Sea Canal through Amsterdam in a light evening-breeze. But it took us some time to get accustomed to the wonderful absence of shipping, all now at a standstill. By nightfall we had arrived at a big swing bridge through which all the liners have to pass, and it is a strange sight to watch them backing and filling in charge of tugs till the huge span swings clear and they are free to go forth on their way. In company with a small fleet of Marken *botters*, we moored here for the night, making fast to a dolphin. But the wash from such few steamers as were not affected by the strike made our berth no pleasant one; and the same drawback will be found when you are moored at the yacht-*steiger* by the

Amsterdam yacht clubs.

A bright, sunny morning with the same light wind saw us beating along this broad waterway, which will shortly be deepened to about forty-two feet, and is already wide enough for a little craft to make good long tacks. It was a long leg and a short leg, and then in answer to our fog-horn the bridgeman on the Spaarn opened his steel span. It was now a dead plug, yet we just did it with the help also of a line and boathook. But thereafter the canal was so narrow and so shallow that it was most difficult to make any tacks at all. No sooner were you round on one board than you were in shallow water again.

Twice or three times we stuck, had to lower sail, and quant off. But the third time, although we were in almost the centre of the channel, we stuck so hard and firmly that we seemed destined to remain. I had heard how tricky this place was and how regular a thing it was for sailing craft to get ashore, but I scarcely thought it as bad as this. We took out the kedge with forty or fifty fathoms of rope, but the mud was so soft that we could do nothing. And as there is not an inch of tide, it seemed that we should have to take out some of her ballast before we could get off. How we learnt to realise the full value of a tide before we were quit of these tideless waters!

So we sat down to lunch and think about it, when up came a tug towing a couple of lighters. Seeing us, he cast off his tow and offered to haul us off and tow us down to the Spaarndam lock for "half an English pound." The price was not cheap, but seeing that we might remain here forever, and that the canal was narrow all the way along with always a head-wind, I decided to accept his offer, and we soon pulled through the mud and were taken along. You may wonder how it was the tug could float and we couldn't. The secret is this: don't get to the right (north-western) bank, nor keep amid channel. The only deep water is between the left bank and the middle, and even then there is precious little. In case of a head-wind, don't attempt to tack, but tow.

We cast off at Spaarndam lock, and the tug returned to his

lighters while the gates and bridge were being opened for us. And then we emerged on to a pretty sheet of water, well buoyed, that reminded one very much of a Norfolk Broad. You cannot get ashore here if you pay regard to the well-marked channel, but it is a pity the Spaarn itself cannot be dealt with in a similar manner.

And finally, after sailing a little further, we found ourselves at the outskirts of Haarlem, famous for its tulips at the proper season. Down came the sails, for there were at least four bridges to pass through and harbour dues to be paid, and we quanted leisurely through the old city past its ship-lined quays till we came to a quieter and more rural spot. Selecting a big iron *klipper-aak* named the *Johann Nicolaas*, cutter rigged, with its deckhouse aft bright with well-polished brasses, flower-pots, and spick-and-span windows, we asked permission of the skipper to come alongside for the night. The mate and I could thus leave *Vivette* in good hands and explore Haarlem together, for there was much we had to see.

Later in the evening the mate of the *aak*, a well-set-up young man of twenty-one with an open countenance and a fine, healthy stature, came and yarned most interestingly. This was Johann Nicolaas himself, for, twenty-two years ago, his father, the skipper, had married. In that year the *aak* had been built, and the year following there came into the world this son, who took his Christian names from the ship herself. He told us much about Holland and her ships. In the *Johann Nicolaas* they lived winter and summer, trading as far away as Prussia, but he did not like the Germans, though the "*schip*-men" were not so bad. He had just been to England, for he was in the Dutch "marine" (that is to say, the Dutch Navy), and had recently come off the Netherlands warship *Heemskerk*, which came over to represent Holland at the Coronation Review, and her we had passed in Amsterdam busy looking after the strikers.

And then there were the exquisite pictures and antiquities of Haarlem to be examined, the splendid Franz Hals, the Albert Dürers, and many another which were a great treat. There were most picturesque side-canals, too, with leafy avenues for you to rest out of the heat of the day. We were sorry to leave the *Johann Nicolaas* and her namesake, but we must push on. And as we sailed down the tortuous river as beautiful as a Thames backwater, with houses and green lawns running down to the water's edge, we caught sight of the Quo Vadis tethered to her private stage, looking none the worse for her trip to Spit- head. But her crew were ashore, and we had no time to stop. It was a fine, smart breeze, such as usually springs up fiercely about noon on a summer's day and dies down towards evening.

We were bowling merrily along just able to lay our course. Some of the corners were a terrible pinch, and finally they could not be negotiated without tacking. Shallower and shallower grew the water, but we remembered our experience of the previous day and kept over to the left. But it was no good; there seemed no depth anywhere, and we stuck in the mud, and had to get a line on to the windlass of a *tjalk* loading clay before we could come off.

It was very hot and the way narrowed still more round the next bend, where the wind was dead ahead. To tack was impossible, and we were not eager to tow by hand in the heat. We had tried, but it was heavy work against the breeze, so we tied up and waited. If only we could get something to quench our thirst. It was a mere hamlet without a cafe, but over there was a farm and the farmer's wife sold me a litre of fresh milk, which put new heart into one.

Later on came one of those motor-barges bound our way, so hailing her we dangled a rope, shouted the Dutch word for tow—"*sliepe*"—and waited developments. The skipper, a genial, good-tempered soul, with a wizened face like the *botter*-men, stopped his engines, came astern and agreed for a couple of *guelders* (3s. 4d.) to give us a pluck as far as we wanted to go. He was bound for Leiden with a cargo of farm produce and bottled Pilsener, but our route was to the left just before reaching Leiden.

This was a piece of luck, and we kept going in the easi-

QUANTING A LOAD OF HAY THROUGH ONE OF THE HAARLEM CANALS

THE BEST PLACE TO BRING UP AT HAARLEM
THE GROOTE KERKE IN THE BACKGROUND CONTAINS SEVERAL INTERESTING MODEL RIGGED CRAFT.

est fashion for the rest of the afternoon. Most beautiful looked the scenery glimmering in the heat, with neat little villages and an occasional bridge. Scarcely had we started before the barge's skipper began to quench his thirst, and then turning round to look at us astern sent his mate below for four more bottles of "Pilz," which he handed to us as a present.

We had indeed found another friend at the right moment. In fact, it became a daily wonder on the *Vivette* whom we might meet before nightfall that would come across our path and render us most valuable service. Seeing that I was interested in his craft, he slowed down a few miles further and instructed his mate to take me below and see his gas-engine, which was doing its work nobly and never gave any trouble.

For most of an hour we talked about ships and their ways, though I cannot exactly tell how we managed to keep up a conversation, seeing that neither of us spoke the other's language. And presently we turned out of the narrow canal into another of those broads as we are wont to call them in England. This was Brassemer Meer, and it was lovely to see the soft greens of the reeds contrasted against the red setting sun.

There was a little draught of wind now, so the *tjalks* were able to set their sails and make their way across the glistening waters of the *meer*. It would be an ideal centre for anyone wanting a thoroughly restful holiday with a small sailing-boat to while away the time. A mile or two further and the barge had cast off: we towards Leiderdorp along the Oude Rijn, he with his cargo to Leiden.

Thus we quanted slowly through a couple of bridges, and were admiring a nice old house with a terrace and stone steps leading down to the water. It was the high light on a couple of brass domes crowning the iron-work that made me look up as we were pushing our way along. A gentleman and his family were taking tea on the terrace, and I was not conscious that we had been noticed, but before we had gone another dozen yards I was hailed through the trees by a voice in English.

"Where are you going, sir?"

"We're looking for a suitable *ankerplatz* to bring up for the night."

"Won't you come and lie here? You'll find nothing further on."

So, taking our ropes, he very kindly made them fast round a couple of trees and began to talk to us of our travels. A few minutes later and our host had insisted on taking us entirely under his care. We returned to the terrace, were entertained with hospitality as kindly as it was spontaneous; we were suddenly transported from the limited deck of *Vivette* into a delightful old house full of the most interesting furniture, paintings, armour, and I know not what else. Comte Henri de Bylandt was not altogether unconnected with England, and at an earlier date one of his kinsmen had been Dutch Envoy at the Court of St. James.

We talked far into the night of European politics, and of Holland especially, and the *Vivette's* crew look back on this as one of the pleasantest evenings in the whole cruise. The Count also happened to be a keen yachtsman, and took us over his ship, the *Albatross*, lying just astern of us and fitted with an auxiliary Gardener motor. In the morning we were not allowed to depart before two delightful children had taken us to see their pigeons, and then at length both ships got under way, the Albatross and her party for a cruise in Friesland, the *Vivette* to follow her course along the Rhine.

It was a fair wind for us and the river widened out into quite majestic reaches. Another fine day but more pleasing scenery with little traffic. And as we sailed we did our shopping. For, first came a boy in a fruit-boat, and the mate rowed off in the dinghy, to return with grapes and cool melons to console us in the terrific heat which most people will remember during the exceptional summer of 1911. A nice breeze carried us along further, where a detachment of troops on the march were singing as they swung down the road through the trees. Still further on and we came to a pleasant waterside cafe and again the mate manned the dinghy and brought off the beer of the country, for it was unbearably hot even doing nothing. Thus at length we came through Alfen and arrived once more at Gouwe.

There was, even in spite of the Amsterdam strike, a good deal of traffic again by this lock, and we watched a number of incidents that were almost collisions, for the wind had worked round ahead of us, and was too light for us to tack. There was a ship-chandler's, or rather a "*Zeil-makerij*," so we might as well remain here for a while and get the sail-maker on board to make a slight repair to the main-sail before we reached the open sea. He came with his palm and needle, and when the job was done I inquired how much I owed.

"*Niet*," answered the proprietor, "nothing."

Holland is indeed a wonderful country, full to overflowing with the milk of human kindness.

Seeing how unfavourable were the conditions for sailing, I accepted the offer of another motor-barge to tow us down the next few miles to Gouda. She might have been twin-sister to the vessel which had brought us along yesterday, and I think we agreed on a couple of *guelders*, as before. On the way we passed a Dutch *boier* yacht bound the opposite direction, and as she was seen to be flying the British ensign at the stern, we paid special attention to notice her, when her owner or charterer, and *Vivette's* mate, suddenly recognised each other as having cruised together in Essex waters.

We cast off from our motor-tug just before we got to Gouda, and then quanted through to the lock, where the usual muddle was taking place. But, as before, we were extraordinarily lucky. For there was not room for a big *tjalk*, and she had to back out although she had been waiting a long time. There was just space enough for one more craft, and *Vivette* fitted it. Out once more into the tidal waters of the Ijssel, we took the last of the ebb down, and when darkness fell and the tide came up, anchored as near as possible to the bank.

Turning out next morning at 3.30, we got under way just as the darkness was clearing away and the tide was beginning to ebb. By a stroke of good luck, the wind had gone northerly, so we had every condition in our favour.

We had our first meal somewhere about dawn, and several more breakfasts as we sailed on through sleeping villages. We had done so well that by the time we were out of the Ijssel and into the Rotterdam river the strong tide was still coming down the Maas, but we had a spanking wind, and cheating the tide all we could we tore over it. Then turning to the right, we bowled past Smit & Co's. basin, where we had anchored last year, past Alblasserdam and Papendrecht, and so to Dort, where the tide was just about to begin flooding against us.

Here again, however, we had good fortune. There was still a drain of ebb, the port hand bridge was just going to close, but we blew our fog-horn loudly and continuously, shot through at a great pace, overtook a small fleet of *tjalks* and *klippers*, and were roaring down the Kil with balloon stay-sail set spinnaker fashion. I had not forgotten little Wilhelmina, and I should have liked to have heard her once more read with her great deliberation, without stopping to take breath, "Old—Marley—was—as—dead—as—a—door-nail." But the fair, bonny breeze, and the open bridge were the greater temptation. It was a sail in a thousand.

Down the Kil we went, out into the Hollandsch Diep, and soon after one o'clock we were moored in Numansdorp once more, having done forty or fifty miles since breakfast, with tide against us for the greater part of the way. In another hour we should have had the ebb to take us through Hellegat, and before night we should have been at Veere, and a hundred-mile run accomplished between sunrise and sunset.

This we could have done easily, but we had had such a tiring time the day before in the hot sun, had had only three or four hours' rest last night, and were so sleepy with the bracing air of today's sail, that we could not keep awake; and it would never do to go through that channel sleepy-eyed. So although the day was so young, I decided to enter our old haunt, and as soon as sails were stowed slept on the deck, until the harbour-master's men woke me up by shouting to go and give the usual particulars as to destination, &c. In the evening I walked up to the village to see the old man who had looked after me the previous summer, but I was too late, and the village had turned in early.

We had to be up early again the next morning to catch our tide through Helleeat, and this time we chose the western channel as providing a change and being wider. We had come out with another northerly wind, but just as the tide got hold of us the breeze dropped, and we had a more anxious time in this flat calm than we had the previous year coming through in a strong wind. The tide was like a mill-race, and the roar it made as it went tearing past the buoys was almost terrifying. Occasionally we would have a little whisp of wind, get steerage way, and then it would die down again. But by the time we had Hellegat well astern and out of the way, the true northerly breeze sprang up, and the tide having now turned strongly against us, we ran into the quaint harbour of Zijpe, which is a most convenient little spot.

There were several hours to wait for the turn of the tide, so we walked over to the small fishing village of Bruinesse, which we had just passed. Imagine to yourself a day of days—hot sun, blue sky, not a cloud anywhere, and a pleasant cooling breeze from the north. Conceive, too, a genuine fishing community with their little harbour packed full of *hoogarts* (fishing-boats), so that there was not a yard of free space. Fronting the harbour were the rows of cottages belonging to the fishermen, and at the back, below the level of the sea, and behind the grassy dune which alone prevents the sea from flooding the land, came a fair stretch of meadows with black grazing cattle and a few dykes dispersed here and there.

At the back of the village rose the village church, from whose belfry the Angelus was ringing out across the water as I walked in. Some of the hardy old fishermen were on board busily mending their nets; others were yarning to each other in little squads ashore. I counted most of a hundred masts with their pennants waving at the top like so many lances. There were a few more that I got tired of counting, and I went back happy at having seen an ideal Dutch fishing village, where everyone looked contented, where ships and men seemed to have been made of the right sort. Bruinesse made a deep impression on my mind, and I thought of it many times when I returned home. And then two months later I saw an odd paragraph or two in the London papers which filled me with horror.

Perhaps the reader may remember the very heavy gale which occurred at Michaelmas of 1911. October came in like a lion, and at that weekend there was one of the worst storms of the autumn and winter. There were disasters on most of the coasts of Northern Europe, but Holland and the neighbour- hood through which we had just passed suffered most. The Bruinesse fleet must have been out as usual, and the numerous *tjalks*, *klippers*, and other trading craft were certainly about in the Keeten Mastgat and other parts of the Scheldt, through which we had passed but a few weeks before. The following, however, which is taken from the *Evening Standard* of October 3, 1911, gives the first telegrams detailing the catastrophe:

> Loss of Life in Holland.—Advices delayed by the interruption of communication with the province of Zeeland state, says a Reuter's message from Amsterdam, that 120 vessels out of the fleet of 130 mussel-fishing boats belonging to the village of Bruinesse were lost or received considerable damage during Sunday's storm.
> The Queen will visit Bruinesse today. Forty-five inland vessels were wrecked on the waterways between Dordrecht and the North Sea. Most of the crews were drowned. It is reported that twenty-eight bodies have been washed up near Steenbergen.

This was followed by a later telegram saying that in consequence of 120 Bruinesse fishing vessels being wrecked in the gale, 240 families were destitute.

At Stavenisse 24 boats, with crews, went down.

The following version appeared in the *Daily Mail*, and con-

(1) AND (2) THE HARBOUR AT BRUINESSE
SHOWING THE FISHING FLEET WHICH FOUNDERED IN THE MICHAELMAS GALE OF 1911.
(3) THE HOOGARTS FISHING FLEET IN FLUSHING HARBOUR

firms the other announcement:—

Rotterdam, Tuesday.

"Practically the entire fishing fleet, numbering over a hundred vessels, of the village of Bruinesse, was destroyed in the weekend gale, and intense suffering has been caused to the inhabitants.

Queen Wilhelmina today visited the village to inquire into the extent of the disaster and to offer her sympathy to the bereaved families.

A large number of vessels were thrown against the dykes and wrecked in the waterways of Zeeland, many lives being lost.

News reached Flushing today of the wreck in the North Sea of a Belgian pilot schooner. It is feared that the crew of twelve, all residing in Flushing, have lost their lives. The body of the captain of the vessel has been washed ashore at Middelkerke.

Many dead bodies and a large quantity of wreckage came drifting down the Scheldt, and in addition to five sea-going steamers which drove ashore, eighty river craft were wrecked in the East Scheldt. Forty sank and a large number of men were drowned. It must have been a thousand hells in Hellegat in such a gale as that, but it is sad to think of so many fine fore-and-aft seamen, so many ships and neat little craft swept off, leaving Bruinesse, that had looked so bright and happy, now a village of widows and weeping mothers.

CHAPTER 15

To the English Channel and North Sea

We left Zijpe in the early afternoon with a northerly wind and the ebb tide just about to begin, and made a quick passage down the Keeten Mastgat, passing a number of Dutch fore-and-afters in, fine style. The little harbour of Stavenisse, just alluded to, soon sunk astern, and then we had a glorious race to catch up an *aak* which was a mile or two ahead. There was a fine, strong breeze, and we were soon up with her. Turning into the Engelsche Vaarwater, of course, we met the ebb pouring out into the Keeten Mastgat with fierceness. By this time the wind had become N.E., so that we were both on a wind. If the latter held consistently we could cover these three miles against the strong flood, but we needed a slashing breeze to do it.

It was a ding-dong race. The *aak's* skipper had jammed her up to windward from the time we approached him at the first gas buoy, and he did his best to keep me from overhauling him. *Vivette* having no alternative but to go to leeward and be blanketed or get picked up by the shoals, we ran dead level, neck and neck, for quarter of an hour, with the balloon stay-sail, and everything drawing splendidly.

After that I saw we were so nicely to windward of our course that I could afford to bear away just a little. That was the little that made so much, and at once we ran right away from him, entering the Zandkreek leaving him a good mile astern, which

"There was a fine strong breeze and we were soon up with her".

we presently increased still more. We had been busily watching the seals gambolling on the half-covered sandbanks, and finally ended up by a most exciting and exhilarating sail, close-hauled, through the narrow passage up the Haringvliet into Veere at night against a hot three-knot tide in the rain with the glass tumbling back and every sign of a dirty night.

This channel contracts so much that it is quite difficult in daylight, but at night, when there was no moon and it was very dark and clouded, it was touch-and-go. There is a small lighthouse ashore, but the channel must have altered a good deal since its institution, for its red and white beams seemed to indicate shoals and deep water promiscuously without any discriminating method. However, by steering a careful compass course and by the smart look-out on the part of the mate, we got through without even smelling the ground, bore up between the two green lights of Veere, and after much blowing on the foghorn for the lock-gates to open, passed through, and moored for the night at our old spot.

Here we made the acquaintance of two delightful American artists, whose paintings of Dutch scenes are well known to most picture-lovers. They were spending the summer in the *Tulip* houseboat, at whose stern the stars and stripes were flying in the summer breeze. We were rejoiced to be back at Veere again. Polderman came down to the jetty as usual with his farm produce.

"WATCHING THE SEALS GAMBOLLING ON THE
HALF-COVERED SANDBANKS"

I was in the cabin at the time, and instantly knew his croaking voice. Apparently he failed to recognise the ship, but as soon as he saw me his eyes lit up, his unemotional nature vanished, and he was as pleased as if we were buying up his entire wares.

"Ho, *kaptein*," he said, thrusting a horny hand into mine. But the rest of the sentence was lost, though I understood. The mate also had sought out the owner of the *hoogarts* model and remarked that it had been re-rigged since last year with gaff and boom instead of sprit. The landlord of the café had not forgotten our admiration for this little craft, and was much impressed by a return visit. But we were short of time, so the same evening we took advantage of the fair wind down the canal, sailed past Middelburg, sweltering in the heat, and arrived at our old mooring spot in Flushing harbour. Great excitement was being exhibited ashore, for the annual *kermis* or fête was being held, which included an aviation meeting.

As we came down the Middelburg canal, the Walcheren children were wild with interest, and the little girls in their quaint costumes ran along the banks calling our attention to the monoplanes.

"*Oh, mijnheer, mijnheer*," they shouted, "*de vlie-schip, de vlie-machine.*" But one "flying Dutchman," seeing that we were the only craft in that part of the canal, thought to give the crowd an exhibition of his skill. So swooping down he came immediately over our heads, and at such an amazingly low altitude that I expected every second that he would foul the top of the mast and either come crashing down on us or capsize us.

We had now come through Holland in less than a week, and after stopping a day to get in stores and to yarn to a couple of British yachts just arrived from England and bound North, we were up bright and early ready for sea on July 27. But there was a long wait at the lock, so it was half-past eight before we had got the other side and were running out into the Scheldt. There was the lightest of easterly winds, which soon fell to a flat calm, and throughout the day the breeze continued to be unsatisfactory.

The *Vivette* and the "Flying Dutchman" in the Flushing Canal

At times it would be a nice sailing wind, then it would die down suddenly and return as quickly. So we were kept busily employed with sail-drill, changing from square-sail to balloon stay-sail, and then stowing that for the working fore-sail. Finally, having been becalmed for most of the way, we arrived inside the pier heads of Ostende, when a Belgian lady passing in an open motor-boat courteously proffered to tow us up the harbour.

As the wind had practically entirely gone, we gladly availed ourselves of yet another of those kindly actions which had so distinctly marked this cruise. We moored between the dolphins at the Ostende Yacht Club, and I strongly urge all cruisers to do likewise instead of enduring the nuisance of entering the lock-gates. Another advantage is that in the former case you have no dues whatsoever to pay.

The next day—July 28—we decided to spend lounging ashore in the almost tropical heat and sunshine. This and the 29th of July the reader will probably recollect as being marked by the most exceptional phenomena in England. These phenomena were duly reported in the papers. It will be remembered that in the West Bay, after a warm, close wind from the S.E., a very heavy and sudden squall came up about 4 p.m. from the south, followed by a tidal wave. At Bridport the sea immediately rose three feet, rushed into the harbour and rushed out again.

Similar experiences were noted at Salcombe, Plymouth, Falmouth, the Bristol Channel, and elsewhere. The glass was observed suddenly to fall from 29.95 to 29. 8, followed by a tremendous thunderstorm, lightning, rain, hail, and wind. At Hamble numerous vessels were driven ashore during the squall. But so soon as the squall had passed, agree all the accounts, the barometer as quickly rose again.

During the former of these two days we were in Ostende, and on the second day we found in Dunkerque, as hereafter to be related. ourselves It may be at once stated that early in the evening on the 28th a sudden, rushing wind swept down with a great vehemence, but as quickly vanished.

It was lucky we were lying in harbour and not under way, as

will be seen presently. I noticed no tidal wave, as I fancy it was about high-water. The next day we were up at 6.30 a.m., were under way at 7.15, and had cleared Ostende harbour an hour later, the wind being N.E. light. Presently it freshened when oft Middlekerke and shifted to N. by E. After another bright sail in the broiling sunshine, having passed through the fishing fleet, we entered Dunkerque at 1.30 p.m., in spite of the fact that the signals were flying forbidding ships to enter.

There was a dredger at work and a number of liners and tramp-steamers were coming out to sea, but we dodged about till there was a cessation in the long procession, and then anchored in the little bay which goes out of the harbour on the port hand by a shipbuilding yard. The Customs officers rowed off and came aboard full of the keenest excitement concerning the likelihood of war breaking out with Germany. And as we spoke a big ketch was being towed up the harbour with her mizzen broken off half-way.

Later in the day we learnt that it had been carried away during *l'orage* which we had noticed whilst in Ostende. There was another British yacht just ahead of us whose owner told me he had been caught out in that squall with topsail up and had an exciting time, finally having to up-helm and run before it. In the evening the mate rowed me ashore and after exploring Dunkerque, I took tram over to Malo-les-Bains, the little seaside resort just east of Dunkerque.

It was a hot, muggy night, and after dining I decided to walk home by the sea. As I proceeded on my way I noticed that a universal thick black cloud was extending over land and sea; then, hurrying to get back to the yacht, a sudden squall blew with terrific violence from about W. or W. by N. By the time I had reached the forts and barracks it was blowing with exceedingly heavy gusts. It took me another twenty minutes before I had got down to the landing steps, and the mate had caught my hail and come off in the dinghy.

"Is everything all right?" I inquired anxiously.

"Yes—we're all right, but we're aground. We were heading to

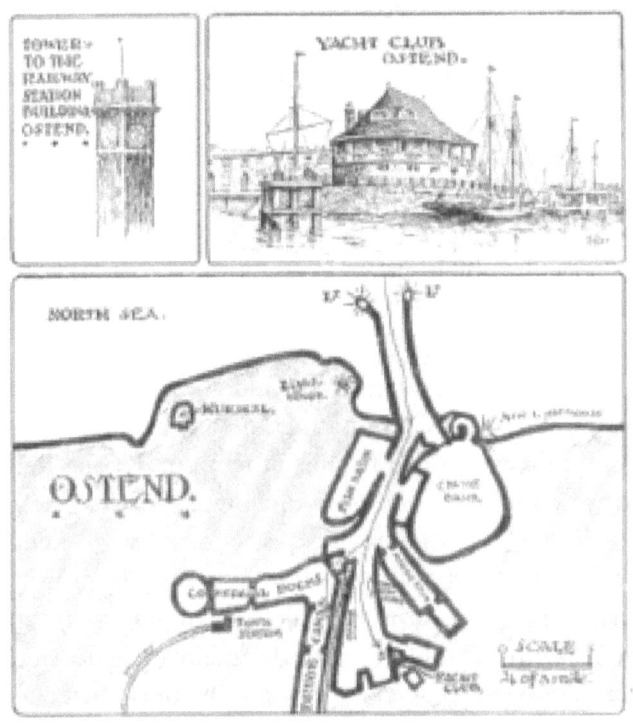

PLAN OF OSTENDE HARBOUR

THE BEST PLACE TO BRING UP IS NOT ON THE STARBOARD HAND IN THE BRUGES CANAL BUT BY THE YACHT CLUB. MOOR BETWEEN TWO DOLPHINS AS SHOWN IN THE SKETCH. THE RAILWAY STATION TOWER - THE MARK FOR LEADING THROUGH THE BEST WATER OUTSIDE (SEE TEXT) - IS SHOWN AS AN INSET ABOVE.

the east when that squall suddenly twisted us right round to the west. Tide's rising though."

As we passed I could hear the other yacht busy with her cable, for she also had swung right round and taken the ground. This squall had occurred at 9 p.m. (within a few minutes). It is interesting to note this fact, and that in Falmouth on the same day it was all over by 2.45 p.m., and at Bridport (West Bay) the squall occurred about 4 p.m., so it was evidently travelling east all the time. But I noticed no tidal wave either in Ostende or Dunkerque. Yet again we were highly fortunate not to have been caught out, for which we were thankful. The following morning we got under way about eight o'clock, left Dunkerque, and against a foul wind beat towards Calais.

Off Gravelines the wind freshened and raised a bit of a lop against the tide. We rolled in a reef or two, but the breeze soon died, and off Oye we had to shake them out. Finally, as the tide turned we could not even hold our own, and were swept back almost to Gravelines. There was just enough air to keep steerage way on her and that was all. In the distance a number of submarine craft were manoeuvring off Calais harbour entrance, and we began to wonder if war had actually been declared. After another tiring day, we were able, when the tide slackened, to get into Calais in the darkness with the aid of our sweep.

We spent a day ashore, and then, after a somewhat sleepless night owing to the noise of one of the cross-Channel packets blowing off steam, making a maddening din for most of an hour, and by the arrival of a steam tramp with a cargo of wood anchoring alongside us, waiting for the docks to be opened for her to go into the Carnot basin, we got under way at 8,30 a.m., not sorry to be out in the open sea.

The tide was just beginning to go to the westward, and the wind was very light from the S.E. We came out with the intention of making for Boulogne, and proceeding from there to Newhaven and the Solent. But the wind dropped utterly and seemed likely to remain quiescent, so having no intention of being made a sport to the powerful tides and the treacherous shoals

DUNKIRK

THE BEST PLACE TO BRING UP IS INDICATED BY POSITION OF *VIVETTE* AND SPIRE IN BACKGROUND (SEE TEXT).

FISHING CRAFT SEEN OFF DUNKIRK

between Calais and Boulogne, I decided to make right across Channel and get hold of the English shore without delay.

We had put the log over and set a course N.N.W., but we had no sooner got about two miles off Sangatte than the flattest of calms came down. At 10 a.m. a light breeze came up from N.E. by E., but that died down again after about half-an-hour or less. I have no wish to weary the reader with a detailed account of this very trying, exceedingly hot and (for the most part) breathless day. We never got a steady breeze the whole time, but an occasional will-o'-the-wisp from all points of the compass.

Our courses varied as frequently, and included practically every bearing from W.S.W. through N. to N. by E. From about 1 p.m. to 6 p.m. we were entirely becalmed, and the Channel was so smooth that you could have crossed from Calais to Dover in a Canadian canoe. I say this expecting to be understood literally. We laboured at the sweep till we were too fatigued to do anything in the heat, and after lashing the helm amidships, and getting the main-sheet quite tightly in, we let *Vivette* look after herself.

Never once had I failed to know my position to a mile, and all the time I knew from the book of *Tidal Streams* where the tide was carrying me, and when it would turn. We took cross-bearings from Cape Gris Nez, Cape Blanc Nez, and other parts of the coast, so. that if the fog which threatened to come on should shut out the French shore we should know approximately our position. The only other fear was that we might get carried on to the Varne, the Colbert, or the overfalls between the two.

Seeing there was no sign of any wind, the only thing to do was to work the tides as best we could. Presently, revived by the juices of some fruit, we laid on to the sweep, and before the west-going tide had barely finished we were by the N.E. Varne buoy. A slight suspicion of a breeze appeared about six o'clock from the S.W., and just enabled us to stem the tide now setting east.

We set first the square-sail, and afterwards changed to the silk

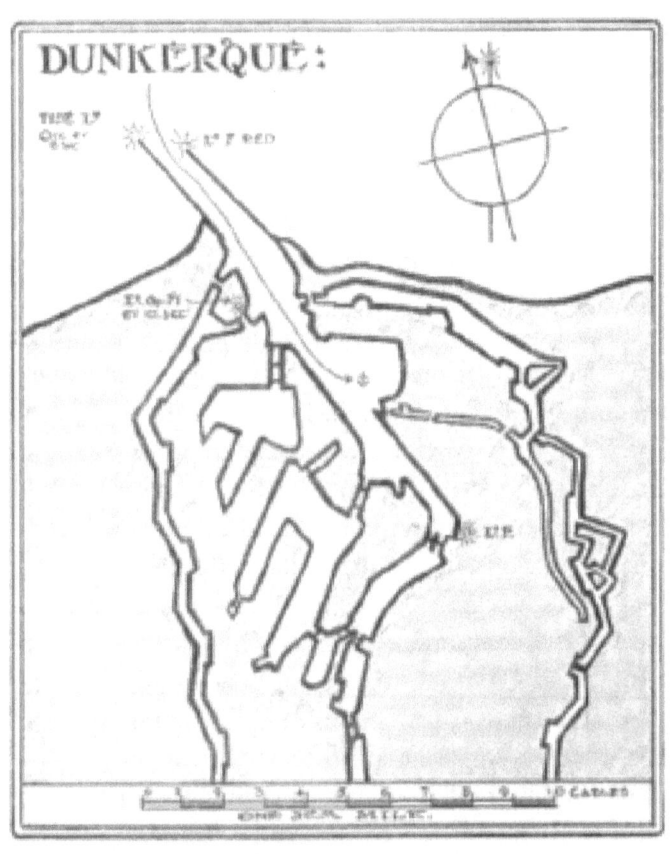

PLAN OF DUNKERQUE HARBOUR

THE ANCHOR SHOWS THE BEST PLACE TO BRING UP.

balloon stay-sail, as the wind was so light, and were just up to the *Preussen* wreck by the east entrance to Dover harbour when we had a partial repetition of those two phenomena which we had experienced in Ostende and Dunkerque. For suddenly the wind began to pipe up in a strong squall, the glass dropped with great suddenness, and the sky over Dover's hills took on the most extraordinary colours, of which yellow and green—the latter especially—predominated.

A nasty short sea got up, so that quickly we had to stow stay-sail and reef down main-sail. Then tacking in through the eastern entrance, we sailed through the flotilla of destroyers, and dropped anchor in about eight fathoms just to the N.E. of the Prince of Wales's pier, with room enough for the next destroyer to swing clear of us at the turn of the tide. The rain came down in torrents as we lowered sail, but, just as on the 29th, the squall soon passed and the barometer instantly rose.

But for that little puff from near the N.E. Varne buoy, and perhaps a total of one hour's very slight breeze, we had crossed without the aid of sail-power. We had rowed practically three-quarters of the way from Calais to Dover in the heat of the day. For this was that memorable summer when more than one oarsman rowed the Channel in an open boat during the next few weeks, and presently Burgess succeeded in swimming across to France.

The track chart of the latter, showing the drift which his body made with the tide towards the westward, was exceedingly interesting, as I found it compared roughly with ours in that direction. Generally speaking, if you draw a line joining Folkestone to Cape Gris Nez, you have the western limit of the west-going tide. I noticed that was as far as we were carried down Channel in *Vivette*, and I believe Burgess was swept no further than this line.

Our ensign was flying at the main, and we were anxious to get cleared, as we were short of water and provisions, and wanted to get ashore to replenish our stores. But neither that night nor the next morning did the Customs officers come out

Vivette in Dover Harbour, 1911

to us, although they now have a motor-launch for use in attending ships in the big harbour. In the morning I rowed off and asked one of the officers to come. Although we waited till the afternoon, he failed to keep his promise, so we got in the anchor and ran round past the forlorn *Preussen* through the Downs—another glorious sail, with a smart S.W. wind, a wine-coloured sea, and brilliant sunshine—into Ramsgate, with the ensign still at the masthead.

Here we were at once given *pratique*, and the mate signed the official declaration as "ship's cook." I had thus altered my plans from going west, for we had had a long spell of north-easters, and now that the wind had settled down in the S.W., it would assuredly remain in quarter for some time. I was in a hurry to be back in town and did not relish beating all the way down to the Wight, so deciding to make a foul wind into a fair, it was resolved to make for an east coast port and leave the yacht there. From Ramsgate, therefore, after wiring to town for some new charts we sailed with a light wind round the North Foreland and Margate.

Just as we came to the Margate Hook the wind came out smartly from the S.W., and we had a very sloppy sail through the Horse Channel, the mate having a pretty wet time forward reefing.

We beat into the East Swale, and brought up midway between the can and conical buoys by Shellness, as the darkness had fallen and we could see no more. At dawn we got the an-

THE ILL-FATED PREUSSEN LYING UNDER DOVER CLIFFS

chor, and, running up the East Swale, let go off Harty Ferry (Isle of Sheppey), where we found a snug and solitary anchorage. It blew hard for a couple of days, and then getting under way from here soon after 9 a.m., we had the grandest sail of the two cruises, making a fitting finale to our voyaging. For with a S.W. wind which gradually grew stronger, we had left the Columbine at 11.20 a.m., and passed the Girdler Lightship about an hour later, where the Queenborough packet boat was crossing on her way to Flushing.

Then having entered the Barrow Deep and set our good friend the square-sail for the last time, we bowled merrily along, doing splendidly, with all sorts of interesting shipping bound the opposite way up the London river—an interesting turret-ship, one of the Admiralty surveying ships making soundings of the Barrow, a fine steamer from the Baltic, a torpedo boat, and many another besides. With a fair tide, a true, steady breeze, a white-flecked sea, a blue sky above, and every sail pulling well and doing its duty, it was one long joy—a day of days.

At 2.15 p.m. the Barrow Lightship was abeam, at 4.45 p.m. the Gunfleet Lighthouse, and then, coming on a wind, we set a

A PRETTY WET TIME REEFING

course N.W. by N. for the Stone Banks buoy off Walton Naze. We were past there by 7.20 p.m. in the falling light, and, squaring away for Harwich, passed the bell-buoy at the harbour mouth five minutes after eight, thus having looped the loop which had been begun in the ss. *St. Petersburg* three weeks since to the day. For we had left that port at 10 p.m. on a Monday, and here we were back from Holland on the Monday at 8.5 p.m.

We sailed smartly up the Orwell in the darkness past the flashing gas-buoys, and then in the moonlight let go anchor off Shotley near the pilot's moorings. A few hours' sleep and we ran farther up the river to that beauty spot Pin Mill, where, after putting *Vivette* on to moorings, we hauled down the burgee, locked the cabin door, bundled our bags into the dinghy—and we had brought our travels to an end.

We had been into the ports of four countries, we had seen many an out-of-the-way place, we had sailed past hundreds of miles of interesting scenery, viewing strange sights, shipping, and happenings. We had fraternised with the seamen of different nationalities, extended our knowledge and broadened our outlook.

We had been everywhere without pilot or paid hand, and found our way by the help of chart and compass, lead and line. We had enjoyed fair weather and foul, gales and calms, sun and fog. The sons of the sea in every port had treated us as their own, and now it was all over and belonged to the things of the past. It was a great opportunity, and no amateur yachtsman's education can possibly be complete until he has seen for himself that flat, windmill country where the first yacht was born.

Winter has since passed, and the first glints of returning sunshine, with the lengthening of the days, have sent one's thoughts out across the chimneys and the streets to the little village, where soon the smell of varnish and the sound of the caulking mallet will show that the time for fitting-out already approaches.

The call comes back to you keener than ever. You have done away with winter's gloom; you are ready for the wandering to recommence.

Anchorage at Harty Ferry in the East Swale

I will go back to the great sweet mother,
Mother and lover of men, the sea.
I will go down to her, I and none other,
Close with her, kiss her, and mix her with me.
Cling to her, strive with her, hold her fast;
Oh fair white mother, in days long past
Born without sister, born without brother,
Set free my soul as thy soul is free.

WE HAD BROUGHT OUR TRAVELS TO AN END

Appendix

SAILING DIRECTIONS, &C.

Note.—For convenience in using this book, it has been thought advisable to collect under one heading the following data, which are likely to be of use to yachtsmen contemplating cruising between Southampton and Amsterdam. The chief value of this information lies in the fact that it is the outcome of personal experience. In most cases fuller details will be found on turning to the preceding pages.

Charts.—*The Pilot's Guide for the English Channel* will be found to contain all the charts necessary until you come to Ramsgate. For the Dover Straits (England to France) get Admiralty chart, No. 1895. Admiralty chart, No. 1872 will take you from Calais to Blankenberghe, No. 120 from there to Hellegat, and No. 122 thence as far as the Ijssel. But I have used with the greatest advantage, and strongly urge others to obtain, the following charts published by the Dutch Ministry of Marine. They are obtainable direct from De Gebroeders van Cleef, Spui, 28a, The Hague; No. 204 (Veere to Bruinisse), price 1 *guelder*, 75 cents, and No. 209 (Zijpe to Dordrecht), price 1 *guelder*, 75 cents. These Dutch charts are on a very large scale, strong paper and very clear. From the mouth of the Ijssel to Amsterdam you must needs obtain a Dutch Ordnance Survey map showing the canals, towns, where the roads cross the canals and rivers, &c. Thorpe's *Yachtsman's Guide to the Dutch Waterways* will be found to be good as far as it goes.

General Hints.—As to draught, there is water enough for any yacht in the East and West Scheldt, the Hollandsch Diep, the Rotterdam river, and the North Sea canal. But it is the smaller rivers and canals which impose the restrictions on the depth of your ship. A fairly safe rule sums the matter up thus. Anything up to 5 ft. draught can traverse Holland, but if you only draw 4 ft. 3 in., like *Vivette*, or, better still, 4 ft., you have no cause for anxiety, though the waterway between the Oude Rijn and the North Sea canal (*via* Haarlem and Spaarndam) is certainly tricky. If you go north that way the chances are you will have a fair S.W. wind, so that you can keep just to the starboard of the middle in the best water. You can usually get a tow when you want it from steamer or motor-barge, but you must make your bargain before you hitch up. And remember that a Dutchman's first offer is capable of reduction.

As to extra-equipment above what the yacht would ordinarily carry, it is essential that she be provided with a quant-pole, at least one long boat-hook, and four good, stout fend-offs made out of rope and covered over with canvas. If you have to tow by hand (we did so only for a few minutes), the best thing is to use a long log-line. Your lead and line will, of course, be needed, as also your fog-horn for warning the bridges to be opened, the usual rule being that you drop ten cents into the wooden shoe which is dangled at the end of a fishing-rod as you go by. The local men use a sounding stick marked with coloured horizontal stripes for feeling their way through the shallows. When approaching railway bridges or locks, you will see either a red or white triangle or globe usually.

If it shows red you must wait till the structure opens; if it shows white, it is already open, and you can go ahead. At certain more important railway bridges, such as Dordrecht and Amsterdam, you may have to wait for a couple of hours, but experience taught us that we could usually expect to find them open at midday for about a quarter of an hour.

Contrary to what most people tell you, I found that it was possible to purchase in Holland jam, marmalade, condensed milk, and English tobacco, although the three are not of the best. The latter I found to be cheaper than in England, although bought in the same packets.

There is a shop in Amsterdam close by the Royal Palace where you can get really excellent cigars at a penny each. In other parts of Holland they are wonderfully cheap, but only just smokeable. Most grocers give you one or two when buying your provisions! It is well to take plenty of consumable stores, including a number of preserved meats, so as to be independent. Fresh milk, bread, butter, eggs, bacon, fruit and vegetables you can get in almost any village. But there is great difficulty in obtaining meat other than veal and pork, and no one wants to eat the latter, in the summer months at any rate.

Only in Amsterdam and Dort could we get beef. If you drink beer you can obtain a kind of lager in nice, stoppered bottles from any of the waterside cafés. Occasionally you may come across dredgers at work. They will display a red and white flag indicating the side on which to be passed. As to buoyage system, as long as you are in British, Belgian, or Dutch waters, leave all conical buoys to starboard, and can buoys to port. In French waters the starboard hand buoys are painted red and surmounted with a cone (with or without even numbers commencing from seaward). The port hand buoys are painted black surmounted with a can (with or without uneven numbers commencing from seaward). The Franco-Belgian frontier is about mid-way between Dunkerque and Nieuport.

Sailing Directions for Foriegn Ports (Calais to Amsterdam)

Calais.—The best time to enter is at either two hours before or two hours after high-water. At H.W. springs the tide sets eastward across the entrance at between 3 and 4 knots, so hug the western pier quite close to. There is practically no tide when once inside. At neaps the stream across the harbour entrance is only about a knot.

Sail straight up the harbour, turning neither to the right hand nor the left, and let go anchor just to the west of the Carnot Basin's lock gates opposite where the cross-Channel steamers bring up. Run out a line ashore to moor by the stern. If the wind comes northerly run in through the gates into the Bassin Carnot.

Note.—The shoals and buoys outside the entrance are sometimes altered, so only an up-to-date chart should be trusted.

Dunkerque.—The best time to enter is at about two hours before high-water, but at half-an-hour before high-water the east-going or flood stream is at its strongest: in the latter case hug the western pier till well inside. In light winds wait till the tide slacks before attempting. The British Admiralty publish an excellent large scale chart of Dunkerque harbour (No. 1352, price 3s.) which is well worth having. Stand straight on up the harbour until you come to a bay, on the port hand, which has a shipbuilding yard on its eastern extremity. Be careful not to get too far in this bay, as it is shallow and full of small fishing-craft, &c. But let go anchor just out of the traffic- line as shown in the plan given on another page. Land in the dinghy at the steps to the southward.

Ostende.—Do not enter the fishing harbour to the right, nor the lock gates, although sometimes men endeavour to wave you into the latter. Ignore all such ideas, and continue to stand straight up the harbour, as shown in plan, till you get to the Ostende Yacht Club by the bridge. Bring up on the port hand and moor stem and stern between the two substantial dolphins which will be readily recognised. This is undoubtedly the only satisfactory berth for small yachts. In entering from outside allowance must be made for the strong tide setting across the piers, especially at H.W. springs. At neaps there is a slighter stream.

Zeebrugge.—Round the breakwater, then steer between the two lines of buoys to the S.W., when you will come to a narrower entrance. Continue straight up, and finally moor a few yards before you reach the lock gates. A berth will thus be found by the dolphins on the port hand, but get sufficiently well in, and out of the traffic-line.

Flushing.—Allow for strong tide which the Scheldt carries past the entrance. Run in between the two arms of the harbour. The lock gates will be seen straight ahead, but if closed a red basket globe hoisted on a pole will be recognised. In that case stow sail, and make fast on the port hand till the gates open. Beware of considerable amount of traffic. When once through the lock a nice quiet berth will be found on the starboard hand a few yards further along, in No. 1 inner harbour.

Middelburg And Veere.—Moor in both cases on the port hand.

Zijpe.—The entrance is very narrow, after which it suddenly bends round to the starboard. A smart lookout should be kept for a steamboat which is frequently in and out of here. Moor at the eastern end of the harbour where a very comfortable, snug berth will be found in clear, clean water. Bruinesse is a short walk from here. No harbour dues.

Numansdorp.—Enter at all states of the tide under easy canvas, as there is not much room for manoeuvring inside. Let go anchor and then warp to a good berth on the starboard hand. A steamer is constantly running throughout the day from here across the Hollandsch Diep to Willemstad.

Dordrecht.—Beware of strong tide setting on to bridge. There is an opening at extreme right and extreme left, but both are very narrow and quickly closed. Stand on, when once through, and take the first turning on the starboard hand past the swimming-baths. Pass through Wollewevers' Haven into yacht basin, where there is no tide, and you will be perfectly comfortable no matter what the weather.

From Dordrecht to Amsterdam a suitable mooring-place can be found at almost any moment. So long as you are this side of Gouda, and therefore on tidal waters, you can anchor, and then sheer in near to the bank so as to be out of the way of traffic.

Above Gouda you are in canal or river water, and can bring up against the grassy banks when and where you please.

Amsterdam.—The big bridge over the Amstel will open on applying at the *kantoor*, which is just the other side of the bridge. Moor temporarily and row off in dinghy to obtain permission. You can afterwards bring up along-side any of the quays, but a far more private berth can be found in either the Oosterlijk Dock, or by the yacht-*steiger* on the Ij close by the two yacht clubs on the port hand as you sail towards Ymuiden. But run lines out as a breastfast to prevent the ship from bumping against the jetty owing to the continual wash made by passing craft.

For this reason some prefer the Oosterlijk Dock, although it is less interesting. Given settled weather and fair wind, a yacht anxious to hurry back to England could then proceed *via* the North Sea canal, through the Ymuiden locks, and stretch directly across to Lowestoft. But the advantage of the route which has here been followed lies in the fact that there is a port every few miles to run for in case of bad weather.

ALSO FROM LEONAUR
AVAILABLE IN SOFTCOVER OR HARDCOVER WITH DUST JACKET

CAPTAIN OF THE 95th (Rifles) *by Jonathan Leach*—An officer of Wellington's Sharpshooters during the Peninsular, South of France and Waterloo Campaigns of the Napoleonic Wars.

BUGLER AND OFFICER OF THE RIFLES *by William Green & Harry Smith* With the 95th (Rifles) during the Peninsular & Waterloo Campaigns of the Napoleonic Wars

BAYONETS, BUGLES AND BONNETS *by James 'Thomas' Todd*—Experiences of hard soldiering with the 71st Foot - the Highland Light Infantry - through many battles of the Napoleonic wars including the Peninsular & Waterloo Campaigns

THE ADVENTURES OF A LIGHT DRAGOON *by George Farmer & G.R. Gleig*—A cavalryman during the Peninsular & Waterloo Campaigns, in captivity & at the siege of Bhurtpore, India

THE COMPLEAT RIFLEMAN HARRIS *by Benjamin Harris as told to & transcribed by Captain Henry Curling*—The adventures of a soldier of the 95th (Rifles) during the Peninsular Campaign of the Napoleonic Wars

WITH WELLINGTON'S LIGHT CAVALRY *by William Tomkinson*—The Experiences of an officer of the 16th Light Dragoons in the Peninsular and Waterloo campaigns of the Napoleonic Wars.

SURTEES OF THE RIFLES *by William Surtees*—A Soldier of the 95th (Rifles) in the Peninsular campaign of the Napoleonic Wars.

ENSIGN BELL IN THE PENINSULAR WAR *by George Bell*—The Experiences of a young British Soldier of the 34th Regiment 'The Cumberland Gentlemen' in the Napoleonic wars.

WITH THE LIGHT DIVISION *by John H. Cooke*—The Experiences of an Officer of the 43rd Light Infantry in the Peninsula and South of France During the Napoleonic Wars

NAPOLEON'S IMPERIAL GUARD: FROM MARENGO TO WATERLOO *by J. T. Headley*—This is the story of Napoleon's Imperial Guard from the bearskin caps of the grenadiers to the flamboyance of their mounted chasseurs, their principal characters and the men who commanded them.

BATTLES & SIEGES OF THE PENINSULAR WAR *by W. H. Fitchett*—Corunna, Busaco, Albuera, Ciudad Rodrigo, Badajos, Salamanca, San Sebastian & Others

AVAILABLE ONLINE AT **www.leonaur.com**
AND OTHER GOOD BOOK STORES

ALSO FROM LEONAUR

AVAILABLE IN SOFTCOVER OR HARDCOVER WITH DUST JACKET

WELLINGTON AND THE PYRENEES CAMPAIGN VOLUME I: FROM VITORIA TO THE BIDASSOA by *F. C. Beatson*—The final phase of the campaign in the Iberian Peninsula.

WELLINGTON AND THE INVASION OF FRANCE VOLUME II: THE BIDASSOA TO THE BATTLE OF THE NIVELLE by *F. C. Beatson*—The second of Beatson's series on the fall of Revolutionary France published by Leonaur, the reader is once again taken into the centre of Wellington's strategic and tactical genius.

WELLINGTON AND THE FALL OF FRANCE VOLUME III: THE GAVES AND THE BATTLE OF ORTHEZ by *F. C. Beatson*—This final chapter of F. C. Beatson's brilliant trilogy shows the 'captain of the age' at his most inspired and makes all three books essential additions to any Peninsular War library.

NAVAL BATTLES OF THE NAPOLEONIC WARS by *W. H. Fitchett*—Cape St. Vincent, the Nile, Cadiz, Copenhagen, Trafalgar & Others

SERGEANT GUILLEMARD: THE MAN WHO SHOT NELSON? by *Robert Guillemard*—A Soldier of the Infantry of the French Army of Napoleon on Campaign Throughout Europe

WITH THE GUARDS ACROSS THE PYRENEES by *Robert Batty*—The Experiences of a British Officer of Wellington's Army During the Battles for the Fall of Napoleonic France, 1813.

A STAFF OFFICER IN THE PENINSULA by *E. W. Buckham*—An Officer of the British Staff Corps Cavalry During the Peninsula Campaign of the Napoleonic Wars

THE LEIPZIG CAMPAIGN: 1813—NAPOLEON AND THE "BATTLE OF THE NATIONS" by *F. N. Maude*—Colonel Maude's analysis of Napoleon's campaign of 1813.

BUGEAUD: A PACK WITH A BATON by *Thomas Robert Bugeaud*—The Early Campaigns of a Soldier of Napoleon's Army Who Would Become a Marshal of France.

TWO LEONAUR ORIGINALS

SERGEANT NICOL by *Daniel Nicol*—The Experiences of a Gordon Highlander During the Napoleonic Wars in Egypt, the Peninsula and France.

WATERLOO RECOLLECTIONS by *Frederick Llewellyn*—Rare First Hand Accounts, Letters, Reports and Retellings from the Campaign of 1815.

AVAILABLE ONLINE AT **www.leonaur.com**
AND OTHER GOOD BOOK STORES

www.ingramcontent.com/pod-product-compliance
Lightning Source LLC
Chambersburg PA
CBHW030216170426
43201CB00006B/104